Dearest Bess

'The Duchess' — Bess in later life.

Dearest Bess

THE LIFE AND TIMES OF LADY ELIZABETH FOSTER
AFTERWARDS DUCHESS OF DEVONSHIRE

FROM HER UNPUBLISHED JOURNALS
AND CORRESPONDENCE

DOROTHY MARGARET STUART

FONTHILL

Fonthill Media Limited
Fonthill Media LLC
www.fonthillmedia.com
office@fonthillmedia.com

This edition published in the United Kingdom 2012.

British Library Cataloguing in Publication Data:
A catalogue record for this book is available from the British Library.

ISBN 978-1-78155-005-2 (print)
ISBN 978-1-78155-145-5 (e-book)

Typeset in Bembo 10.5 on 13 pt
Printed and bound in England.

Connect with us

 facebook.com/fonthillmedia   twitter.com/fonthillmedia

PREFACE

'Never', wrote her kinswoman, Mrs Dillon, 'was there a story more proper for a novel than poor Lady Elizabeth Foster's.' She was right. Yet if such a novel had been written before the publication of the new material in the present book the chances are that 'poor Lady Elizabeth' would have appeared compact of one halfpenny-worth of goodness to an intolerable deal of guile. Posterity has seen her mainly through the angry eyes of Lady Harriet Cavendish, otherwise Hary-O, second daughter of her lover, later her husband, the fifth Duke of Devonshire; and historians and biographers have not unnaturally accepted as a portrait something which is little better than a caricature.

Now that the generosity, of the Duke of Devonshire and Lord Dormer permits me to present 'Bess' in three dimensions, I hope that many of my readers will agree that hers is a far more likeable, and indeed endearing, personality than we had had any reason to suppose.

Let us concede that she was something of a *poseuse*; it was common form among the Devonshire House ladies. A little histrionic she may sometimes have been, as was the wont of the whole charming sisterhood. Yet those are hardly grave defects, and from a biographer's point of view they are almost merits.

It was certainly regrettable that she should have loved the Duke of Devonshire, the husband of her dearest friend; but she loved him faithfully and even fervently to his life's end and beyond. She and the Duchess were undeniably foolish in their exaggerated expressions of affection for each other; but there again it was common form, and an age quite as cynical if less psycho-analytical than our own was able to take such harmless idiocies in its stride.

As for the Duke, who having read his love-letters to 'Dearest Bess' could possibly endorse the general verdict that he was a hopelessly dull fellow?

Lady Elizabeth knew many of the great figures of her time. In her Journal she brings them to life for us, thanks to her observant eyes and her almost Boswellian skill in setting down remembered dialogue. George III, George IV (as Prince of Wales, Regent and King), Marie Antoinette, Count Fersen, La Fayette, Mirabeau,

Napoleon, Berthier, Junot, Nelson, Wellington, Fox, Pitt, Grey, Sheridan, Byron, Lady Hamilton, Madame Récamier, they all cross the stage under a strong new light. But the attention of the diarist was not focused exclusively on these shining ones; she was interested in all sorts of people, postillions and *sans-culottes*, dustmen and watermen, lackeys and abigails, and the good-humoured mass of the London mob.

Apart from providing punctuation and modernizing spelling I have left Bess's text unedited, and I have tried as far as possible to let her tell her story in her own words. It is told with almost startling candour in the autobiographical passages to be found in Chapters II and III. For the guidance of future biographers and historians, I have marked *C* and *D* respectively the material from the Duke of Devonshire's archives at Chatsworth and the Journals and other family records in the possession of Lord Dormer. Footnotes have been supplied for the minor celebrities, and I have italicized the text wherever I have regretfully, and yielding to the urgent request of my publishers, translated into English the anecdotes and epigrams which Bess naturally recorded in the original French.

Some difficulty was experienced in choosing a title. *The Life and Times of Lady Elizabeth Foster* sounds a little ponderous, and for the last fifteen years of her life she did not bear that name. Then the circumstance that she was so often addressed as 'Dearest Bess', by her family, her friends and her lover, suggested the alternative finally chosen. It may not be quite worthy of the historical importance of her letters and journals, but to the lady herself it seems singularly appropriate.

D. M. S.
Kew, 1953–4

CONTENTS

ILLUSTRATIONS

The Prince Regent, by Sir Thomas Lawrence.

CHAPTER I

Prologue: 1791 — The Amazing Triangle — 1783–1784

It is Fanny Burney who sets the scene for us in the month of August 1791, and in the city of Bath, where she was then staying with her friend Mrs Ord to recuperate from the strain of five years' service as Second Keeper of the Robes to Queen Charlotte.

Even Mrs Ord, who always 'thought the worst of the Devonshire House circle', can have felt nothing but gratification when that exemplar of every active and austere virtue, Lady Spencer, called at their lodgings in Queen Square. Her ladyship's looks corresponded to her character: her features were narrow and regular; her upward-swept hair looked as if it had been carved out of wood; her dress, dark in colour and plain in cut, anticipated the slightly mannish 'tailor-made' of the late Victorian period. Both physically and morally her daughters, Georgiana, Duchess of Devonshire, and Harriet, Viscountess Duncannon, were made of other stuff. About them there was no austerity; and their loosely rippling ringlets and wildly towering feathers served to emphasize the unlikeness between themselves and their 'dearest, dear Mama'.

Mrs Ord's mood changed when in Lady Spencer's own lodgings in Gay Street her young friend became acquainted with two of the ladies of the party, one of whom, at least, showed every sign of wishing to cultivate her. 'Lady Spencer,' runs Fanny's Journal, 'with a look and manner warmly announcing pleasure in what she was doing, introduced me to the first of them, saying, "Duchess of Devonshire, Miss Burney."' The Duchess 'made a very civil compliment' to the deeply curtsying diarist; and 'Lady Spencer then slightly, and as if unavoidably, said, "Lady Elizabeth Foster"'.

In Fanny Burney's eyes the Duchess was first and foremost the Queen of that Whig coterie which, based on Devonshire House, had actively encouraged the Prince of Wales in his undutiful conduct during the recent mental breakdown of the King his father. But she was not proof against the engaging charm of her personality. Mrs Ord, who had not come within its range, felt a dismay which she made no attempt to conceal when she and Fanny were later discussing the events of the day. 'I always wonder', wrote Fanny sadly, 'why people good in themselves can make up their minds to supposing themselves so singular.' The trend of that censorious lady's thoughts is clearly indicated in the next sentence.

> Lady Elizabeth, however, has the character of being so alluring that Mrs. Holroyd told me it was the opinion of Mr. Gibbon no man could withstand her, and that if she chose to beckon the Lord Chancellor from his Woolsack in full sight of the world, he could not resist obedience.

Mrs Ord, like many other people, must have been well aware that William, the taciturn, outwardly apathetic Duke of Devonshire,[1] was among the men who could not withstand her. Even in an age of unorthodox family patterns the Devonshire House triangle was regarded as distinctly odd, for there His Grace's lawful wife lived on terms of the fondest friendship with his mistress, and there Lady Elizabeth's two children were sharing the nursery and the schoolroom of the three young Cavendishes.

Seen side by side in retrospect the two ladies have strong affinity with the two daughters of the Vicar of Wakefield, Olivia, 'open, sprightly and commanding', Sophia, 'soft, modest and alluring'. 'The one', says Dr Primrose, 'vanquished by a single blow, the other by efforts successively repeated.'

'Dearest Bess' has long been condemned as a heartless coquette, a calculating and insidious dissembler of whom by some strange, unlucky chance the not-normally-susceptible Duke became enamoured. Yet even without the conclusive evidence of her private journals there are many indications in contemporary memoirs that she could easily have taken unto herself other lovers — two Dukes among them, they of Richmond and Dorset. Moreover, after her wretched little husband's death in 1796 she might, had she so willed, have attained honourable matrimony more than ten years before the widowed Duke made her his lawful Duchess. There is no reason to doubt and there is every reason to believe that she remained, in spite of a few flirtations by the way, essentially faithful to him from first to last.

Lady Elizabeth was born with a prescriptive right to both brains and beauty. Her grandparents were the famous pair of whom it was written that

> Venus herself ne'er saw bedded
> So perfect a beau and a belle
> As when Hervey the Handsome was wedded
> To beautiful Molly Lepell.[2]

Her father was that incredible, fantastic person Frederick, Earl of Bristol and Bishop of Derry,[3] commonly known as the Earl-Bishop: her mother, *née* Elizabeth

Davers, was, if not strictly beautiful, a very delightful woman, intelligent, well read, and sympathetic. As the wife of the Earl-Bishop she had much to endure. God granted her patience under her sufferings, though not always quite as much as the occasion required.

Elizabeth Christiana — to give her both her baptismal names — was born at Horrenger, in Suffolk, in November 1757,[4] the second of the three daughters and the third of the six children of a marriage which, beginning idyllically, ended abruptly towards the close of 1782, when the Earl-Bishop and his long-suffering lady went out for a drive together, apparently on their usual tolerant, not unfriendly terms, and, returning in dead silence, ceased to speak to each other for the rest of their lives.

That was rather the Earl-Bishop's way. He was estranged from his mother, who, though she did not die until Elizabeth was nine years old, most probably never saw her pretty little granddaughter: he was violently at loggerheads with his sailor-brother, the third Earl, whom he succeeded in 1779; but he contrived somehow to remain good friends with his eldest brother, the bachelor second Earl, and it was upon the fringes of Ickworth Park, within easy reach of the still unpretentious family seat, that the first years of his marriage were passed and the lives of his children began.

The small Herveys enjoyed at least one advantage in their infancy — the affection of both their parents. Lady Bristol wrote tenderly in 1778 of her babies as 'little fairies' tripping after her and 'bleating ... that dear word, "Mama"'; and the Earl-Bishop once declared that when he had 'first, second and more children', he never wished to see London, and when forced to visit it thought every hour spent there 'a plunder from his babes and his duty'.

The same spirit of restlessness which later sent him wandering all over the Continent soon deprived his sons and daughters of any settled home, for they found none in the grandiose palaces, pillared and domed, which he afterwards erected in his dear adopted land of Ireland — a land in which he succeeded in winning the affectionate regard of Protestant and Catholic alike, and where perhaps better than in any other the rich absurdity of his proceedings would be tolerated and even approved.

The elder children went abroad with their parents in 1765, and towards the end of that year Mary and Bess, the two elder girls, were placed in the care of a Mademoiselle Chomel at Geneva, to whose tuition they probably owed the skill in French and Italian of which their letters give abundant evidence. From the indulgent, slightly compassionate tone of the allusions to their second daughter in the correspondence of the father and mother it would appear that 'poor dear little Bess' had already something wistful and pathetic about her — the same quality which was later to inspire the sobriquet of the 'poor dear little orphan'.

Six years later the Earl-Bishop installed his wife and children dispersedly in Bury St Edmunds while he took his eldest son, Midshipman Jack Hervey,[5] for a Continental tour. Bess and Frederick William[6] were placed at 'Dr. Mandeville's lodgings in the Market Place at Bury'.

Almost without exception the Hervey family loved Ickworth, both in life and in death. Yet Bess does not allude to the place at any time with any affection. Perhaps it was associated too intimately and too intolerably with the unhappy months she spent in 1780–81 at the house which her father had inherited with the earldom in 1779 and which was afterwards replaced by the present vast and grandiose building. By the dubious expedient of penning them together for several months in that congested and inconvenient abode the Earl-Bishop had endeavoured to reconcile her and her young husband, John Thomas Foster, the son of his old friend, the Reverend Dr John Foster of Dunleer, and a Member of the Irish House of Commons.

They had been married at Brussels in December 1776, five months after Mary's marriage to the widowed Lord Erne, and at first things seemed to go well, though Dearest Bess found the rural solitude of Dunleer a little melancholy and gravitated to Dublin more often than her father thought judicious. When she faced with a faint lack of enthusiasm the prospect of early motherhood, her own mother wrote offering to take 'the dear little creature' off her hands and make it 'as hardy and active as a Magilligan kid': but it was probably growing disillusionment with the father rather than reluctance to welcome the child which chilled the spirits of young Mrs Foster; for it was now clear that 'little f.', as he was called to distinguish him from his reverend father, had almost all the qualities needed to make a bad husband; he was parsimonious, exacting, irascible, intemperate, and unfaithful.

Their first child, Frederick, was born in Dublin on October 17th, 1777; Bess was expecting a second during her stay at Ickworth, where there was another baby imminent. Her sailor-brother, Lord Hervey, had chosen that rambling, far from commodious dwelling as a suitable place for the confinement of his Scottish-Canadian wife, *née* Elizabeth Drummond of the ancient family of the Drummonds of Megginch. Their only child, the much-loved Eliza of her Aunt Bess's later years, was born on August 17th, 1780; and on December 4th General William Hervey noted in his diary that his niece, Lady Elizabeth Foster, had been 'brought to bed of a son' — the future Sir Augustus. Five months later the Foster marriage disintegrated beyond possibility of repair, and Bess was left, as she herself wrote fourteen years later,

without a guide; a wife, and no husband, a mother, and no children ... by myself alone to steer through every peril that surrounds a young woman so situated.

Looking back, she indulged in a little self-analysis.

... books, the arts, a wish to be loved and approved; and enthusiastic friendship for these my friends;[7] a proud determination to be my own letter of recommendation; these, with perhaps <u>manners </u>that pleased, realized my projects and gained me friends wherever I have been.[8]

She spoke truly, both as regards her desire to be loved and her innate power to translate that desire into reality. Her mother had noted the first trait long since, and had uttered a gentle word of warning.

Strangely enough, 'little f.' was anxious to have the custody of the two children of the broken marriage; and — even more strangely — he seems to have filled the role of father with tolerable credit. The boys were placed in the charge of a family named Marshall at Dunleer, where their good old grandfather kept an eye upon them until his death in 1784. They were not, however, sent to Ireland before the summer of 1782. Fourteen years would elapse before their mother saw them again.

Lady Spencer must sometimes have recollected rather ruefully that it was she who first brought about the threefold conjunction between her daughter, her son-in-law, and the irresistible Lady Elizabeth. She had had some acquaintance with the Earl-Bishop, who had visited her at Althorp and inspected with enthusiasm her various charitable works in the village; she knew and sympathized with his unfortunate wife; and it would have been characteristic of her to suggest that Georgiana should pay some little attentions to the two eldest daughters of that now-sundered couple, Mary and Bess, who were living rather bleakly together in London.

Mary's marriage to Lord Erne had been only a few degrees less unhappy than Elizabeth's to John Thomas Foster. Her husband was a difficult, unpredictable man, and they were now, so to speak, semi-detached; but she had the consolation of keeping with her the charming little dark-haired Caroline, otherwise 'Lal-Lal', who had been the sole issue of the union.

On May 22nd, 1782, Georgiana wrote to her dearest Mama that the Duke had gone with her to see 'Lady Erne and Lady E. Foster'. On June 1st Lady Erne and 'Lady E.' were their 'chief support, else it would be shockingly dull for the Duke indeed'. Two days later poor Lady Erne was very ill, she had had influenza, which 'her thin carcase could not well support'. 'Lady E.' was also a victim, but her chief affliction was that her poor little children were just going from her. The Duchess, herself longing for a child, was full of sympathy. Already it seems as if she found her dearest Mama less well disposed towards her new friend than might have been expected. Did Bess feel this also? The Duchess's next words suggest that she did. That most devoted of daughters was naturally delighted when her new friend declared that she was sure, from what she had heard, that the religion practised by the Dowager, while it diffused happiness to all around her, must secure it most to

herself. ^C With charming delicacy she asks Mama to say to Lady Bristol that she
and the Duke were very happy at seeing a great deal of Lady Erne and 'Lady Eliz.',
and she hoped thus to make that strange man, Lord Bristol, ashamed of doing
nothing for his second daughter.

Conscious, however, that Lady Spencer was far too shrewd to waste compassion
on self-pitiers, Georgiana adds that neither of these ladies 'talks about it at all'.

The whole party were together at Bath later in the month of June, and Lady
Bristol, writing to Bess of their imminent return to London, dwells upon the
'heavenly conduct of the Duchess when her friend had found herself in urgent
need of ready money pending a remittance from the singularly negligent Earl-
Bishop. For poverty was added to the other misfortunes of Dearest Bess, who
had to maintain herself upon a totally inadequate average income of £300 a year.
This circumstance redounded more to the discredit of her wealthy father than
of her not-particularly-well-to-do husband; and Horace Walpole, who had been
devoted to Molly Lepell and thought poorly of that punchinello prelate, her third
son, commented waspishly upon it in a letter to Horace Mann.

Towards the end of June Georgiana and Bess were seized with a craze for
drawing. Between them they produced a picture of Prospero's island at the very
moment when he says to Miranda

> The fringèd curtains of thine eyes advance.

Georgiana was responsible for the figures, Lady Elizabeth ('who draws very
well') supplied the sea and the trees. ^C

The numerous sketches which adorn Lady Elizabeth's Journals show that she
drew quite as well as the average lady of fashion at that time. The landscapes are
feathery and — when colour is used — rather dusky; the figures are conventional.
Only on two occasions does she achieve anything remarkable in the way
of a portrait: a thumbnail head of Napoleon as First Consul, with all his hair
violently blown forward, and the lovely wash-and-pencil likeness of the Duchess,
reproduced in Chapter V of the present book.

Well might Lady Bristol comment that her second daughter's summer was
'most happily allotted' for the year 1782.

In July Bess was with the Devonshires at Plympton.[9] The Duke read aloud to
the two ladies from *Hamlet* and *A Midsummer Night's Dream*. When he rode into
Plymouth they made him do some commissions for them, and were very much
delighted with his buying some Italian gauze. Then we catch a carefree glimpse
of Bess playing with a comical black-and-white dog and jumping off walls. ^C She
shared the Duke's love of dogs and many years later she exasperated his undoggy
second daughter almost to frenzy by her enthusiasm for a new litter of puppies.

Still striving to incline her mother more favourably towards her fascinating friend, the Duchess proudly reports that they had both risen with the lark and gone to church; but her natural honesty constrained her to confess that she did not get there 'quite for the beginning'. Nothing, said Lady Elizabeth, ever looked so happy to her as a country church. She was perhaps more familiar than the Duchess with the three-decker pulpit, the high pews, the rude forefathers of the hamlet scraping their fiddles in the gallery, the cold bright light from the unpainted windows slanting on to recumbent worthies carved in alabaster. Such things were to be seen and heard neither at St James's, Piccadilly, nor in the gilded and velvet-cushioned setting of the private chapel at Chatsworth.

Shortly after this the Duchess fell ill, but so tenderly was she nursed by the Duke and 'Lady E.' that it was quite a comfort to need their ministrations. Then, as the fateful summer waned, it was Bess whose health caused alarm. She had a violent cough, a persistent pain in her side, some spitting of blood — in short, many of the recognized symptoms of consumption, including a stubborn refusal to confess to being anything worse than 'nervous'. [C]

Lady Spencer expressed a polite concern, but threw out a strong hint that 'Lady E.' should be left behind at Bristol — then a very popular spa — when the Devonshires returned to town. [C] The doctors did not agree; but it was felt that going abroad for the winter months would be vastly good, and her friends set about devising some means to enable her to go.

At this time a visit to Althorp was pending. 'Will Lady E. come with you when you come?' asked Lady Spencer. 'I do not know', she added, 'what we shall do if she does, for your father is too ill to see a stranger with any comfort.'[C] Georgiana countered with an appealing picture of the 'poor little soul', the 'quietest little thing in the world', sitting and drawing in a corner of the room, or going out of the room, or doing whatever Mama pleased.[C10]

Apparently the visit passed off well enough, for in December Bess was touched and flattered by Lady Spencer's goodness to her in conversation with Lady Mary — that is to say, Lady Mary Fitzgerald, the Earl-Bishop's sister, who had been converted to the most lurid and gloomy school of evangelical Christianity 'on the correspondence system'.

The Duke, the Duchess, and Bess had now reached that stage in their friendship when a formal mode of address ceased to seem appropriate, and nicknames were adopted — a very usual Devonshire House development. The dog-like merits of the Duke won for him the sobriquet of 'Canis'; the peaked, anxious face and melting eyes of Bess qualified her to be called 'Racky', short for 'Racoon'; but it is not clear why Georgiana should have received the less agreeable name of 'the Rat'.

Neither Canis nor the Rat could rest until arrangements had been made for their dear Racky to winter abroad, but the means devised were such as to shock

Horace Walpole, for it was as governess and guardian to the Duke's illegitimate daughter by a pretty young milliner that Lady Elizabeth was to travel. Left rudderless by her own lack of children, the Duchess had made a sort of pet and plaything of 'Charlotte William',[11] but Lady Spencer now began to feel some misgivings, especially as there was at last reason to hope that the long-desired Cavendish grandchild might be on its way into the world. The Duke, too, may have felt that the situation at Devonshire House promised to become a trifle peculiar. Just how peculiar it would ultimately become no one could then have foreseen.

Bess and her young charge set off on December 29th, 1782. She at once began to keep a diary, a habit which she continued, with occasional pauses, at least until the year 1819. Some of the volumes are small and compact, bound in white vellum now tawny with age, but by far the greatest number consist of ordinary exercise-books with marbled paper covers, crimson, yellow, or blue. The pages are stiff, and seem more suitable for sketching than for writing upon. Some of the earlier journals contain dried leaves, myrtle, olive, and other sub-tropical plants.

Bess was a born diarist; she had a selective eye and a remembering ear. Take, for example, the very first entry of all:

> As the ship bore away I could still observe the thoughtful Englishmen walking slowly on the shore; but when the vessel sailed into the harbour at Calais the confused clack of many voices spoke the different temper of this happy but petulant people.[D]

She noted the contrast between the men's dress and the women's. Almost every man wore a muff and a fur-lined coat. The women's cloaks were long; they wore no hats but powdered hair, ear-rings and necklaces gave them a well-dressed appearance. At Saumur the postillions wore nightcaps under their hats 'and the most enormous boots'. In an age peculiarly insensitive to the sufferings of the brute creation she wrote compassionately that these postillions 'always looked as if they would overpower their miserable horses'.[D]

Of Paris she thought but poorly, with its narrow streets, its absence of any pavement for foot-passengers. She blamed the 'insolence of the servants and thoughtlessness of the masters' which caused many of the poor to be 'daily run over'. An introduction from the Duchess of Devonshire to the Duchesse de Polignac[12] opened the doors of Versailles, where the visitor was rather shocked to see 'little stalls with all sorts of articles of dress, books, etc., in the gallery leading to the apartments of the royal children'.[D]

The friendship uniting the young Queen Marie Antoinette and Madame de Polignac was in its essence not unlike that which now united Georgiana and Bess — a sentimental friendship, rather exaggerated and immature. It was to be most cruelly

interpreted by the Queen's enemies in the time to come. No creeping shadow
fell upon the mind of Bess, who noted that though the place of the Duchesse
as *Gouvernante des Enfants de France* was a very great one, the first in the land, her
'merit was equal to it'. Nothing escaped those big, hazel-brown eyes of hers; the
glass door between the rooms of the *Gouvernante* and the Dauphin; the good looks
of the little Prince; the King's two beds, one all white and gold and 'railed off like a
Communion Table' for the *coucher du Roi*, and the other in which he actually slept;
the unforgotten face of Monsieur d'Adhernan, who had been French Minister in
Brussels at the time of her marriage. She confesses that she was pleased when she
heard that at the theatre the Queen had asked who she might be. No doubt it was
on this occasion that the court hairdresser had dressed her hair, putting on 'feathers
and chiffon' and begging her to tell people that it was he who had *coiffé* her — the
French court had adopted with ardour the fashion of skyscraping plumes brought
into vogue in England by the Duchess of Devonshire. Bess's romantic soul was
charmed by the notion that there might still be hermits dwelling in the Forest
of Fontainebleau; but her pitying eyes noted the wretchedness of the thatched
cottages, the care and want upon the faces of the 'lowest order', all of whom wore
black gowns or black cloaks. New impressions did not efface the memory of her
friends. She was a regular correspondent and from Coudrieux she sent to the Duke
of Devonshire some of the 'sun-dried grapes' for which the district was famous.

In the meantime the Duchess had been pouring forth letters of lyrical affection
to her friend, sending her chintz and muslin and chip hats, begging 'on her knees'
that she may have some share in Bess's spring dress and good looks, and adding tea
for full measure, in case no good tea was to be got at Nice.[C]

Three months later she was much agitated by the suggestion that the Duke
should go as Viceroy to Ireland, where his father had once filled that difficult office
with marked success. Characteristically she resolves that if the thing happens she
will make Mr Foster give her Augustus, the second boy. Signs of amiability in a
recent letter from him have sent her, as she puts it, 'wild' about another scheme.
She conjectures that, being a vain man, he will be actuated to behave better now
that he realizes that his good or bad conduct to his wife will be known beyond the
confines of her family: and she suggests that on her return to England Bess should
write to him and point out that as Frederick, the elder son, will be provided for,
Augustus will probably be obliged to embrace either 'the professional lives of the
Army or the Navy'. In that case, she is to say that she thinks it is a pity that he
should not by being sometimes with her cultivate the friendship and acquaintance
of relations and friends in whose power it would be to serve him. The Duchess
begs Bess to recall that this plan would be for the advantage of this dear child, and
for the unspeakable consequence that the having an object would be to herself.
Her brother Canis and her Georgiana urge practical help upon her; if she does
not accept it, she will be not worthy of the names of 'sister' and 'friend'.[C]

In a second letter the Duchess further develops her 'scheme', flying from one idea to another with a generous ardour all her own. Her baby is expected in July; if Bess were to return before then the resulting agitation might be too great, but when she does come, she is to come to Devonshire House. It is conceded that what she playfully calls her friend's 'little pride' and other circumstances may make it as well that she should not absolutely live always in the house with her brother and sister, but she will look out immediately for a house for her near them, on condition that she should be less in it than at Devonshire House. The summers she should pass at Bolton Abbey or Chatsworth, the winters in London. 'Am I too presuming', asks the Duchess, 'in making myself and Canis the principal movers in this scheme for your future life?'^C At this point one seems to hear Canis growling amiably in the background. Bess corresponded with him as well as with Georgiana, for he writes to her about this time: 'I have not had a letter from you this great while but am in "whops". I shall have one soon and shall hear that you are better.'^C

A fictitious brother-and-sister relationship was common form in this circle. Did not the Prince of Wales subscribe himself the Duchess's 'Brother and Friend'? Real brothers and sisters[13] often used terms of affection which now seem rather excessive, and women friends were almost invariably each other's 'Dearest Loves'. Emotion was pitched high, but good breeding demanded that religion should be kept on an even keel. Nobody — not even Lady Spencer — wanted to be suspected of 'enthusiasm'. As for Bess and Georgiana, there is probably much truth in what Lady Elizabeth wrote from Naples in 1784: that the nature of the circumstances that had attended their affection for each other and the strong similarity of their characters 'had formed a stronger friendship ... than perhaps ever before united two people'.^C Even when the circumstances altered, their friendship remained the same.

A passage in the Duchess's second letter gives a clue to the cause of her anxiety that her 'angelic friend' should have 'an *object*'. It was Molly Lepell, Lady Hervey, who coined the word 'flirtation', and never was there a more exquisite exponent of that agreeable if sometimes dangerous art than her granddaughter Elizabeth. For this reason the Duchess urges Bess to seek every amusement that would not be either hurtful to her dear health or imprudent: for it was certain that the line of conduct she had used, young and beautiful as she was, was absolutely necessary.^C Poor Lady Bristol, too, was exhorting her to 'lay down the coquette without adopting the prude'.

It was during her stay at Nice that an episode took place which her mother described cautiously as 'a rural compliment very well turned' but which caused the Duchess much anxiety on account of the 'ridiculous stories' which were made about it. This was the dedication of a fountain at which Bess was publicly crowned with flowers.

It was here, too, that she attracted the admiring attention of the local peasantry when one day, wearing a befeathered hat and 'a white riding uniform habit', she rode up a richly wooded slope leading to the modest abode of the parish priest. He himself was not there to behold the vision of an *Inglese oppure un Angelo*,[14] but hearing from his flock of the beautiful lady who had got on and off her equally beautiful horse with an agility which seemed to them supernatural, he decided to go and make personal inquiries in Nice. There he soon identified the white-habited horsewoman, whom he begged to honour his poor dwelling with a visit. This she did more than once, partaking of raisins and figs and fully appreciating both his artless conversation and his venerable looks.[D]

There could hardly have been a more innocent adventure. But she was the sort of woman round whom gossip tended to gather, and presently she was forced virtuously to resolve 'never to receive any gentlemen at home'. It was a resolution she often made — and broke as often.

At Nice she made the acquaintance of a deaf but lively Dowager, Lady Rivers, a great friend of her pious aunt, Lady Mary Fitzgerald. Lady Rivers looked on beauty as 'essential to one's happiness and advantage, one should almost think to one's salvation', and therefore talked to Bess of hers as she would have done of her health or her fortune, 'not as compliments but as the most interesting and important topic' to talk to her upon.[D] The attitude of Bess towards her own good looks was disarmingly frank and unaffected at this time and for long after. Her looking-glass confirmed what her friends so often told her, and it is to her credit that under the influence of such reiterated assurances she never became an insufferably vain woman.

Occasional raids by the Moors caused much alarm in Nice, though this was slightly allayed by the arrival of a frigate and three galleys from Genoa. Bess rowed round them, but had not the heart to go near, 'so horrid appears the situation of these creatures,[15] whose chains you hear from afar'.[D] She was at Geneva when she received the exciting news that a daughter had been born to the Duke and Duchess — their first child, Georgiana Dorothy. ''Tis almost a dream to me,' she wrote, 'and so difficult is it for a heart oppressed and long accustomed to sorrow to bear up under joy, I quite sunk under it.'[C] How happy, she mused, were those who had a right to be the baby's official godmothers! 'But I,' she adds, 'am to be its little Mama. Canis said so.'[C] Six years earlier Lady Bristol had written that she feared her Dear Bess had inherited her own anxious temper about those she loved. It was true. Dear Bess was going through agonies of apprehension not so much for Georgiana the elder as for the 'little frail life', lest it should be no more even while she was writing. She was reassured by letters from the Duke, in one of which he wrote that he had forgotten to tell her that the Duchess thought the child was just such a little thing as her, and he thought so, too, except that she was not so naughty, or so apt to be vexed.

Well might the 'little Mama' observe to the real one that she was glad Canis still loved his little Bess.

Before the year ended he wrote to her from Bath something which deserves to rank as an authentic love-letter, a letter which marked a long forward stage in his still nominally fraternal feeling towards her.

> This place has been very unpleasant to me compared with what it was a year and a half ago. For then I had the Rat and Bess and good health and fine weather, and now I have had none of them till a day or two ago the Rat and her young one came down here. There are many places in Bath that put me so much in mind of you that when I walk about the town I cannot help expecting upon turning the corner of a street to see you walking along it, holding your cane at each end and bending it over your knee, but I have never met you yet and what surprises me likewise very much is that somebody or other has the impudence to live in your house in Bennet Street. [C]

Then, as if suddenly conscious that he is going rather far, he concludes:

> I must finish my letter, or I shall grow giddy for I have just been drinking two large glasses of water. [C]

Unlike her idolater, Mr Gibbon, who spent fifteen years within sight of the Alps and hardly glanced at them, Bess responded ardently to the double appeal of the rugged and the romantic. She even clambered a little way among the rocks of la Meilleraie, described by Rousseau in *La Nouvelle Heloise*, though she had not the strength necessary to climb as far as the rock upon which the name of Julie was said to be visible still. A violent thunderstorm cut short the sentimental pilgrimage, and the pilgrim was pleased to find that fear had no part in her. Charlotte, as usual, was with her, but we are not told what were her sensations when God demonstrated His might by striking with lightning two houses in the vicinity.[D]

It is curious that Gibbon's name should not be mentioned in the Journal about this time. He had just returned to Lausanne from a ten years' sojourn in London as a completely mute Member of Parliament. While there he had become acquainted with 'Lady Eliza Foster', granddaughter of his old friend, Molly Lepell, Lady Hervey 'a bewitching animal', as he called her in a letter to his stepmother written in May 1782. On November 14th, 1783, he wrote to Lord Sheffield, 'Your later flame and our common goddess, Eliza, passed a month at the Inn — she came to consult Tissot,[16] but she appears to have made no conquests and no fountain has been dedicated to her memory.' According to Tom Moore, Tissot said one day to the historian, 'When you have made Milady ill with your nonsense, I will make her well again'; upon which Gibbon retorted, with his characteristic slight stutter, 'When Milady has died of your medicines, I shall immortalize her.'

Mr Gibbon was mistaken in thinking that Milady had made no conquests. A Monsieur (or Count) P., a certain 'Chevalier', and a 'Mr G.' other than Mr Gibbon soon surge up to perturb at long range the anxious Duchess. The fourth conquest was innocuous and rather pathetic — 'an old officer sunk with illness' whom Bess went to visit.

> I suppose my countenance expressed pity for him, and a similar fate to his–his nerves being violently affected, his sensations were strong and he fancied me something uncommon and was near throwing himself at my feet. My Angel, am I not born to have strange adventures! C

She had promised to dine with him on the following Saturday surely no great indiscretion! But the Duchess was thrown into paroxysms of anxiety by some of her angelic friend's more unconventional proceedings. She wrote from the Spencers' house at Wimbledon on August 19th, 1783, expressing the view that the innocence of Bess's conduct and intentions did not make her aware enough of the danger of her situation. After all her resolutions about not receiving men, she had been for a day with Mr G. to Vevai [sic] and had allowed him to drive her out. That was in itself nothing; but supposing, urged the Duchess, Bess had somewhere seen a beautiful young woman arrive, travelling alone, who, though there was nothing against her, had had imprudences laid to her charge; supposing she had seen this young woman giving parties and living with two men,[17] both supposed to be in love with her, would she not 'with all her candour', think her imprudent?

She solemnly assures her 'sweetest Bess' that she does not fear 'the essential' with her for one moment; but she reminds her that the opinion of the world is of so much importance to their future scheme (to persuade 'little f.' to give up one of the boys to her) and adds 'so many of our women have lately gone into Switzerland and Italy when in scrapes that you should be doubly cautious to show you are not that kind of person'. C

She begs Bess to live with women as much as she can, 'let them be ever so disagreeable', she begs her impetuously to forgive her 'idolizing G.'.

In her reply, written from Turin on September 8th, Bess meekly thanks her best beloved Angel for her friendly reproof à propos of the excursion to Vevai with Mr G. and also — it appears — Monsieur P. 'I own', she says, 'there being two with me blinded me to the imprudence, and as Charlotte never quits me the consciousness of the openness of my actions and conduct deceived me.' When she went by water to Lausanne to consult Tissot she thought it better to have Monsieur P. and Mr G. with her than to be at the direction of the boatman. Mr G. as a sea-officer was a natural protection; but she fears a 'sad dose' from her mother. C

The mysterious P. is, it is true, in Turin, where she has continued seeing him out of pity for his melancholy and infirmity, the more because she did not like him; but she will tell him she cannot receive him in future. The Chevalier is not expected for another week; him she will receive only once upon his first arrival.[C]

To augment the Duchess's anxieties it appears that Bess is kept in the dangerous city of Turin by lack of funds. 'Good God, good God,' she ejaculates, 'and all from my fault!'[C] Needless to say, she took immediate steps to remedy this state of affairs.

Charlotte William was not neglected. In this same month of September her temporary preceptress wrote that she began 'to have hopes' because for the first time the little girl had been 'affected in reading *Telemachus*'; and her 'present method' with her is thus laid down:

> First the cold bath and a little walk. Then breakfast. She then reads to me. When the lesson is done I make her repeat what she has read as accurately as she can and I then help her to put [it] in writing. Dancing comes after, and after that getting by heart in the Italian grammar. Another walk. Dinner always with me and in the afternoon walking and some little work for her doll. Sunday her catechism.[C]

It is a plan which does credit to Bess. Unfortunately Charlotte William failed to profit fully from it.

Lady Bristol had felt comprehensible misgivings when she heard that her daughter's wanderings would extend to Italy. It was one thing, she pointed out, to take 'Miss W.' with her 'for health to a place of retirement' and another 'to act as a mother to her all over the world'.[18] But Bess, with 'Miss W.' in tow, continued her way unmoved.

She was not unnaturally flattered when the Duchess of Modena expressed a wish that her 'young ladies' should imitate her style of dressing; as she entered Rome by the Flaminian Way she was properly impressed by the first far-off glimpse of the cross on the dome of St Peter's; and in Rome itself she felt 'almost incapable of leaving the Apollo Belvedere'.[D]

She was in Rome when news reached her of the death of Lord Spencer. It must have been with curiously mixed feelings that Lady Spencer — now by that death a Dowager — heard that Bess had promptly donned a suit of sables.

At High Mass in St Peter's the black-mantled lady had the satisfaction of contemplating two reigning sovereigns — the Emperor Joseph II and that epicene, extravagant Francophile, King Gustavus III of Sweden. The Emperor, she noted,

> had a great contempt for Gustavus and always did everything as different as possible from him. The Emp. travelled with two attendants only — the King of

S. had twelve gentlemen. I met the Emperor one day in St. Peter's. The Pope came to say *Ave Maria* in one of the small chapels. The Emperor followed. The Pope directed a handsome velvet cushion to be given to him to kneel on — but he knelt on the marble flag. After prayers he came and asked me what I thought, '*What do you think of him?*' pointing to the Pope. '*He plays his part well;*' I said. '*Yes, that's it — it is nothing more than a part.*' [D]

A triple tiara and a cardinal's hat balanced the imperial and royal crowns in the design of Bess's life at Rome. She met Cardinal de Bernis,[19] who had befriended and entertained her father there five years before, and who now not only called her his *fille chèrie*, and presented her to the Pope, but prudently desired the Princess de Santa Croce to 'go about with her'. The Holy Father raised her up when she attempted to kneel and questioned her 'with kindness and interest about her solitary travels. They were less strictly speaking solitary than he imagined.

She now begins her excellent habit of noting down any interesting anecdote or epigram that may come her way. For example, she relates that when the Austrian Emperor asked the Abbé Raynal[20] where he 'got his statistics', the Abbé replied, '*From Customs archives and from the best authorities he could find.*' '*And your opinions?*' '*Sire, out of my head.*' '*Happy man*', said Joseph, '*whom your King permits to keep both your head and your opinions.*'

Among the twelve gentlemen in attendance upon Gustavus III was one whose name was destined to ring down the valleys of history like

> the voice of that wild horn
> On Fontarabian echoes borne.

It was the name of Count Axel Fersen, the Swedish Knight Errant whose undissembled devotion to Marie Antoinette had already caused tongues to clack, and who had then only recently returned from a period of service in America with the French expedition sent to aid the 'rebels' in 1779.

When he and Bess met in Naples a few weeks later she seems to have seen nothing unusual in his falling in love with her; either she had not heard the gossip of the French Court, or she had accepted the more charitable view that his devotion to the unhappy young Queen was wholly chivalrous and strictly platonic.

CHAPTER II

Count Fersen — Italian Interlude —
The 'Archi-Prêtre des Amoureux'— 1784–1785

Having bought mourning for Earl Spencer so recently it can hardly have been necessary for Bess to make further funereal purchases when towards the end of January 1784 her mother wrote to tell her that her good old father-in-law, Dr Foster, had died at Dunleer. Her mind flew at once to her 'two darling boys'. Mrs Marshall writes that they are well, but that 'f' is 'in a state of total folly'. Pouring forth her fears and longings to her 'sweet friend', she reveals that she has at once ordered her sons' pictures to be done for her. It might, she adds thoughtfully, be inconvenient for Mrs Marshall and the painter to wait till she could pay. Would her angelic friend add to her numberless obligations and send her a 'draught' when the pictures are done? 'Adieu', she concludes, 'ever dearest — I adore you and dote on Canis.'[C]

The next letter from the Duchess is touching in its tenderness and poignant in its unconscious irony. Her dearest, loveliest friend and the man whom she loves so much and to whom she owes everything are united like brother and sister. She imagines them ensuring each other's happiness until, she hopes, a very great old age. No shadow of misgiving darkens her ardent mind.

When Bess returns she will find a small house for her very near to them, but she must every now and then sleep in the red room.

At Naples Lady Elizabeth conscientiously noted that Vesuvius threw out volumes of thick smoke and had snow to the very top; also that the picturesque and celebrated laurel still grew beside the small round ruin which was Virgil's tomb. But her mind was not fixed upon either smoking volcanoes or laurelled tombs; it did not even brood steadily over Dunleer; for in the foreground now stood the figure of the 'very, very amiable Count F.'. He said sometimes that he wished he had never known her, and yet would not now relinquish having done so. He was respectfully tender; and he seems to have made a dint, though not a deep dint, upon the heart of Bess, who confessed to the Duchess that she did not understand her own feelings. But her sweet love had no cause to fear for her, because she lived for her and would act for her happiness's dear sake.

When Fersen drove her to Pompeii she was fearful that the Duchess should think her so strange, so light, to feel anything like partiality, after what she had lately saved her from. What this was may be conjectured from a later allusion to an importunate wooer whose identity is masked by the letter 'H'.

The other morning, Bess continues, Count Fersen came before the other gentlemen who generally came to walk or drive with them, and she confided in him that she was very uneasy at the part her father played in politics. She asked if the King of Sweden had mentioned him, and the Count replied that 'he had — a good deal'.^{C} Another King — George III — was also mentioning the Earl-Bishop a good deal in secret correspondence with his ministers, describing his conduct as factious if not treasonable, and himself as 'this wicked prelate': but this Bess could not know. She put forward the view that her father's 'unfortunate uncertainty of character influenced him in everything even in her own marriage and situation'. When she told him that she was not allowed to write to her children, Fersen burst into tears. 'I was *émue*,' she writes; and she begged his pardon for loading him with such things. She was indeed *émue*, not only by his sympathy but also by his restraint — so unlike her former admirer, 'H.', who had immediately sought to endanger her principles by the wildest expressions of the most violent passion!

Georgiana in her reply urged Bess to come back to England without delay; and Bess responded with alacrity. She was well enough to return; she would return. And though she could but little contribute to the happiness of her friends because she was a foolish little thing, the mite she could contribute she would. The parable of the Widow's Mite was familiar to the Devonshire House circle, and the Prince Regent himself modestly invoked it when assessing his own share in the events leading up to the downfall of Napoleon.

During this visit to Naples Angelica Kauffmann painted the head of her picture of Bess[21] in a broad shady hat — the figure being finished later in Rome. The pretty, pensive face half shadowed by the hat seems to reveal something of the wearer's mind at this time. She was full of fears. Supposing someone should attempt again to reconcile her and her husband? Charlotte, too, was a source of uneasiness. The unattractive little girl had not, she felt, improved in any respect as she had hoped that she might. There were moments when her constant — and, indeed, very necessary — presence seems to have rasped on Bess's nerves. When she escaped from it by going to a masquerade, she felt 'very low' afterwards.

But had the Duchess really nothing to fear? The next passage in the letters suggests that Fersen had made a deeper impression upon the heart of Bess than she herself would acknowledge.

> You know the person I have so long named to you — the other evening he
> was a little while alone with me, and I was very low, and leaning on a chair with
> both my hands on the frame and my head resting on them. He stooped down

Lady Elizabeth Foster, painted
by Angelica Kauffman in 1784.

and kissed my hands, and at last — oh, dearest G — my cheek. Pray, pray, don't
be angry. I neither started nor was angry, but took his hand and said, 'This must
never be again.' He said 'No' — he was very melancholy — so was I.[22C]

The next day he drove her out and again 'owned his regret that he had not met
her before her fate was decided'. 'I think better of him', she wrote, 'than anybody
I have ever seen.' Thereafter until they parted he never ceased to reiterate, with
tears in his eyes, '*I only ask you never to forget me, and always to do justice to my*
feelings'.[C]

No wonder the Duchess was worried. And to add to her tremors it was
reported that the Prince of Wales was going abroad. 'If', she wrote to Bess, 'he
comes anywhere near you I shall write to you volumes to guard you.'[C]
Two years later Fersen paid his second visit to England — the earlier had
been in 1774–75. Bess was then abroad, and the Duchess wrote to her describing
her excitement at first seeing him and piously thanking God that she herself is
not in love with him. As it was well known that 'Mrs B.'[23] liked him, there was
disappointment in this country because he was not spectacularly good-looking,

Count Axel Fersen.

but it was allowed that he had delightful eyes and a most gentlemanlike air. He and the Duke seem to have avoided each other by tacit consent, for Canis merely peeped at him and he merely peeped at Canis — through the jalousies, when His Grace was out riding.

In March 1784, Bess received from Georgiana a letter which must have given her food for much anxious thought. In it the Duchess reveals her 'long-kept secret' that she is in desperate straits for money. Canis must not know that she has told her. She must give no hint to him that she knows that everything that has come to her had flowed from him. She cannot name the total sum — 'many, many thousands'. The 'little expense' caused by Bess is like a drop of water in this sea. A month later Georgiana was again begging her to come home. She was certain that poor Canis's health and spirits depended upon her soothing friendship. He was urging her to write to Bess; he was asking why she would not come. She should, he declared, return for the winter, and for the summer months Chatsworth was as good a climate as any.

This letter was written during the turmoil of the famous Westminster election of April 1784, when both the Dowager Lady Spencer and her son-in-law the Duke were shocked and distressed at the activity with which the Duchess and her sister, Lady Duncannon, had gone canvassing for Charles James Fox. The story that the Duchess bought a vote from a butcher with a kiss may not have been true, but it went all round London and was almost everywhere believed. No wonder that poor Canis required soothing.

After some hesitations and delays Bess set off. Mr Gibbon wrote to Lady Sheffield that 'the Eliza' had passed through Lausanne on her road from Italy to England 'poorly in health, but still adorable'. He had enjoyed some delightful hours at her bedside. In July the travellers arrived, and the Duchess wrote to Mama that 'Lady E.' would first go down to Ickworth, while she herself brought Charlotte to Newmarket. Bess's educational methods had in one way proved their worth; Charlotte spoke French and Italian fluently and was 'vastly clever'.[C]

Before long, Lady Elizabeth was once more an integral part of the Devonshire House circle. Her *flamme* for Count Fersen seems to have burnt itself out and the Duke remained in sole possession of the field. Later, when writing down some circumstances connected with the flight to Varennes, she omitted to mention that Count Fersen, dressed as a coachman, had driven the lumbering yellow berline which had so nearly carried the French Royal Family to safety. In September 1791 he wrote to her, laying the blame for the sufferings of that family upon the 'silence and ambiguity' of England: she mentions this quite simply, without comment, nor does the report that he is going to serve in the Duke of York's expedition in 1793 kindle any faint spark of the old fire. In July 1810 she either kept no journal or destroyed what she had kept. Perhaps she had lost interest in him when she became convinced that, as Bonaparte put it rather crudely, he went to bed with the Queen; but surely she cannot have heard unmoved of the cruel death at the hands of a Stockholm mob of him whom she had once called the 'very, very amiable Count F.'.

Lady Elizabeth, for all her frail beauty and her soft, caressing ways, was a pertinacious woman. In spite of many rebuffs she continued to woo the Dowager Lady Spencer assiduously. In a long postscript to a letter written by the Duchess in October 1784, she expatiates upon the beauty of their 'dear little Lady Georgiana', who now (at the age of one year and three months) 'distinguishes letters and aims at words'; she avows her anxious desire that the Duchess should have a son; and assures the Dowager that when writing about her friend she feels that she has a claim on *her*, and owns that she is irresistibly attached to her with all a daughter's affection.

The Dowager's response could hardly have been more frigid. In her next letter she prays the Duchess to thank 'Lady Eliz.' for her postscript and adds that from the account Lord Spencer gives her of that lady's cough she could not help wishing she were 'safe in a warmer climate'. She hints bodingly at the November fogs in England; asks if Charlotte is to go abroad again; fears that the child's little head might be turned by a foreign education; and finally conjectures hopefully that

'Lady Eliz.' will try to instil as much solidity and humility into her as she can.[24]

Not until the end of the year did Bess leave England, and when she went Charlotte did not go with her. She was pregnant, and the Duke of Devonshire was the father of the child.

As the Duchess was also expecting a baby in the summer of 1785, the triangle was becoming more and more peculiar. And Lady Duncannon was yet another hopeful mama that year.

The diary-keeping habit had taken so firm a hold upon Lady Elizabeth that even in deep distress she did not wholly relinquish it. After an interval of several months she began at Turin on March 25th, 1785, a Journal which is also an intimate fragment of autobiography. Her flowery phrases remind us now and then that she was a student of *La Nouvelle Héloise*, to say nothing of *Les Liaisons Dangereuses*; but in the main it is a candid and moving chronicle, and bears upon many of its pages the marks of almost intolerably poignant truth.

After four months spent at Paris in all the amusements which the best society and the gayest court could afford us, how does my situation hang over me like impending ruin! — And how have I spent these four months? In shutting my eyes on all that could reveal what I apprehended, and giving way to illusions: in preserving indeed entire my faith and love so lately given and proved to the D. of D——e[25] but in listening to the attachment of the D. of D.[26] and not encouraging it — that I never did — but I allowed him, whilst I declared I could not love him otherwise than as a friend, to cherish a warmer sentiment for me — I suppose that woman's vanity requires more fortitude than we like to exert to resist it — in surmounting or resisting a great passion we know how much merit will be attributed to us, and this flattering our pride supports our courage, but in suppressing the little movements of vanity which actuate us to the attainment of what we think adds to our glory, the merit is all secret, known but to ourselves, and remains unadorned with any trophy to grace our success.

I have felt less vanity since my love for the D. of D——e and I think if I know my own heart, had I been his, or could I live near him, I should feel no desire of conquest — but my isolated situation and continual absence from him, my privation of all the ties so natural to a heart like mine, particularly the loss of my Children, the only one which my fate allowed me to feel the tenderness of, all have exposed me at times to give way to the pernicious desire of attaching people to me — yet even this desire whilst I was with the D. of D——e was quite annihilated within me so totally did I love him. — I left Paris with the tenderest friendship for Madame de Polignac who I have every reason to think has the same for me; with gratitude to the Queen who has loaded me with distinctions; and with the satisfaction of seeing myself regretted by all those I had known.

My brother[27] had joined us before we left Paris, and I had hoped my amiable but unhappy sister-in-law, would be eased of the uneasiness my Brother's infidelities had caused her. But now I see nothing but the overthrow of the fair fabric of fame and character I had raised to myself in the world, of comfort and consolation to my mother and family, joy and pleasure to my friends — despair has seized on my mind. Once I had resolved to hazard all, and at Lyons to entrust Miss A. —— with my secret; and I tremble to think it came through my mind to try by exercise to destroy the cause of my fears. — I weighed the criminality of the act with the great object of saving my mother, family, and friends from the sorrow I should bring on them — again I made an offering of all to God — yet praying I might be spared. — At La Pailliasse I fainted away — I thought fatigue had operated what I could not voluntarily do — but my misfortune was but ripening — and from the moment my babe had life tho' sorrow did not forsake me, yet tenderness often blunted the sting.

We arrived at Lyons — I saw Miss A. — settled her affairs, made her happy, but could tell nothing and continued miserable. My soul could not yet stoop to be in any one's power — oh God — oh God! We left Lyons the 13th — the first day I felt a kind of calm, which I attributed to having resigned myself — I resolved to trust to fatigue and looked on all suffering as trivial compared to the horror of ignominy — 14th — arrived at Chambéry; went the 16th — and after incredible fatigue on the Alps in taking care of my little niece, we arrived at Turin 23d. I arrived heated, ill, and exhausted. I was blooded — deceived my Physician out of necessity — it was a miracle so copious a bleeding did not occasion a miscarriage — I half hoped, half dreaded it — Nature as if to torture me more, spoke all a Mother's language within me — Alas, alas, my soul was ever open to her dictates! could I be forgot by the world I would none thee, my child, and bless thy birth, and he who gave it thee; but to have thee born to Heaven knows what fate, a misfortune perhaps to thyself and others, nay, not daring to own thee, yet anxious for thy safety — oh till this hour I knew not what misfortune was.

Oh, may thy too dear, too beloved Father never know the pangs which rend my heart.

My acquaintance at Turin receive me with joy and every mark of distinction and attention — The English Minister scarcely leaves us and speaks already the language of gallantry. My heart is dead to all and longs only for obscurity and retirement. At times I would have told my brother — then I could not — dared not — and I resolved to suffer in silence and try my fate till Naples. — 27th we left Turin — arrived at Milan 29th — go out, see company — all civil to me, but I am wretched — oh God, great God — what shall I do——

Florence April 6th

Every day increases my torment and misery — I know not how to bear up under such oppressive circumstances — the dread I have of my situation being known makes me endure bodily fatigue and pain that would seem impossible to me at another time.

On the 4th — when we arrived here — we spent all the night under the town walls, in our carriage: but I feel to deserve all suffering and I ought not to complain — the worst is to me the praise I meet with, the esteem and consideration of all those who knew me when I travelled through Italy alone and yet escaped all dangers. They know not how I have fallen — oh, ondeserved praise is death to my heart. I dread a confinement I may not be able to conceal — yet my soul yearns to cherish the dear Babe I bear. Oh I could bear all but giving my mother pain. She has had sorrows enough. I know not what to do. Oh, God pity me. How could I bear to let the D, of Dorset be attach'd to me, to think me virtuous![28] I shall write to tell him I don't deserve his love.

Would I could fly the face of human kind — yet I could not bear not to see my loved friend again. She has been my comfort and happiness, tho' her unthinking kindness has hurried me down the precipice. Perhaps she thought I was still attached to the Comte Fersen — I did like him once, never as I do D.D., never was led an instant to what even now I wish I had not done. I then thought D.D. indifferent to me, that his former love had only been a sensual one. Yet even so, the thought of him was a check to my feelings, and the desire of his esteem was more than prudence or principle to me. Oh me — oh me—

Pisa — 12th [April]

Went every day to the Cashine with Ldy Hervey where I had walked formerly when unhappy, but not wretched as now. Would I could have opened my heart to her as she did to me! We sat on the banks of the Arno watching the stream as it glided along, gathering violets and wandering along that charming wood which forms so beautiful a solitude — the Country Girls weaving the straw hats was our only interruption, and the solemn creaking of the lofty Pines the only noise besides the Arno—

Leghorn — 13 —

Beautiful Country — but nothing can please or soothe me—

Rome — 16th

After a fatiguing journey we arrived here, at Rome where I had bought 'golden opinions' from all ranks of men.[29] I had never strayed from any rule Virtue or prudence cd. suggest — every principle was strong within me and I felt all the delight of self-approbation — and now — yet my heart is not changed — still I love Virtue tho' I have wandered from it. The Cardinal de Bernis shewed me if possible more kindness and affection than ever, more tender and real pleasure at seeing me — all have testified regard, partiality and esteem. Oh I could feel comfort did I not feel shame! All that woman's vanity can wish for I meet with — but can praise and adulation silence the true tho' secret voice of conscience? I should think myself an hypocrite to speak the sentiments so little suited to my faults, did not my heart remain unalter'd, and my severest judge.

Sometimes I look at myself in the glass with pity. Youth, beauty, I see I have; friends I know I have; reputation I still have; and perhaps in two months, friends, fame, life and all future peace may be destroyed and lost for ever to me. If so, my proud soul will never, never return to England — Cruel friend — when I could not stay to be supported and comforted by you, should you have plunged me in such misery? But it was not his fault. Oh no — his nature is noble, kind, tender, honourable, and affectionate. Passion has led us both away — his heart suffers for me I know—

Naples May 4.

We left Rome the 2d and after a fatiguing journey arrived at 4 this morning — My companions, dred and impatient, could not conceal their being so, and I had in this instance a new proof of Shakespeares just remark, 'where the greater malady is, the lesser is scarcely felt.[30] So I — the weakest, in a bad state of health, and in a situation to increase each corporal pain, yet from the greater pain of my mind, suffered with patience, and bore all in silent suffering. God knows how all will end — *in un mare di tante pene, sventurata che farò*[31] — may I at least escape causing sorrow to my Mother, and I shall be resigned.

Arrived a courier from the Dss. — nothing particular — A long letter from the D. but mysterious from necessity — my heart wanted the comfort of reading the expressions of his tenderness, but prudence forbid his writing them — patience, oh, my soul — he tries to encourage and support me.

16th

The courier goes — I can no longer calm the agitation of my mind — dangers seem to multiply around me — my shape increases every day — my health grows weaker — I know not what will become of me — How I long for the solitude of Ischia———

23d

I have been ill several days. My God, my God assist me — help me to hide my shame and sorrow from the friends it would afflict — I must undeceive the D. of Dorset in his opinion of me — it is too good a one — yet how do it, and not endanger my secret? I hate to deceive — yet here it is a virtue. What can be greater misery to a feeling and delicate mind than to lose the Virtue it cannot cease to love?

June 11. We dined at Mr. Morris's at Portici — suffered here both bodily and mentally — the heat intolerable and the conversation was all concerning the misfortunes of Lady Ossory,[32] with a thousand observations and remarks on such a situation as hers was, the cleverness of some women in concealing their being with child, with all that she went thro' and that she said herself that she scarcely knew how to support her misery — that she read without understanding what she read, and that she had lost all repose — and all this I was obliged to listen to with an appearance of tranquility and with a distracted mind — what will become of me? I do not, cannot guess — but all must end soon — to be away too from him, for whom I suffer — Oh heavens, have pity on me——

Ischia June 21.
I left Naples yesterday with my Brother, and came to this little Island which I am not perhaps to leave except deprived of life or honour — my sister-in-law, and my little niece cried at taking leave of me, but it was without knowing what I was going to be exposed to. The passage was tedious — we did not arrive till midnight. The night was fine, the sky clear — no noise around but the rude voice of the Sailors, and the splashing of the sea against our boat — I scarcely uttered a syllable — I could not — the fatigue was almost too much for me in my situation. My Brother's kind attention supported [me] and I concealed from him my despair — At last we landed and wandered a little while on the coast, the other boat with the servts. not being arriv'd. How beautifully serene the sky! — Arrived at the house we eat a little morsel[33] to recruit our strength, and threw ourselves half dressed on beds not ready to receive us. Today at ½ past 9. he left me I could not check my tears, though I concealed the cause from him — I remained in bed as stunned with my situation — At last I rose — I am then alone — a prey to the most bitter reflexions, an almost broken heart, and a mind in despair — Miss Ash[34] is to come in a few days — I think I shall trust her with what as yet no one knows — I must exert myself — another month must I pass thus — what will become of me and the innocent creature I bear? Heaven have mercy on me and relieve my torments — this Island is beautiful and tranquil — I shall wander about, sometimes perhaps find relief, but cannot find rest——

July 10th, 1785 —
It is done — I am in the power of my servant, and I have caused sorrow and grief to a beloved Brother — the 7th I told Louis of my danger — we consulted on the necessary measures I had to take — he went the next day with a letter

to my Brother — he received my confession with kindness and tenderness and will come to soothe me — but I must quit my little island — I am observed here, known by the Poor, and some workmen I had employed to cut seats in the rock, by the Peasants who used to conduct me about the Country — besides different families from Naples are expected: I am not safe here — I must expose myself to new fatigues and dangers. Weak and ill how shall I support these Last days passed in such fatigue and pain? For I must go near 100 miles at sea and in an open boat — I must go amongst strangers, perhaps leave my Infant with them. Patience, patience; my punishment is just — 'tis even gentle. My Brother is kind — my Servant faithful — and perhaps the Almighty will protect and save me from disgrace and infamy — I can bear all but that — and the loss of his love for whom I have sacrificed myself. — How calm the Sea is — it scarce is heard as it beats against the rocks. the air is perfum'd with herbs, the sky is clear, at a distance blazes Vesuvius — oh, were I happy!

11th

My dear Brother came to see me — we were a long time without speaking, clasped in each other's arms — we passed the day in forming plans and settling our excursion — he is not very well — As for me I could not — dared not name the dear Author of my child's existence———

12th

My Brother has left me — I felt comforted by his tenderness, but weak and oppressed———

13th

Not well. Oh, how full of fears I feel———

16th

Better again — a year today that I left Paris to return to England. How different then my situation! Oh, what would I give these few remaining days of trial and expectation were passed and to see an end one way or the other to the dreadful state in which I find myself———

18th

Today a year that I landed in England — Oh, sad remembrance for me now———

nessun maggior dolore[35]

How different the times———

Lady Elizabeth Foster,
by Ozias Humphreys.

19th

A year today that I was restored to my beloved friends — Oh, I felt that the D.D. had ever influenced my conduct — 'Tis true I thought myself attached, I was attached to Count Fersen: yet nothing could efface the impression the other had made. My return proved it too well — Could I have foreseen the ills that awaited me, I believe I should have avoided those dear friends, tho' so tenderly loved. I am better in health — but my mind feels terrified——

> *Mi dispera il passato*
> *Il presenta m'opprime*
> *L'Avenire mi Spaventa*——[36]

Tomorrow I expect my brother. Sometimes I own I dread the thoughts of dying — dying without the comforts of friends, far from those I love, with the fear of shame, leaving my beloved Child as soon as born, and surrounded by strangers — the fear of a discovery is the worst of all — the dread of adding to my Mother's sorrows, and causing grief to my family and friends — oh God, protect me.[D]

July 22nd.

    I go — the boat waits for me — God protect and assist me———

From Ischia, Bess had written to Georgiana a 'secret letter' which appears to have been destroyed. Whatever its gist may have been, it made the recipient the happiest of creatures and made 'poor Canis a very happy dog, too'. The Duchess's gayer mood is pleasantly reflected in the anecdote of the Prince of Wales's newly appointed courier, who said, 'I had rather have belonged to Lady E. Foster — I *aime* her so much.'[C]

On July 12th the Duke wrote to 'Dearest Bess' very happy to hear that she is in better spirits, but is in the utmost impatience to hear how Ischia agrees with her.[C] She had been asking him what was said about her in England, and he answered that all that he has heard has been in her praise; but if she has heard of something that has been said of 'a contrary nature' he hopes she has philosophy enough not to be distressed with it, but to bear patiently the fate which is hers in common with all other people— 'at least with all those who don't pass their lives in obscurity'. He had nothing more to say to 'Mrs Bess', except to reiterate his impatience to hear that Ischia agreed with her (probably a code sentence to announce the birth of their child) and to assure her that absence could never lessen his friendship and affection for her.

On August 4th he is complaining that he has not heard from her this great while, and imparting the information that the Rat was so big she could hardly waddle, and thought she would have twins. If that should happen, he says, 'we intend to make you a present of one of them'. They were going to Chiswick and were very unhappy not to have her 'monkey's face' with them there. Affectionate allusions to her 'monkey's face' or to herself as a '*Simia*' often occur in the letters of her friends. They suggest that there might be a puckish as well as a pathetic quality about her beauty at times, but few of her portraits show this unless it be the mop-headed one by Reynolds painted in the year 1788 and now at Chatsworth.

It was from Chatsworth that later in this same month of August the Duke wrote to 'Dearest Bess', describing with unexpected ardour how much he missed her there. 'The Rat', too unwieldy to take the journey, had been left behind in London, and the Duke, alone in the great magnificent house, was constantly reminded of his absent mistress. In the drawing-room he saw the couch on which she used to sit, surrounded by her sighing lovers. He strayed into her bedroom, and gazed at the blue bed in which she used to sleep. If he went out, he saw her pony, 'little Mr Phaon', at grass in the park. He informs her that he is going to shoot at Bolton Abbey, if he can find time, and that he will then prepare the place for her against next summer, when he proposes to take her there whether she likes it or not, let the consequence be what it will.

In his next letter he is still impatient for news, obviously uneasy, and peremptorily demanding a very circumstantial account of herself and all her plans. He had, he observes, told her some time ago, in answer to some question of hers, that he had heard no reports concerning her. This, he now confesses, was not strictly true, though pretty nearly so, for he had heard very few, and those few were only the same kind of things that were said at Chatsworth concerning her and himself, and by the same people, or, at least, by people who were there at the same time. He ends 'the foreign post has just come in and I cannot bear not having a letter from you — Good-night, dear Mrs. Bess'.[C] A postscript informs her that after a long labour the Duchess has been brought to bed of a girl. This was Harriet,[37] self-dubbed Hary-O, that solid, forthright, implacable, authentic Cavendish, who, perhaps because she took so markedly after his side of the family, was never a favourite with her father. Time, and a happy deliverance from the Devonshire House environment when it had been made painful by her beloved mother's death, released her better qualities, her wit, her intelligence, her fidelity in love and friendship: but she was in her youth a very prickly young person indeed.

'Mrs Bess' was now upon the verge of such woes as would have wrung her lover's heart to hear. She could not even set them down in English, but upon September 4th she began to write her Journal in French.

It would be hard for any pen to depict the terrible condition in which I passed three weeks after quitting Ischia — I took leave of my maid and of Madlle A. with an indescribable pang in my heart. As I went sadly away I looked back at the little retreat which I had hoped might be my place of refuge. My knees trembled under me and it seemed to me that either I should never see these people and this shore again or that I should see them when I myself was tarnished and dishonoured. — The moment draws near — the boat, thrust onward by a wave, moves towards the shore — I climb aboard with difficulty, half-fainting — my brother follows, and clasps me in his arms. Faithful Louis leaps aboard, and fixes a sad gaze upon me. We set sail — the land recedes from our eyes — my servants walk slowly up to my deserted house — and I am on the open sea, expecting the final moment of pregnancy. We touched at the Island of Procida to deceive the crew; we said we wanted to go to Capri. But presently the wind began to rise, forced us to change our plans, and bore us far from the Cape of Sorrento.

Sea-sickness was added to her sorrows, but her brother supported and comforted her. Next day she was so exhausted they had to halt at un *petit endroit* for refreshment and repose.

We had to set off again. We decided that I should change boats at Marsa, where I would embark with Louis only, and that my brother would not visit me till two days later. We thought that by then everything would be over.

It was a terrible moment. I had to part from this dear brother of mine not knowing whether I should ever see him again — I had to pass myself off as the wife of Louis and, in a condition which needed so much care, I had to submit to a thousand discomforts — However, I resolved to risk anything to hide my fault and to spare my family the sorrow of my shame. I gave my beloved medallion,[38] to my brother and parted from him with despair in my heart.

We reached the little harbour of Salerno — I was still very ill and weak. We hired a *calèche* and arrived at Vietri.[39] We had to go downhill to reach the street where our '*Archi-Prêtre*' lived.

The term *Archi-Prêtre* gives a grim clue to the functions of the proprietor of that sinister and ambiguous abode.

My heart almost failed me as I traversed the little streets, narrow and dim, leaning on my servant and compelled to pass myself off as his wife and the light o' love of my lord and brother. With no woman at hand, encumbered by the weight of my child, enfeebled by long ill health, fearing every person I met, and, for the first time in my life, wishing only to hide myself, I arrived at last.

Imagine a little staircase, dark and dirty, leading to the apartments of these people. The family consisted of the *Archi-Prêtre des Amoureux*; his woman-servant, a coarse, ugly, and filthy creature; the doctor, (his brother) and his wife — the doctor an honest man, the wife everything that one can imagine of wicked, vulgar and horrible; two young girls, pretty enough but weeping all day; a married elder sister — who was the best of the lot; the nurse who was to take charge of my child; and some babies which cried from morning till night — there you have the family of the respectable *Archi-Prêtre*, who had a sort of seraglio round him.

We entered. They clustered about me, and, seeing how weak I was, they installed me on a sofa, but could not refrain from making a thousand comments upon myself and my supposed husband. Some of these remarks related to my being his master's mistress — I was too delicately beautiful for a valet's wife. 'Look', they said, 'her features are more royal than the Queen's[40] — what modesty and sweetness!'

I heard everything but pretended to understand nothing. I wished to escape from their comments and went to bed — but not to sleep. My faithful servant wept for me and wept that he was compelled to forget that he was my servant in the familiar terms upon which we had to live. — How many things increased my unhappiness! I had to dine with him, and to endure the odious company of these people; I had to live in a house which was little better than a house of ill fame.

My brother came to see me. We wrote letters to Naples, full of imaginary incidents[41] — everyone was taken in and believed us to be a hundred and fifty miles from where we were.

A week passed, and I was much troubled at having to part from my brother before my confinement. I had moments of acute pain, when I prayed to God with bitter tears to end my sufferings. Every moment I expected to hear that everything was discovered. It was a terrible moment for both of us when I had to part from my brother. I gave him a letter — all my papers were in order — I waited patiently for death, regretting only my child, and its father, and my friend.[42]

Fifteen days were passed in waiting — and at last, just as I was thinking of looking for another refuge, on August 16, at 9 o'clock in the morning, after strong but short pains, I gave birth to a daughter.[D]

Eighteen years later she wrote in her Journal on that date Prospero's words to Miranda:[43]

> O, a cherubim
> Thou wast, that did preserve me! Thou didst smile
> Infusèd with a fortitude from Heaven
> When I have decked the sea with drops full salt,
> Under my burden groaned; which raised in me
> An undergoing stomach to bear up
> Against what should ensue.

CHAPTER III

Caroline and Clifford — Selina Trimmer — Versailles — 1785–1789

The little daughter to whom Elizabeth Foster gave birth in the squalid den at Vietri was welcomed by her as warmly as 'the little brown girl' born at Devonshire House in the same month and year was welcomed by the Duchess.

> ... the moment I took her in my arms I felt only a mother's tenderness. With tears in my eyes I commended her to God. I kissed her — I conned her features — weak as I was, I took her into the bed and tended her myself, seeing the ignorance of those about me.[D]

She was torn to and fro by a strange conflict of feelings; sometimes she was almost ready to risk discovery in order to keep the child with her; then a vision of her own mother in tears gave her the strength to part from the baby. So rapid was her recovery, she thought it almost miraculous; and on August 22nd, at six o'clock in the morning, she quitted Vietri in a wretched hired conveyance and went first to Castellamare.

To leave the child behind nearly broke her heart, even though it was to be only for a fortnight. She put no faith in the fair promises of the people with whom she left her, and she flung herself 'quivering and weary' into the corner of the *calèche*; but she was not so weary that she did not hear and remember the remarks of the peasants to whom she said that she was a Calabrian. 'No,' they answered, 'you are too beautiful and too fair — there is none like you in Calabria.'

At last she reached her brother's house at Naples and was received by her sister-in-law in a manner which at once assured her that nothing was known. The faithful Louis brought her flannels for her breasts every day, and everything else necessary to hide the traces of her recent experience; she took back into her service the maidservant whom she had formerly dismissed; and on September 6th she noted with excitement that Louis had gone to fetch her little daughter. It was a hard moment when she knew that the child was so near and yet might not be seen by her; it was harder still when she discovered how badly it had been neglected. But it was now in good hands, and Louis went to see it every day.

On September 23rd the Duke wrote to 'Mrs Bess' that it was impossible for anybody to be more uneasy than he was for many months about her, but knowing that she was apt to think everything worse than it really was, he thought it best not to assist her in magnifying 'any disagreeable circumstance'.[C] She had, it seems, reproached him for being too much at his ease!

'Mrs Bess' was more resilient than he realized. Mingled with pathetic entries about her baby are such interjections as 'The fleet is in port — a magnificent sight' or 'The Queen overwhelms me with distinctions.'

Lord Bessborough's recent researches when editing the Duchess's letters have brought to light the hitherto unknown origin of the surname home by Lady Elizabeth's daughter — St Jules. A certain Comte St Jules, then living at Aix en Provence, was apparently willing to be regarded as the father. Of Christian names the infant received three — Caroline Rosalie Adelaide. Another Caroline was playing with her coral in the winter of 1785 — the pretty elf to whom Harriet Duncannon gave birth on November 13th. On September 10th Bess went by stealth to visit her baby. Were its temporary guardians deceived by the story that this gracious agitated lady was the 'protectress' of her manservant's child? Her emotion must have been obvious when, seeing how the delicate little limbs had been chafed by neglect, she ordered that finer linen should be obtained without delay.

Having once held Caroline in her arms it was impossible for Bess to keep away from her. 'Sometimes', she writes,

> I go to see her as her protectress in her own house, sometimes I arrange that she shall be taken for solitary walks where I myself go on horseback, and where I dismount and gather her into my arms.[D]

She wavers once more upon the question of the child's immediate future, but fearing the arrival of her father, the Earl-Bishop, she followed the agreed plan and allowed Louis to take Caroline away and place her in the care of his own family.

A fortnight later she is ashamed of herself because she is allowing the Russian Ambassador to make love to her. 'Misfortune', she says ruefully, 'cannot cure me of my vanity', and it is, she declares, only from vanity and from lack of other interests that she encourages the amorous but amusing envoy. His excessive passion flatters her — but ought she to be flattered? 'Oh, non!'[D]

On December 8th she played the harpsichord at a concert, and while she was actually sitting at the instrument a letter from Fred North[44] was handed to her, saying that Louis's journey and the cause of it were both known, but that a report had been spread that it was Lord Hervey's child. 'I almost fainted,' she confesses.

Lord and Lady Spencer were then at Naples, and Bess wrote to the Duchess a slightly malicious description of her ladyship's deportment when they both called upon her. Georgiana, who had little liking for her sister-in-law Lavinia, must have been vastly diverted by Lady Spencer seeming to raise herself three feet in order to look down on Bess, almost turning her back on her while she addressed all her conversation to the Ambassadress, and then departing without a civil word. When they met again the next day that most supercilious of women passed by with a toss of her head and a brief, perfunctory curtsy.[C]

A few weeks later Lady Elizabeth records, amongst other social gossip, that George III's unsatisfactory brother, the Duke of Cumberland, is in Naples with his vixenish Duchess, *née* Anne Luttrell. 'He seems', she says, 'to be in love with me — one cannot be suspected of encouraging him.'[45] There was also the attentive and sympathetic 'Captain B.' — clever, entertaining, extremely ugly and *guère dangereux*.[C] Perhaps it was because she distrusted her own fortitude that she welcomed an invitation from the Earl-Bishop to spend Holy Week with him in Rome.

If it were not for the abundant corroborative evidence one might be inclined to dismiss all these stories of eminent persons sighing like furnaces as the wishful thinking of a vain and self-deluding woman, but that evidence is overwhelming, and cannot be discounted.

During the first half of 1786 she moved about Italy, admiring prospects, contemplating fragments of antiquity, and gradually recovering her usual, though never very robust, health. On May 16th the Duke wrote to 'Dearest Bess' that whatever happens to her in other respects he is sure she has no reason to despond so much, at least if she is as much attached to them as she used to be and as much, she might depend upon it, as they would always be to her, at all times and in all situations. 'The Rat', he says, 'does not know the chief cause of your uneasiness and I, of course, shall never mention it to her unless you desire me, but I am certain that if she did she could not think you had   been to blame about it after I had explained to her how the thing happened."[C]

At Rome, wrote Bess later, when summarizing these months for which no detailed Journal seems to have been kept,

> my attention and feelings were chiefly occupied for others, distress at my father's strange conduct, which made him be censured, the desire to obtain something from him for my brother, the anxiety of my sister-in-law to soothe, and the future interests of my younger brother to manage.[D]

The elder brother, Lord Hervey, was causing his wife much distress by his intrigue with a youthful Neapolitan beauty, the wife of Prince Roccafionta: but it is to be feared that his strayings from the narrow path led him in other directions as well; otherwise how was he able to guide his second sister to the lair of the *Archi-Prêtre des Amoureux* at Vietri?

At the end of May the family party dispersed, and Bess set out for Venice in company with Mrs Anne Seymour Damer, the future inheritrix of Strawberry Hill and one of the least *simpatica* of the figures upon the contemporary scene, in spite of her undeniable talents as a sculptress and her undoubted woes as a wife.

'At Cento', writes Bess, 'I had the misfortune to be in the same house with my father without his consenting to see me.'[D] She described the episode more fully in a letter to Georgiana. 'Poor dear Frederick came out and said, "He won't see you."'[C] He could not bear the agitation of knowing her in the house — if she came back he would be injured by it — the least anxiety brought about a return of the complaint in his bowels. He would not even put her up for the night *without* seeing her.[C]

In June, Bess wrote from Venice to the Duchess in her most emotional vein. She could not live away from her; they were losing the most precious thing in their lives by being separate. The hint of a possible threefold meeting at Spa had made her half wild with delight, but it never materialized, and, disembarking at Southampton a month later, she continued the story in her Journal.

I landed with transport — Alas, my heart, too fondly devoted to the D. of D. forgot all past sufferings and felt nothing but joy. My friend[46] was at Southampton — I fear I was glad. I arrive — he had dined out but left a note; he came; Oh, heavens, such moments do indeed efface past sorrows! — yet it was happiness mixed with fear and agitation——[D]

A strange, incoherent, staccato chronicle follows. We see Bess making Lady Melbourne's acquaintance and liking her much. We witness the 'sad scene' when Georgiana had to tell the 'D.' that she had again lost an immense sum. 'How nobly, kindly, touchingly did he behave.' We learn incidentally that General Fitzpatrick[47] is inclined to make love to Bess; he was also inclined to make love to Lady Bessborough, and his heart was not fixed upon either lady. Now Sheridan accuses her of being in love with 'the D.'. Now she confesses to having been capricious, jealous, and quarrelsome with her lover, who none the less found it in his heart to forgive her. 'Every day', she writes, 'my tenderness for him increased and so, I think, did his confidence and affection for me. We wish for Caroline, but know not what to do.'[D]

Still wooing the Dowager Lady Spencer, Bess wrote to her in August apologizing for the apprehension she had had the misfortune to cause by a recent illness. She mentions that their dear little Georgiana was on her lap, 'laughing and amusing herself as usual'.[C]

Another crisis soon arose in the chequered life of the Duchess, whose long-suffering if unfaithful husband now decided that a five years' exile from his hearth, if spent in seclusion and economy, might correct (if not cure) her follies. The Spencers offered to harbour her at Althorp, but fond though she was of her brother, she wilted in the presence of her sister-in-law Lavinia, nee Bingham, that woman of strong character and decided views, who seems to have been able to win and hold the affection only of her husband and her children — an important qualification but not helpful to Georgiana. No wonder that the Duchess pleaded that she might go instead to her 'dearest M.' at St Albans. In the event the Duke dropped the plan — only to revert to it later in a more drastic form.

It was during this year, 1786, that another crisis had arisen in the Duchess's life — an emotional crisis; her meeting with Charles Grey, the brilliant, good-looking boy seven years younger than she, who became, according to herself, her one and only lover. His leaving-portrait at Eton gives a better idea of what he must have been than the more familiar bald-headed statesman of later years, 'Grey of the Reform Bill', a bland and unromantic figure. Always sensitive to atmosphere, Bess knew that the tension had heightened between Canis and the Rat. She makes no explicit allusion to the cause of it, or to the scheme for separation, but it is impossible to resist the conclusion that it was owing to her mediation that things were patched up before the end of the year. Writing in February 1788, and looking back on the events preceding her second unhappy departure from England, she says that passion — her love for the Duke — could never make her forget the kindness of the Duchess, their mutual friendship, their 'strict ties':

Depositary of both their thoughts, I have sought, when her imprudences have alienated him, to restore him to her, and when my full heart has mourned over her avowal of his returning caresses, I have checked and corrected the sensation.[D]

In October 1786, the air at Chatsworth was clear again. The Duchess writes merrily to her mother that they had been out riding, and that 'Hare' had made them laugh.

He said to Bess, 'I wish you would fall in love with me.' And then he said, 'Tell me, because I must be in town the 29th.'

'Hare' was James Hare, wit and Whig MP 'The tallest, thinnest man I ever saw,' wrote Sir Augustus Clifford, 'his face like a surprised cockatoo, and as white.' The Duchess and Bess collaborated in a flowery, grandiloquent epitaph when he died, to the general regret of the Devonshire House circle, eighteen years later.

In July 1787 Bess was asking the Duchess to impart a great secret to the Dowager — namely that she had been able to secure a good post for her brother, Lord Hervey, who had been living abroad on nothing. When the Duke of Richmond mentioned that Mr Fawkener[48] was not going to Florence after all, she directly asked for her brother. The Duke promptly went to Mr Pitt and other Ministers; Lady Bristol, instigated by Bess, wrote to Pitt on behalf of her son. And that night the Duke of Richmond came to announce that the King had consented, and the thing was done. It must not, however, be talked about till they send officially for Hervey, as it is 'one of their best places, 2500 or 3000 a year'. Bess, a good sister if ever there was one, was 'wild with joy';[C] but why she should have expected the

John Augustus,
Lord Hervey, by
Gainsborough.

Dowager to be pleased — or even interested — it is not easy to determine, unless it were for the sake of poor Lady Bristol.

At this juncture the Duke of Richmond took his place in the long queue of Lady Elizabeth's admirers. This was the third Duke, a childless widower of fifty-three. At the Coronation of George III he had carried the sceptre with the dove; in 1765 he was appointed Ambassador Extraordinary to the French Court, and in 1782 he became Master General of the Ordinance. As late as 1796 the Earl-Bishop was making arch remarks about the Duke's admiration for his daughter, but Bess seems to have adhered to her first opinion — that it was impossible she should like him except as a friend.[49]

The breathless, disconnected story of that summer proceeds:

I go for a week to Tunbridge — return and am foolish and capricious because they dined out — but suffered severely by the D. taking it very ill of me. We made it up at Chiswick and have never quarrelled since — passed a happy week there — returned to town — my friend jealous of the D. of R — indeed without cause; how should I like him? We go to Bolton Abbey, a long-laid plan — a delightful journey, beautiful place and we are all happy and contented — but oh, I fear it was a fatal journey to me. After a week passed there, we returned to Chatsworth for a day and then to the Derby races — I staid two days and then was forced to leave them — I had no presentiment of my misfortune — but, alas, was I less culpable? I spent a month with my Mother at Ick. I soon had cause to apprehend my misfortune — I grew very ill — we came to town. Still ill.[D]

It must have been about this time that the Duke wrote to her from Chatsworth:

Your room here is very warm, and I believe you will be much safer from catching cold here than in London, especially as I hear you go to plays. Take care you do not catch cold by going with the coach-glasses down.

Yours, dearest Rack,

C.[C]

'Dearest Rack' can have had little heart for play-going. She had been forced to reveal her fears to her physician in London. The narrative hurries on:

I grew a little better and went to Chats. With what joy did we meet! Found only a few people there. Mr. S.[50] still observing to the Dss how attached I seemed to be to the D. It was a strange conduct in him!

The D. hardly knew the ill I had hinted to him, and asked me if it was really so. I confirmed it. We regret this new anxiety, but yet I felt a kind of pleasure that supported me. — How kind he was to me, how soothing and endearing![D]

They stayed in Bath, all three of them, for two months, and then after a week together in town it was decided that Bess, 'as if for her health', was to go abroad again. The Duke and the Duchess came to Dover to see her depart and stayed for two days. They walked together on the beach, and seemed, as she observed ruefully, to be 'actuated by the same sentiments'. When the Duchess embraced her,

oh, it was bitterness of grief to lose her — but him — his last embrace — his last look drew my soul after him — I remained motionless — even now, it is present to me. I see him — he is fixed in my heart — this guilty heart — Oh, why could I not love him without crime? Why cannot I be his without sin? My soul was made for virtue and not for vice.[D]

It would be rash to dismiss this as mere novelettish nonsense. It was an age of sentiment which when it was not hotly spiced was heavily sugared; but through these outpourings there runs none the less a narrow stream of genuine and poignant emotion. Taking stock of her feelings, she realizes that she hardly felt a pang that did not originate in absence from the Duke or fear of causing him pain. All other considerations had lost their power over her — he could tune her mind to joy or sorrow as he pleased. Yet at the same time she is angry with herself for 'plunging again into such errors'.[D]

This part of the summarized journal was written at St Quentin on September 4th. 'I live retired', she notes, 'for I fear all eyes. My little dog is all my comfort.' At Lyons on September 20th she sets down how she revealed the truth to her maid, Lucille.

Yesterday I told Lucille — for three days I had fixed each day as it came to do so — but still as she came into the room, my courage failed me — at last, last night just as I was going to bed I call'd her and told her — Heavens how my heart beat, how my voice trembled — Why, why, have I put myself in such situations, why reduce myself to esteem my own servant more than myself? She too is parted from her husband, is young, pretty, yet innocent — and I — and does not even my contrition come partly from fear?[D]

Her next halt was at Marseilles, where she spent five weeks receiving 'distinctions, attentions and marks of regard' which she did not deserve. In the meantime she was still a prey to remorse, complicated by a degree of calm self-assessment unusual in one so passionate.

I have great cause to be thankful and I am so — yet if it is a crime to love him for whom I have erred, I have that doubly to answer for: first as loving him with undiminished affection, and not wishing to love him less — Yesterday and today I had a return of vanity too. I looked in the glass, and seeing health and beauty returning to me, I felt glad, and wished I might be seen by *him* handsome as he had once thought me. This must be wrong in a creature so deep in error as I am — I try to turn my thoughts to resolving on no further connection with him at my return — but how rebellious are my thoughts![D]

On April 5th she went from Bordeaux to Toulon where she met the faithful Louis and settled everything with him for the removal of her 'little darling',

Caroline. Is it necessary to add that there was an attentive swain in the offing? It was the 'sensible and amiable Lord B.', but his attentions were 'irksome' to her.

Then, on April 26th, she had the desire of her heart — she saw her Caroline, whom she found 'gentle, lovely, and like her dear, too dear father'.

> It was by stealth I saw her — such are the consequences of errors, the Mother could only see her Child by stealth. Oh, how dear she is to my heart — how I gazed on her dear little innocent face and pressed her in my arms — she looked at me with an enquiring eye and did not shew any fear — oh, I could not have borne the misery of seeing her avoid me — Sweet Innocent — may the plan I have formed prove to thy advantage, as it promises. May I be enabled to watch over thee with a mother's fondness and anxiety, and compensate for the error which gave thee birth — Bless her, oh, my God, and punish not her with my faults.[D]

That prayer was both heard and granted, for never surely was there such a reconciler of clashing personalities as Caroline St Jules, of whom the Dowager Lady Spencer would write 'I love her and sincerely wish her happy', and for whom the affection of her mother's implacable enemy Harriet Cavendish would never wane to their life's end.

The next passage in the Journal reveals what was the 'plan': simply to install her with little Georgiana and Hary-O in the nurseries at Chatsworth and Devonshire House. It has been suggested that by acquiescing in this plan Duchess Georgiana purchased pardon from her husband both for her extravagance and her infidelity: but the next words of Bess herself do her more justice: 'My darling friend will be kind to her — oh, I know the goodness of her heart, she will be kind to her, and if I am taken from her she will be a mother to my innocent child!'

> I tore myself from her, for I had sent out my maid and Mr. B. to walk and could only seize that moment to go to her — I dreaded their return and their finding me in [Mrs] B.'s room with her and Louis' wife — At last I got away in time, and they returned — I took leave of Monsr. B. and left him at Castelandari to take care of my little treasure to Sorège — He only knows her as a Protestant Child my friends and I wish to educate, and who is to be removed in Septr. to Paris — Louis and his wife went to Sorège for the first week till she was accustomed to Monsr. B's family — my joy at having seen Caroline supported me for two days. I felt nothing, neither fatigue, nor apprehensions, nor even the sorrow of having left her, so glad was I to have seen and removed her — dear, dear little Angel — I passed through Toulouse, Montanton Agen, Birli, and so to Bordeaux — the 30th of April — a beautiful country, which sometimes I could force myself to be pleased with, but arrived so tired and full of pain, I begin to fear I never can reach London—[D]

Her mind is tossed to and fro between affection for the Duchess and love for the Duke, between good resolutions and an inward consciousness that they are unlikely to be kept.

> I deserve to suffer, and will not complain — Oh, may I see my beloved friends again, for they are dearer still to me than all else in the world! — She is the kindest, dearest, best most beloved of friends — and he is and must be ever the very soul of my existence — I will cease to live in error with him, tho' with shame and blushes I confess it, one moment passed in his arms, one instant pressed to his heart, effaces every sorrow, every fear, every thought but him — but this must not be, shall not be — no, I'll live for him, but as his friend; still will I share, if he will let me, his every thought, his cares, and his anxieties, or his happiness, still will he find my heart adopt and make its own whatever can interest him, still will his pursuits be mine, whatever he likes or dislikes, will be pleasing or otherwise to me, for not only are my natural inclinations like his, but the instant his are known they become mine without a thought to make them so.[D]

She prays anxiously that he may never doubt the strength of her affection if she should alter the tie which united them.

The next entry is dated 'Rouen, May 25th', and endorsed 'this is the day on which I expected to be confined, yet I do not think I shall'. She had arrived there on the 15th, alone with Lucille: on the 16th she went to Dieppe where the Duke had sent 'Dr G.' to meet her with a letter which revived her courage, strength, and spirits. They decided together that it would not be safe for her to go to England, to which she gave way more readily because she had found that 'from Prudence the D. had decided to be out of London'.

> Dr. G. came back to Rouen. Make acquaintance with a sensible humane Physician, who procured me an apartment, and I followed the next day — Here then have I been 6 days, thought to be Dr. G.'s niece, but he was obliged to return to England. The apartment tolerable, but in a close confined street on one part and a stinking court at the other — The Physician comes to me sometimes, but else poor Lucille and Lill[51] are my only resource — but I have reason to bless the goodness of Providence, in that I am here, safe, with every necessary assistance near me, I only pray all may go well, and nothing discovered — the length of time I bear my little burthen is surprizing, yet even this tho' distressing proves my strength, and I ought to be thankful — But should I pass the 28th what will the D. think, when that is the last day I was with him, and did not return till I was above two months gone? Yet I could as much set about clearing myself of murder as of clearing myself of any infidelity to him, to whom my

faith and love is pure and unspotted as the love of Angels. It is impossible I think that he should suspect it an instant — he must see and know how truly, tenderly, and fondly he is loved — he knows my heart is wedded to him, and he will not suspect its faith and truth.[D]

She need not have feared. The next entry runs:

On the 26th of May, 1788, at 3 in the morning I was taken ill and brought to bed of a son at six — a dear, dear little boy whom I pray to God to preserve and bless with his father's virtues and merits — my labour was short but severe, but my recovery surprisingly quick, considering my anxious state of mind, and the dreadful noise and bad air of the house I am in — I bless the mercy of God, and will try to deserve it. I suckle my darling Child who is loveliness itself. Erring as I have been, yet my heart can feel nothing but tenderness and joy at the sight of this dear Child — I only wish now that my dear friend had a son also — Lucille I have sent for my letters, and trunks, and I wait anxiously for her return — pray God all may be secret and unknown, I shall be too happy — yet I must then part with my Boy, and I feel already the bitterness of that moment; God bless him—[D]

Again the prayer was granted, for this child was the future Admiral, Baronet, Gentleman Usher of the Black Rod, and close friend of his half-brother, the sixth Duke of Devonshire.

To him was given a name more boldly revealing his Cavendish origin: 'William' after his father, 'Clifford' after his father's mother, who had been Baroness Clifford in her own right. 'Augustus' and 'James' were thrown in for makeweights, the first being very usual in the Hervey family.

The Duke of Dorset wrote to the Duchess from Paris on June 18th, 1788, with unconscious accuracy that 'that abominable *Scimia*', of whom he had heard nothing, was playing her monkey tricks somewhere, '*perdue dans quelque coin*'.

Less than a month later the much-chastened *Simia* was back in England, though not yet at Chatsworth. Her first weeks were spent at Ickworth with her mother. In the meantime the Duchess had, through the good offices of the Dowager, engaged Miss Selina Trimmer as governess to the Ladies Harriet and Georgiana.

The name of Trimmer was well known in the serious circles which the Dowager frequented. Selina was the daughter of that admirable woman, Mrs Sarah Trimmer, whose *Story of the Robins*, so beloved of Pet Marjorie, had appeared three years earlier with a dedication to Princess Sophia, fifth daughter of George III. This little book, though it contains much that modern child-psychologists might deprecate, quickly reached the rank of a nursery classic, which it held well into the nineteenth century. It represented one of the earliest known attempts to inculcate in the infant mind the importance of kindness to animals.

Lady Elizabeth Foster in 1788. Miniature after the
painting by Reynolds.

Selina was, perhaps, rather less accomplished than one might have expected an
instructress of the Dowager's choice to be, but 'visiting masters' supplemented her
slightly *bourgeois* curriculum. It is certain that she won and kept a high place in
the regard of the lady to whom she owed her promotion, and whose particular
turn of mind she perfectly understood. The feelings of the Duchess fluctuated,
and were chequered by a comprehensible jealousy of the ascendancy acquired by
the demure Selina. G., as the elder Cavendish daughter was soon called, and her
sister Hary-O, became sincerely attached to 'dear Selina', though they sometimes
deplored her habit of 'administering a little bitter into one's cup'. Under a discreet
and correct deportment Miss Trimmer only half concealed very strong opinions.
These were founded on the same moral code that the Dowager considered indis-
pensable to salvation. It is hardly surprising therefore that from the very first she
should have been deeply antagonistic to that ambiguous member of the circle
whom her pupils called 'Lady Liz' — or even 'Liz' *tout court*.

It seems inconceivable that a great lady of a character so hard-set as the
Dowager's should have been seriously influenced by a person in Selina Trimmer's
position; but it is at least curious that her first open move against Bess should
have been made so soon after the new governess took up her duties. On August
8th, 1788, she wrote to her elder daughter a grave letter which was obviously a
follow-through from certain painful episodes.

She reminds the Duchess of her anxiety to make her happy and to show her
regard and gratitude to the Duke; she assures them both that she has asked no
advice about her own conduct, nor has she ever thought of discussing 'this' with
anybody — 'this' being 'Lady E.F'. She reverts to scenes at Chatsworth which she
was unfortunate enough to witness. She confesses that, finding she had so little
power to command herself when she was deeply afflicted, she thought it better to

avoid all opportunities of acting in a manner that might distress them all. But she means to behave civilly to 'Lady E.F.' whenever they meet, and she hopes — 'of late especially' — that she has done so. She had never, she wrote firmly, avoided speaking to the Duke on any subject; if he should mention 'this', she would listen candidly to him, and tell him truly, if he so chose, what her sentiments were.

Most unfortunately the Duchess was at that time even more than usually eager not to annoy her husband. One financial crisis had been piled upon another. Neither Calonne,[52] the ex-Controller General of Finance, nor the wise and kindly Thomas Coutts had been able to help her in the face of her reluctance — or, more probably, her inability — to name the staggering sum-total of her debts. Her one hope was to placate her husband by giving him an heir.

All that she could do for the moment was to promise that her mother should not encounter Bess at Devonshire House, except occasionally at dinner in the presence of others, and to offer to arrange her engagements to fit in with this plan. The storm died down, only to break out again two years later.

On June 19th, 1789, the Devonshires set out for Spa by way of Paris. It was hoped that the Spa waters might relieve the Duke's gout and promote the pregnancy of the Duchess. Bess went with them. Also Charlotte William, whom they would leave behind in Paris, with a worthy couple, Monsieur and Madame Nagel. There was only one other little boarder in their care, 'a very young lady from the provinces' whose name was Caroline St Jules. Monsieur Nagel was, unfortunately, an arch-bore, but that defect would be less apparent to the two small girls than to their elders.

Though they had been warned that the rising ferment of popular unrest might prevent them from reaching its focal point, the Palace of Versailles, Georgiana and Bess found themselves dining there very shortly after their arrival.

The dinner, noted Bess in her journal, 'was silent and thoughtful such as I have never seen at Versailles'. It was known that the populace was clamouring for the dismissal of Madame de Polignac, who was accused of every wickedness from shameless peculation to secret Lesbianism.

Conducted by the Duc de Polignac the English ladies also attended *la messe du Roi*. In the gallery outside the Chapel Royal the King spoke to them both. He was less fat than they had expected: but the Queen, alas, had lost both her figure and her hair.

Bess showed, not for the first time or the last, a fund of solid good sense in her comments upon public events. The surrender of the noblesse in order to save the King was, she observed, 'a triumph to a set of people who, having nothing to lose, there was everything to fear from': and she later described the Revolution as 'seeming to have been brought about more for the sake of degrading the King and finding their own advantage in the general confusion than from hopes of the public good'.[D]

The Duke now bestirred himself sufficiently to don full fig and go with the Duke of Dorset to Versailles, there to be ceremoniously presented to all the French royals in turn. When Dorset remarked to Bess that 'the Queen ought to have another son', and the remark was translated, Marie Antoinette retorted bitterly, '*Why should I? So that Monsieur d'Orleans can have him killed?*' So well had she summed up the character and the purposes of Philippe Egalité in that fate-laden summer of 1789.

Less than a fortnight later the Bastille fell.

Marie Antoinette.

CHAPTER IV

The Continent in Revolution — Marie Antoinette and her Son
The Dowager Intervenes — Emma's 'Attitudes' — 1789–1791

All the traditional imperturbability of the Cavendishes must have been needed to enable the Duke to keep his womankind on the Continent during times so unquiet. Even before they left Paris for Brussels many episodes had taken place which might have made many people head for home. Bess relates a variety of examples, some grim enough, some grimly gay. Ladies walking in the Palais Royal were surrounded by hostile crowds who sniffed at their scented powder and muttered, '*That smells of the noblesse.*' When the mob stopped Baron d'Éscarts at Versailles and demanded money with which to drink the health of the recently recalled Monsieur Necker,[53] 'the Father of the People, the Father of the Poor', he said to them, '*My friends, go to your father and tell him that you are ill clad, ill fed, and even worse bred.*' They laughed and dispersed.[D]

On another occasion a similar gang of ruffians announced that they were about to burn the house, the wife and the children of a certain Monsieur d'Espremenil, but were deflected from their purpose by a wag who got up and said, '*Messieurs, in my opinion we ought not to burn the house of Monsieur d'Espremenil, because it is not his, and only the poor landlord would suffer; nor his children, who are not his either, nor his wife, who is everybody's.*'[D]

Then officers wearing hussars' uniform were mobbed, and two of them escaped in women's clothes. When the Duke and his party set off for Brussels they were pursued all the way by rumours and alarms.

The flight of the Duchesse de Polignac to Switzerland was perhaps the most shattering single event of the hour. 'She pretended', says one French historian, 'to bow to the storm'; and certainly none of her English friends ever doubted for a moment her loyalty to the Queen. The National Assembly was baying for her blood, and she must have hoped that by absenting herself, if only for a time, she might deflect some of its fury from the head of Marie Antoinette. Four years later, when the news of the Queen's death reached her in her place of exile, she pressed both hands to her heart and died.

Her departure raised anew the problem of Caroline St Jules, who was nominally under her protection. In November 1789 the Duchess of Devonshire was writing to her mother from Brussels about the desirability of finding 'a proper French girl' as a companion for G. and Hary-O. She wished, she added, that she could send her over the little St Jules girl. She was a sweet child, and would be quite Georgiana's little Hermia.[C]

In the meanwhile the longed-for grace had been granted, and a third lawfully begotten little Cavendish was on its way into a world prepared to receive it with appropriate magnificence. The Duke's attitude seems to have resembled that of Henry VIII in 1537 when Edward VI was imminent — 'I must have my heir.' He would not hear of the Duchess returning to England for the child's birth, and it does not seem to have occurred to him that even a stormy sea-crossing might be less dangerous to his hopes than land journeys upon a Continent seething with revolution. Brussels would surely be a safe spot. Was not the Archbishop ensconced tranquilly in his palace at Laeken?

None the less many of their experiences were startling enough. For example, Bess writes on October 7th, 1789:

> ... Just before St. Trond we were very much alarmed indeed. We passed by several of the country people with their coloured cockades and one of them got up behind the carriage. The Postillion very imprudently struck at him with his whip — he was driving four horses in hand and had just time to get up on his horse again when the man levelled his pistol at him, swearing and threatening very much, but [I] did not hear it go off. The Postillion said the man fired at him. I was much alarmed at seeing the pistol but concealed the motive of my fear from the Duchess of D. till we were out of his reach, for she was with child and I was in dread of the fright it might occasion her.
>
> The Postillion galloped on, and though they ran after us we got out of their reach and soon joined the Duke, who had walked on. He had heard a great hallooing which I suppose was these men following us.[D]

The Duke's calm disregard of the tumult, even though it proceeded from the direction along which his womankind were travelling, was characteristic. On another occasion he serenely watched some people pillaging a house in Brussels 'in so quiet a manner that he thought it was an auction'.

There were humours as well as horrors to be set down. An officer being reprimanded for being at Brussels when he had been told to remain at Alost said, '*It is true, Monsieur, that you ordered me to remain at Alost — but my men would not remain there with me.*'[D]

On December 29th, 1789, the Duke set out for England alone. In a postscript to a letter written to Bess from London early in 1790 he says, half in English, half in French, 'Caro is in the right, *je t'assure*, in thinking *que je pense à elle*.'[C] He had made the acquaintance of his little unacknowledged daughter and was clearly pleased with her. A few weeks later the Duchess wrote to the Dowager that on their return 'Charlotte W.' would be 'out of the way' except occasionally; 'Madlle St. Jules' was another story. Though very lively, she was a remarkably orderly little creature and would be of great assistance to G. and Hary-O in their French. [C]

On January 5th, 1790, Bess went to the Théatre de la Monnaie in Brussels to see Voltaire's *Mort de Jules César*. The veteran General Van der Merch,[54] who had defeated the Austrian Imperial troops at Turnhout in the previous October, was the hero of the hour, and when his battered countenance was recognized in a small side-box there were cries of '*le voila!*' and he had to come forward.

> Every line that could be applied to him was repeated again and again and his name substituted to that which was in the play, and all who were on the stage joined in the chorus; at last the principal actor got up by the stage box and put a wreath of Laurel on his head. The bursts of applause doubled and continued an amazing while but he looked, tho' pleased, embarrassed and in the simplicity of his heart asked if he must leave it on. They told him that he must a little while, and he sat down perfectly unconcerned, indeed probably not knowing that the knot which tied the wreath ought not to hang down before on his poor, scarred, weather-beaten face, but there he left it till, having got leave to take it off, he put it in his pocket, stroked his wig which he seemed to think more about than his Laurel, and soon afterwards took leave of us all and returned to his wife.[D]

One happy result of the Duke's trip to England was the arrival at Brussels of his two daughters, shepherded by Miss Trimmer. In a letter written to Calais to greet them the Duchess tells G. that she has got a charming little companion for her, who, as she could speak no English, would teach her and Hary-O French 'in play'.[C]

On May 6th the Dowager arrived in Paris with the grave news that Dr Warren had been sent to her by 'a person whose authority and intelligence could not be doubted', to warn them that they must quit Brussels and that Spa likewise was out of the question.[D] A week later they all joined her and Lady Duncannon, and installed themselves at the Hotel de l'Univers. For the moment there seems to have been a tacit suspension of hostilities between the Dowager and 'Lady E.' of whose devotion to her daughter the Duchess she had daily ocular proof. Harriet Duncannon, too, had yielded to the Hervey spell, and would be held fast by it — with one brief intermission — till her life's end.

The Duchess did indeed need all the comfort that love and friendship could give her. Apart from the distresses of a singularly difficult pregnancy, she was in an agony of uncertainty about her financial affairs, and galled by gad–fly rumours that she was not pregnant at all. For these rumours her husband was largely to blame.

Very natural surprise was caused by the circumstance that this important baby was to see the light neither at Devonshire House nor at Chatsworth. How strange, too, that instead of being attended by the well-known Dr Denman, who had brought the Ladies Cavendish into the world, the Duchess should enjoy the services only of Denman's son-in-law, Richard Croft, an *accoucheur* of far less experience and not yet thirty years of age.

Surprise begets speculation; and speculation begets legend: but it was not until twenty-seven years later that the seeds sown in 1789–90 would spring up into a crop so monstrous that the briefest impartial scrutiny would make it wither away. This was nothing less than the story that the child born in France was the child of Lady Elizabeth Foster, foisted upon the world as the lawful Cavendish heir. One thing nobody attempted to explain — how there could be any previous certainty as to the sex of the changeling.

While the Duchess enjoyed the comfort of Mama's society and the presence of her little daughters, her husband, actively abetted by Dearest Bess, hunted for a suitable house, large enough, secluded enough, and yet near enough to be reached without a long jolting drive over the very bad French roads. They found one at Passy, and on the morning of May 20th Mrs Bartho, the midwife, came to tell Bess that Her Grace had been unwell throughout the night. Two housemaids were immediately dispatched to prepare the house and a few hours later the Duchess and her friend were driven carefully and slowly to the scene of action.

That same night, opera-glasses were levelled at the box in which 'the beautiful Lady Elizabeth' was sitting enjoying the performance in the company of that gayest of old rakes, Lord St Helens.

Bess got back to Passy in time to be present when, on May 21st, 'the Duchess of Devonshire was brought to bed of a son, to our inexpressible joy'.[D] The statement[55] that the Duchess 'made a good recovery' is not borne out by Bess's Journal, in which she noted on June 14th that they had had many days of the greatest anxiety and misery about her.

In the meantime the diarist resumes her chronicle of things heard and seen.

Madame de la Sale saw a young boy of fashion whom she knew only by name surrounded and threatened by the mob for having no cockade. They said they would hang him instantly. She conjured them on her knees to spare her son (so she called him to interest them) but they only replied, '*All the better — we shall rid ourselves of two of you.*' She continued however entreating them to spare his life till she got him into a coffee house, when, seeing that he was safe, she turned round and said, '*Now that my son is safe, I hold my own life of no account. Let us see if* _you dare kill me. You are all cowards, murderers, unworthy to be called Frenchmen, you are hired assassins, you are cannibals greedy for human blood.'_

In speaking thus she traversed the Tuileries and got into her coach, no one daring to strike her.

I must add that this extraordinary woman is about 6 feet in height and proportionately large.

On June 3rd Lady Spencer, Lady Duncannon and Bess witnessed the _Fête Dieu_ procession, and soon saw fresh evidence of the spirit of the times.

When the procession first began the drummers, who went before, tired of a little stop there was, threw down their drums and sat upon them to rest. The officers said to the soldiers, '_Please be good enough to a keep a little nearer.'_ And the soldiers swore at the officers, and kept at a distance.

The Queen was dressed simply, but in full Court dress. She walked with dignity and firmness and smiled at such as she knew in the _Balcon_ and smiled at us.[D]

On another occasion Marie Antoinette took the Dowager to a window which commanded a far-stretched view of Paris.

Lady Spencer expressed great admiration of the beauty of the prospect. '_No,'_ said the Queen. '_It is an extensive view, but it is not a beautiful one.'_[D]

The wearing of a cockade in the hat was fast becoming as necessary as the bearing of heraldic dignities was becoming dangerous. A decree of June 19th abolished armorial blazons. 'It is really affecting and distressing', writes Bess, 'to be with some of the great families — to hear them giving orders for effacing the arms on their carriages, relinquishing the respected names they have borne.'[D]

On July 2nd, 1790, she recorded:

We went today to St. Cloud. The Queen had desired us to go to Madame de FitzJames, where she would come to us —The Duchesse de FitzJames has never left the Queen and a friendship of above ten years that the Queen has honoured her with is, I think, a proof that this unfortunate Queen has not the lightness of character attributed to her, and knows how to value a real friend. — When she enquired about Madame de Polignac of Lady Erne, who was just returned from Italy, her voice faltered so that she could hardly pronounce the name, and when I told her that I was to write next day to Madame de P. she said in a low, trembling voice, '_Tell her that you have seen a person who will love her till her life's end.'_

She then turned to the Duchess of Devonshire's little infant son, who was sent for, and caressed and kissed it, enquiring after his sister, who had been so ill.[D]

Poor G. had indeed been very ill, but devoted nursing by Miss Trimmer and Bess gradually wooed her back to health.

At St Cloud all the ladies were charmed with the Dauphin[56] — 'tall, well-made, his countenance full of spirit and sweetness'. The Queen said of him, '*How lucky he is to be only five years old. And yet*', she added, '*there are times when his light-heartedness makes me shudder.*'[D]

Some days later the Duchesse de FitzJames, returning from St Cloud to Paris, was stopped by a procession of labourers shouting, '*We are on our way to dig the aristocrats' graves!*'

Public feeling ebbed and flowed well into the summer of 1790. It was particularly unpredictable towards the Queen. One day they would cry, '*String up the harlot*', another, they would give her bouquets. When she appeared on one occasion with the Dauphin in her arms, some of those present played the air, '*O Richard, O my King, whom all the world forgets.*'[D]

After a reaction of this kind early in July Bess heard that Madame Elisabeth had written to the Comte d'Artois that she feared the King their brother was '*too inert to profit by it*'.

Some of the word-pictures of French notables in this part of the Journal are excellent.

Of Mirabeau Bess writes:

> His features and figure seem to agree with his character — a bold and hideous countenance, a daring and threatening look, a sallow complexion, an ungracious form and a bad manner. In his conversation, which is certainly lively and entertaining, he seeks to surprise his hearers by the boldness of his principles.[D]

She could hardly be expected to look with a favourable eye upon Madame de Polignac's most bitter enemy, but she records his admiration for both Fox and Pitt.

He endeavoured to pay court to Pitt by disparaging Fox: but Pitt answered, '*Oh, Monsieur, you have never seen the Wizard within the magic circle.*' A Frenchman said he turned to an Englishman who was listening to Lally-Tollendal[57] and said, '*Monsieur, that is the Pitt of France.*' The Englishman not answering, the Frenchman repeated it, on which the Englishman said, '*That may be. But I doubt whether Mr Pitt would care to be called the Lally-Tollendal of England.*'[D]

On August 19th the whole party returned to England, 'this odious country' as the Duchess calls it. They walked about at Dover, where 'the common people seemed quite delighted to see an heir to the Duke of Devonshire'. The Duchess was nursing the child; and early in September Dr Croft recommended her to take the three children to Eastbourne. Dr Warren, however, advised St Albans. She wanted dear Mama to give her at least two days at Eastbourne. She was sure that her dearest M. would come to her if she followed her own inclination; but she looked upon her as one of the most biased persons she knew — though she was sure she did not know by whom. This was a little touch of innocent artifice. She had already perceived that Selina Trimmer was the element which caused her to lose ground when she was absent from her much-loved but none the less formidable Mama.

The Dowager was grieved at the Duchess's distress, but could then do nothing to help her. It was the old trouble of 1788 breaking out again with fresh force, and the circumstance that her wishes and counsels had been flouted for two years hardened her heart. She also resented the charge that she was biased, an intolerable suggestion to one who had long and rightly prided herself on her calm and steady judgement. So aloof is her habitual attitude, it is almost startling to find her now describing as 'torture' what she had endured as the result of 'Lady E.'s' continued presence.

In her reply the Duchess reveals that the question of a separation between herself and the Duke has surged up once more. He has given her some months for the sake of her baby son, but if she is to be vexed in this way, her dearest M. had better tell her so, and she will wean William at once.

She had, of course, suspected the reason[58] why the Dowager had not joined her at Compton Place; but Mama was wrong, 'grossly wrong', upon this unalterable subject. She often wishes she would talk to the Duke, who would prove to her that she was wrong, and would also show her how resolved he was that no lies in the world could ever make him authorize them by abandoning a person he had every reason to esteem and think well of. She is convinced that 'this subject' ought not to affect her mother, and that it would not affect her without the help of malicious and flattering people. This implied doubt as to the Dowager's ability to distinguish truth from falsehood was hardly tactful, but Georgiana is deeply hurt because Selina Trimmer, a young person whom Mama has known for only two years, should be better acquainted with her ladyship's plans than she was. For Selina had been so indiscreet as to proclaim as one having authority that the Dowager Lady Spencer would not go to Compton Place.

Almost like an unwilling witness under the influence of a drug, the Duchess repeats what must surely have been

The drilled, dull lesson forced down word by word.

The Duke has often told her that, if they should continue to live together, he would certainly be far from wishing 'Lady Eliz.' to live with them if she had a moment's uneasiness about her, nor would the lady herself wish it. So far is this from being the case, she and the Duke have the highest regard, respect, and esteem for her, 'as well as love'. She pleads with 'dearest M.' how cruel it would be to expose her to the malignant ill-nature of the world for what they both knew to be unjust and false.

The Duke had just remarked that, 'granting Lady Spencer the fact', it seemed almost as if she were hurt that her daughter was not made unhappy by it.

Well might the Duchess exclaim that she was born to a most complicated misery. She was anxious about her delicate first-born; she was nursing her poor boy, and when she weaned him it might well be the end of all happiness for her.

The Dowager's heart was touched; and, though she still repudiated the charge of bias, she confessed that she was grieved from her soul to have given her child pain. Making prompt use of this softened mood, the Duchess wrote that, kind as the Duke was to her, she feared he must be weary of her errors. His health was indifferent, his nerves were shaken, and quiet and gentle society was now of consequence to him. This he found in 'Lady Eliz.', but the Dowager's unfortunate prejudice must either deprive him of her society or herself of her mother's. 'Prejudice' was hardly the appropriate word, but from the Duchess's point of view it was assuredly 'unfortunate'.

In May 1791 the whole party, Devonshires, Duncannons, and Bess, went to Bath. They were there when on June 26th a servant of the Duchess's came and told Bess that there was a report that the French Royal Family had succeeded in making their escape. Lady Duncannon soon heard that the fugitives had been stopped and the frontier closed. French *emigrés* in Bath crowded to the Dowager's house, clamouring for news, but Dr Fraser 'dashed all hopes' with the intelligence of the King's arrest. He added that the municipal officer who had made the arrest declared that he arrested not Louis XVI, King of France, but Louis, a traitor to his country, going to join an army of rebels. They also put a crown of flowers on the Dauphin's head to show that his father was deposed.[D]

On July 2nd it was known that Sheridan was going to St Anne's, Fox's country house near Chertsey, to prevail on him to write to Barnave,[59] the moderate-minded French Deputy, and inform him in what a detestable light they would appear to all Europe and to this country in particular if the Queen's person were insulted or violently used by the public. 'I hope', wrote Bess, 'this letter is now gone but I fear it will not be in the power of the National Assembly to protect her.'[D] Lady Melbourne, arriving a few days later, reported that the general feeling in London was that the Assembly would not dare do anything violent against the Queen. None the less the capital was seething with a strange conflict of emotions. A dinner to celebrate the anniversary of the fall of the Bastille (July 14th) was arranged at the Crown and Anchor tavern in the Strand, that notorious haunt of the disaffected; a party of 'democrates', assembled at Lord Lansdowne's, rejoiced at the arrest of Louis XVI; Mr Sheridan wrote 'that he wanted to insure his life and that he was refused till after the 14th', and Bess could not be sure whether he was in jest or in earnest. Lord Pembroke reported that there had been mutinies in certain

English regiments. He thought that their pay ought certainly to be increased, 'but not now, as that might look like fear'. From Paris, Lord Sheffield wrote with fatuous optimism that while the Queen was well guarded at the Tuileries, he could not conceive that there was any danger. 'All the chiefs must be massacred first, La Fayette,[60] Noailles, Barnave, etc.' But a letter signed by a thousand people had been read in the National Assembly, demanding that *le brigand couronné* should be tried for his life — and at Lille the Bishop of Winchester was insulted 'and the rose cut out of his hat'.[D]

Lady Sutherland, also writing from Paris, had a curious and disquieting incident to relate. It occurred on the Champ de Mars, where the Altar of Reason had been set up.

> Two young men concealed themselves under the altar in which they had tried to bore a hole so that they might see through it. The alarm was at once spread that it was intended to place gunpowder there and blow up the deputies at the Federation. The wretched men were dragged out, hanged, and their heads cut off and carded about. Martial law was proclaimed, the red flag was hung out, and La Fayette obliged to lead the National Guard to the Champ de Mars, where for the first time the mob resisted them, and the troops were forced to fire on them, killing several.[D]

Nearer home the news was of a totally different complexion. The Duke of Bedford said that the Prince of Wales had told him of an interview he had had with the King and Queen concerning the Duke of York's projected marriage with Princess Frederica of Prussia. The Prince then told the King that 'if his friends' attempting to bring forward his debts could be any difficulty in the way of his brother's establishment he should give His Majesty his word of honour that he would never consent ...

> and that though he thought he owed it to himself not to bind himself never to marry, yet he thought it probable he might not, as he should like to marry a woman he loved, for from having lived a great deal with women he should like a domestic life and could not, did he not know the Person, expect to meet with so much good fortune as his Majesty. The Queen was so affected she burst into tears and they both embraced the Prince. The P. of W. added 'should I like the Princess and that she behaves well to me and that I grow fond of their children, I very probably may bind myself not to marry, but not now I can't.'[D]

Unfortunately Mr Ewart's messenger with the account of the marriage[61] came before the Duke of York's express, 'which the King was hurt at, but the Prince of Wales explained it and made it up'.

The Devonshire House circle were surprised to hear from the Duke of Bedford that the Prince of Wales did not seem dissatisfied with the Duke of York's marriage.

> Some time ago the P. of W., D. of Y., and D, of Clarence were at dinner together and lamenting their distressed situation, when the D. of C. said he must do something for the family. The two other Princes remarked that it was certainly very necessary to do something, but what did he mean? 'Oh; said the D. of C. 'marry somebody who is rich.' 'Who would marry you?' said the P. of W., and as he said this he observed that the D. of Y. coloured very much and seemed embarrassed. The P. of W. called on his brother the next day and asked him if he had ever had any intentions such as the D. of C. had expressed. 'Why,' said the D. of Y., 'If I had, should you think I had as little chance of success as Brother William?' — The Prince asked him if he had ever thought of any person in particular. Then the D. of Y. said he had seen and liked the Pss of Prussia when he was last in Berlin and though there might be handsomer women, yet that he liked her, and thought her very pretty and pleasing.[D]

Poor Brother William's efforts to find a well-dowered bride were to be renewed twelve years later with serio-comic results, but it is at least curious that his mind was already tending that way in 1791, when his *liaison* with Dorothy Jordan was in its earliest and most ardent phase.

In the midst of all these alternations of social gossip mid blood-chilling rumour the party at Bath enjoyed an unexpectedly entertaining experience, which may have made some of them forget for the moment the evil colour of the times.

Sir William Hamilton, His Britannic Majesty's antiquarian Ambassador to the Court of Naples, was staying in Bath. With him was the opulently lovely creature whom Horace Walpole unkindly called his 'pantomime mistress', and whom he was to marry in St George's, Hanover Square, a few weeks later. Bess takes up the tale on August 10th.

> Having just seen the celebrated Mrs. Hart, who by an extraordinary talent has, as Lord Charlemont says, found out a new source of pleasure to mankind, I cannot forbear mentioning the impression which she made upon me. She was introduced last night to the Duchess of Devonshire by Sir W. Hamilton. She appeared to be a very handsome Woman, but coarse and vulgar. She sung, and her countenance lightened up — her *Buffo* songs were inimitable from the expression and vivacity with which they were sung. Her serious singing appeared to me not good — her voice is strong, she is well taught, yet has a forced expression and has neither softness nor tenderness. Her voice wants flexibility.

This morning she was to show her attitudes. She came, and her appearance was more striking than I can describe, or could have imagined. She was draped exactly like a Grecian statue, her chemise of white muslin was exactly in that form, her sash in the antique manner, her fine black hair flowing over her shoulders. It was a Helena, Cassandra or Andromache, no Grecian or Trojan Princess could have had a more perfect or more commanding form. Her attitudes, which she performed with the help alone of two shawls, were varied — every one was perfect — everything she did was just and beautiful. She then sung and acted the mad scene in *Nina* — this was good, but I think chiefly owing to her beautiful action and attitudes — her singing except in the *Buffo* is always in my mind a secondary talent and performance———

In the evening she came again but we ought to have closed with the morning. She looked very handsome certainly, and she was better draped than the first evening, but her conversation, though perfectly good-natured and unaffected, was uninteresting, and her pronunciation very vulgar. In short, Lord Bristol's[62] remark seems to me so just a one that I must end with it: 'Take her as anything but Mrs. Hart and she is a superior being — as herself she is always vulgar.'

I must however add, as an excuse for that vulgarity and as a further proof of the superiority of her talents that have burst forth in spite of these disadvantages, that Mrs. Hart was been and lived in the lowest situation till the age of 19, and since that in no higher one than the mistress of Sir W. Hamilton.[D]

It is hardly surprising that with so many rival claims upon her attention Lady Elizabeth did not pause to record that during the same month of August she had briefly encountered the celebrated authoress of *Evelina*. She had many causes of anxiety, too, as the year waned. Lady Duncannon, to whom she was devotedly attached, had been in a precarious state of health for some time, and, disregarding the tumults which threatened to rive the Continent asunder, Dr Warren recommended that she should spend the winter in the South of France. Her mother would be with her, her sister, the Duchess, the two little Carolines, Ponsonby and St Jules, and, of course, Dearest Bess.

Bess set sail last of all, with the Carolines, and they were detained a whole week at Dover by contrary winds. During that time she had no news either from the other travellers who had gone ahead, or from the Duke whom she had left in London, 'God knows with what sorrow.'

When they *did* sail, they reached Calais in four hours. A storm arose soon after, and they were 'happy at being in port'. Colonel St Leger brought her many civil messages from the Duke of York, who with his Duchess was also waiting for favourable weather.[D]

Next day they left Calais. Finding no letters at Abbeville to direct her route, she adhered to the 'first plan they had conceived' and went round by Dieppe and Rouen.

Georgiana, Duchess of Devonshire, drawn by
Bess in 1791.

There a sensible man to whom she talked expressed the view that 'the better
sort were apprehensive that the Revolution would go to greater lengths than any
of them had intended'. It rained so hard that she could only show the children
from the window of the Inn the tower of the ramparts 'which our Harry the 5th
built'.[D]

When Bess and her little charges reached Paris it was found that they had missed
not only the letters which the Duchess had sent to wait for them at various inns
but also the courier dispatched to meet them.

> I drove however to the Hotel de l'Univers and to my great comfort found
> them and Mr. Hare, and Lady Duncannon was rather better. Some necessary
> repairs to my coach made us stay some 5 or 6 days — during this time I saw
> a vast number of people of my acquaintance, all of whom appeared fearful
> and apprehensive of future events. The Queen was so good as to send Madlle.
> Bertin[63] to me, to say she would not ask to see me then, because she knew the
> distress we were in on Lady Duncannon's account, and that perhaps it might
> endanger us.
>
> Madlle. Bertin gave some particulars about the return from Varennes, and said
> the Guards scarcely let the Queen go into a warm Bath without seeing her in
> it.[D]

Writing to his father, Lord Bessborough, to explain why the Duchess and
Bess did not join the rest of the party at Nice till March 11th, Lord Duncannon

informed him that 'they stayed behind to see some relations of that little French
girl whom you have seen at Devonshire House, who were very desirous of seeing
her'.

In sober truth, Georgiana had gone abroad in 1791 for the same reason that
dearest Bess had gone in 1785 and again in 1788: but she was fortunate in escaping
the horrors of the den of the *Archi-Prêtre* at Vietri and the squalor of the inn
at Rouen. Only eight years had passed since the Duchess wrote to her friend
reminding her that so many Englishwomen had gone into Switzerland and Italy
'when in scrapes' and urging her to be doubly cautious in her conduct to show
that she was 'not that kind of person'.

Marie Antoinette with her daughter Marie-Thérèse Charlotte, and her son the
Dauphin, Louis Joseph.

CHAPTER V

'Good Duchess' and 'Wicked Lady' — Gibbon — The Abbé Edgeworth
Crops and Queues — 1791–1796

Mrs Ord and Emma Hart would both have been interested if they had known that the gracious lady whom they saw in Bath during the late summer of 1791 was to leave England before the year's end a banished woman, soon to bear a child of which the father was not her husband the Duke, but her lover, young Charles Grey.

In Mrs Ord's eyes the knowledge would merely have fitted in with all she had heard and suspected of the Devonshire House circle; but with what emotion would the ever dramatically-minded Emma have realized the narrowness of the line dividing her and the Duchess in the sight of heaven! Indeed, the highly coloured creature so soon to be the wife of Sir William Hamilton might have pleaded that her transgression was not mentioned in the Decalogue.[64]

How much the Duke knew it seems impossible to determine. In 1791 Georgiana's figure was already so unwieldy that her pregnancy would not noticeably alter it, and their *vie intime* may have been running in divergent grooves since the birth of the heir. Yet there seems a touch of retributive sternness in his decree exiling her from his home and from the society of their children for a period deliberately left vague.

Her extravagance was an old story, and she had more than once been mangled with that word banishment; but this was something different from an enforced sojourn at Althorp or St Albans. Now the Alps must sunder her from G., and Hary-O and Hart.

Some gossip about Charles Grey can hardly have failed to reach the Duke. When Lady Holland wrote in 1793 that this 'fractious and exigeant young man was the Duchess's *'bien-aimé'*, she was merely setting down something which had long caused Whig chins to wag and Whig lips to be pursed up. Bess's soothing influence was clearly needed here; but she went abroad with her 'angelic friend'. Who better than herself could cherish and comfort that most forlorn of pilgrims?

Lady Bristol, writing from Bruton Street to give Bess news of her boys on January 22nd, 1792, is obviously puzzled as to her actual whereabouts. 'I have just sent to Devonshire House,' she says. 'How vexatious that your poor little *muse*[65] is not there, and where is it? For that I cannot figure to myself.' Mrs Bellew had been to see 'the dear little Fosters', and found them perfectly well although Frederick had for a time suffered from very severe chilblains.

On January 11th the party split up, the Dowager and Lady Duncannon staying at Hyères while the Duchess, Bess and the two Carolines went on to Aix. In letters to her mother Georgiana describes herself and her friend rising early, reading Blair's sermons and Shakespeare, going for walks. It is difficult to realize that during this time — on February 20th, to be exact — there was born in the house of the Comte St Jules the child who would be brought up at Howick as 'Eliza Courtney', the child of Georgiana and Charles Grey.[66]

There is a significant blank in Bess's Journals, and she does not appear to have resumed a regular chronicle till the autumn. Her name, however, constantly crops up in the letters which the Duchess poured out to the children for whom her heart hungered. We catch glimpses of her sitting drawing with Lord and Lady Duncannon while the Dowager arranges her *Hortus Siccus*; suffering badly from cold during the crossing of Mont Cenis; and studying botany 'very much' with 'dear Grandmama and Aunt'. The hostility of the Dowager seems to have slumbered; nor does one see it in active eruption again until 1809, three years after her unhappy daughter's death, when the Duke decided to 'make an honest woman' of his mistress.

On May 30th, 1792, Mr Gibbon wrote to Lord Sheffield from Lausanne, 'the Dowager Lady Spencer is arrived and the Duchess of Ancaster is expected, but I am less anxious about those matrons than for the good Duchess of Devonshire and the wicked Lady Elizabeth Foster who are on their march'. The historian spent a happy summer in what he calls 'familiar intercourse' with these noble ladies. He was playful and indulgent with the two Carolines, rather cumbrously *galant* with Georgiana and Bess, but always, one feels, excellent company.

There is no allusion in the Journal to the oft-related story that during Bess's previous visit to Lausanne the historian had fallen on his knees before her, uttering 'violent protestations of love' and was unable to rise unaided. Monsieur Artaud, who was French *Chargé d'Affaires* in Rome at the time of Bess's death, gives her as his authority in the article contributed by him to the *Biographie Universelle*. The circumstance that the same story was told in various forms and about different people has not deterred his more recent biographers from accepting it as substantially true, though it has been suggested that the real source may have been a garden frolic, a sort of mock-chivalric charade, staged by Gibbon in 1792. A year later he wrote from an hotel in Cork Street to Lady Sheffield, 'the Duchess is as good and Lady Elizabeth as seducing as ever': but his grotesque shadow never falls at any time upon the pages of the Journal, and his death elicited only the comment 'he was always very good to me'.

To Maria Holroyd, Mr Gibbon announced regretfully in November 1792 that 'Eliza' and the Duchess were 'now flown beyond the Alps and would pass the winter at Pisa'; he dwells with pleasure upon the very pretty drawing 'taken' by Lady Elizabeth from the door of his greenhouse and including 'the poor acacia now recovered from the shears of the gardener'.

It was during their sojourn at Lausanne that Georgiana was suddenly impelled to draft her Will. Addressing the Duke, she reminds him that everything she has is his. She leaves him for remembrance nothing but a green antique ring given to her by Bess. And to Bess she begs his leave to give 'the prints of the Vatican and Raphaels' given to her by her brother, Lord Spencer, and the picture of the Duke himself which she carried in her pocket.

Bess's Journal starting on October 21st, 1792, bears on its first page an impassioned note in another hand, obviously a man's: '*To make someone begin the story of your travels who will not be able to share them with you is not like your wonted kindness.* The writer charges her to recall how recently she had been told that she was 'the incarnation of kindness'; and he concludes, '*Try, Milady, to deserve those words by some little recollection of him by whom while he lives you will never be forgotten.*'[D]

After this romantic prologue the first pages of the Journal seem rather tame, and too strongly reminiscent of a guide-book; but the diarist's interest in contemporary events soon reasserts itself, and she transcribes the gist of a letter written by her brother Lord Hervey from Florence, where the Grand Duke of Tuscany had declared the neutrality of the Duchy. The French *Chargé d'Affaires* had thereupon promised that his territories should be respected, but when 'a portion of the French Fleet appeared off Leghorn the merchants there were so much alarmed that they begged Admiral Goodall[67] to remain a few days longer. An English captain arriving from Nice told Hervey that the French were loudly proclaiming their intention of going to Rome, extorting money from the Pope and ravaging Italy — an intention carried out later by the young Napoleon Bonaparte.[D]

On their way from Lausanne to Florence the Duchess and Bess had been squired by Mr Thomas Pelham, ultimately second Earl of Chichester. According to Lady Holland, he imputed a long illness from which he afterwards suffered entirely to the strain caused by 'the whimseys of two capricious ladies'.

The first months of the New Year of 1793 were passed between Pisa and Florence. Bess's Journals are full of disconnected patches of news from France and England, none of it otherwise than deeply disquieting; with these are mixed equally disconnected patches of landscape, ruin, art, and archaeology.

The shattering news of the execution of Louis XVI was slightly softened by a baseless rumour that the little Dauphin, running after his father, had been lost in the crowd and possibly rescued by '*some virtuous hand*', but the shadow of the Revolution tinged everything with a sinister gloom.

At Viterbo on March 10th Bess began a Journal addressed to Caroline in French, and evidently intended to impress upon the mind of the little seven-year-old girl some of the places of interest they had visited together. The elder pilgrim was indefatigable, but the younger seems occasionally to have wilted, as when on the summit of the Palatine Hill she became weary and desired to go home. Again, on March 15th, she preferred to remain with her sick friend[68] 'rather than to enjoy the pleasure of seeing St. Peter's' — a sacrifice to friendship for which her mother hopes to reward her later on. In April, Caroline's mind is further enlarged by a visit to Pausilippo, where Mama quotes Strabo, and they see a dog put inside the *Grotto del Cane* to demonstrate the mephitic vapours within. We are glad to learn that 'the moment it appeared to be suffering' they caused it to be brought out, when it soon began to run about. At the Piscarelli they visited the hot springs and cooked eggs in the bubbling water. Caroline ate the eggs, and, Bess adds affectionately, *'you enjoyed your outing so much that morning'*. At Portici the child collected *pierres de lava*: at Herculaneum she was made to contemplate with attention the ingenious machine set up to restore the antique MSS. discovered there; at Pompeii she was charmed with the baker's shop. She was also encouraged by the kind assurance that some day, when she is a little older, she shall read Virgil's account of the descent of Æneas into the nether regions.

The children seem to have been left at home when on May 14th Sir William and Lady Hamilton conducted the Duchess and Bess to the royal silk factory, where they were much pleased by the benevolent manner in which the King[69] patted the five-year-old operatives on the head and called them by their names. Older operatives who wished to marry had cottages built for them, where they could continue to ply their craft. Bess tells Caroline all about it, and dwells upon the charming cleanliness of these cottages, where you might see the husband weaving on one side, the wife embroidering on the other, and perhaps a baby sleeping near them.[D]

Two days later they all paid a visit to Vesuvius, crossing the great stream of lava which first flowed from a cleft at the foot of the volcano in 1769. 'Sir W. Hamilton', remarks Bess, 'was on the mountain at the time, and had to run for his life to escape from the fire.'[D]

They reached the halt known as the Hermitage easily enough, and the Dowager, the Duchess, and Lady Bessborough[70] went up to the crater's edge, but Bess, who had already been there often, would not let Caroline go near the flames. They halted where they could hear the distant thunder of the volcano and see the column of black smoke curling up from the summit. Caroline ran to and fro, gathering flowers, but the thunders of Vesuvius startled her and brought her to a halt. *'By degrees'*, Bess reminded her, *'you became accustomed to the noise — you even liked listening to it.'* The three more enterprising pilgrims came down with scorched eyebrows and handkerchiefs marked with fire.

This warm affection of Bess for her little daughter constantly breaks out in such tender interpolations. On the next day, after noting how she sat sketching on the seashore while Caroline gathered flowers, she adds, '*How happy it made me to see you so happy!*'

May 1793 had its gay moments. The two Carolines dined with the King and Queen of Naples, and were very proud, and behaved very well. Two days later Bess and her particular Caroline dined with the King of Naples at his hunting-box at Cardetelli, when the younger guest was enchanted by the table which descended to the lower story and then came up loaded with provisions. Ferdinand's notoriously unlovely table manners can hardly have afforded a good example to 'Mademoiselle St. Jules'.

Instructive as ever, Mama, contemplating the moonlit sea, quotes the eighth Book of the *Æneid* and reminds Caroline that Domitian was *un mauvais Empereur*. The Dowager lends her *bourrique*[71] to the little girl when Bess takes her for a charming walk to Lago d'Albano; but that day's journal ends with the wistful remark that Mama regrets that her Caroline 'is not of an age to appreciate the great historical interest of all she sees'.[D] One is irresistibly reminded of Anna Seward attempting to strike sparks from the equally sweet and equally unresponsive mind of her little friend Marianne.

In June they were all back in Rome, where Bess was able to transcribe a letter written to Madame de Narboune by the sister of the Abbé Edgeworth, describing the last hours of Louis XVI. As this letter differs in several respects from the accounts hitherto known it is here summarized at some length. The Abbé's sister cautiously describes him as her *ami*, not as her *frère*.

The King, foreseeing his fate, had asked the Abbé some time previously if he could count upon him, or, if he did not feel equal to the trial, whether he would indicate some other priest. The Abbé regarded this as tantamount to a command, but his mother and sister were in great fear. With his habitual serenity he put his affairs in order, and then, to spare the feelings of his womankind, spoke no farewells, leaving it to a neighbour to tell them this alarming news. The sister guessed the truth, but hid it from the mother, to whom they said that the Abbé had gone to spend the night with a sick person. On the 20th January, the eve of the execution, Edgeworth was fetched away from the house where he lodged with his mother and sister, and brought before the Committee of Public Safety who eyed him up and down and demanded whether he was ready to perform this perilous office. Thence he was conducted to the dreary abode of the most innocent and unfortunate of men. The Abbé passed the night with the King — the guard never took their eyes off them. 'Who could describe,' ejaculates his sister, 'my anguish when I realized that he was locked up with a hundred keys and surrounded by thousands of tigers!'

After a moment of quickly mastered emotion the King spoke of various subjects with a coolness that amazed Edgeworth.

He then said that they must speak of something more important. The Abbé thought it might be necessary to hint at some 'preparations', but everything was in readiness.

Apparently Edgeworth then heard the King's confession, after which Louis slept for some hours.

Knowing that his hair would be cut off by the executioner and wishing to avoid this, the King asked for the services of a barber, but these were denied him. The Abbé then proposed that he should celebrate Mass. The King welcomed the proposal rapturously, but doubted whether he could obtain permission. The Abbé then went to the Council,[72] *which was actually in session in the same building, and made the request to them.*

They were surprised, and obstructive, and passed some remarks upon the significance of the Host. The Abbé smoothed away these difficulties. 'If a priest be needed,' he said, 'I am one. If vessels are needed, you will find them in any church; and as to the Host, you can leave that to us.' At last they gave in, and told him to put what he wanted in writing, because for their part they knew nothing about such matters. The Abbé then celebrated Mass, the faithful Cléry[73] *acting as server, and the King communicated.*

There was a knock at the door. 'They have come for me,' he said quietly. It was however some one with a message. He then returned from the door. A second knock. It was to advise him that the time had come. He looked at his watch. 'Yes, indeed', he said, 'It is the hour.'

With a firm step he got into the carriage, accompanied by the Abbé and two fusiliers. He had a book in his hand and was praying the whole way.

When they reached the scaffold, 'Here we are!' said he, and begged the Abbé to take care of himself. Edgeworth gave his hand to help him up. The King walked steadily to the farther side of the scaffold, and it was thence in a voice of thunder that he declared the terrible truth.

'About to appear before God, I declare for the last time that I am innocent of the crimes laid to my charge. I desire that the crime now to be committed may not be imputed to the French people — only a few of them are responsible, but I hope God will forgive them for it, as I myself do with all my heart.'

He would have said more but Santerre,[74] *perhaps fearing the impression he might make, ordered the drums to beat. The King was then silent. They cut off his hair. He unfastened his collar himself. When they wanted to tie his hands, he resisted, but the Abbé, fearing violence, said to him,*

'Sire, by this sacrifice you will achieve a new point of resemblance with your divine Example.' Then the King allowed himself to be bound like a lamb.

My friend stayed beside him to the last — he knelt down and did not depart until his habit was stained with the blood from the head which was being carried round the scaffold amid cries, of 'Vive la Nation!'

Having fulfilled his mission, he clambered down unaided and made his way to a house in the Rue St. Honoré.[D]

Five years later Bess saw the Abbé Edgeworth at her mother's house in town, and declared 'his head and countenance is like a saint of Titian's painting'.[D]

As one reads the chronicle of this summer spent by three English ladies and two English children in Switzerland and Italy, it becomes increasingly clear that whatever the Dowager's attitude towards Bess may have been she was very fond of Caroline St Jules. They spent a whole morning together at Tivoli, and visited 'the famous cascades and the ruins of the Villa of Macaenas', to which they journeyed companionably on horseback.

Meanwhile Lady Elizabeth was enjoying the society of Roman princes and prelates, and showing, as she would show again many years later, that she had a light hand with Cardinals.

After taking leave of the Cardinal de Bernis 'with all the respect and affection of a loving daughter for the best of fathers', Bess jotted down some of the incidents he had related to her, going back to the time when he was a Minister of France under Louis XV. Almost immediately after his appointment he was at Versailles when the King was brought in, badly wounded.[76] 'At least', said his Most Christian Majesty, 'I can count on *you*.' 'Poor Prince,' thought the Cardinal, 'I have been in your service only five days and you count upon *me*.' Pompadour asked him once whether he would advise the King to dismiss her. He replied that he would not mention her. 'But', she insisted, 'if he should ask you?' 'I should advise him', said the Cardinal, 'to hold you in the highest regard as long as he should live — but to send you away.' 'If that is what you think', said Pompadour, 'you would be right to say so.'

Another distinguished person who augmented Bess's store of anecdotes was Baron d'Armfeldt, described by Lady Holland as 'the *ami de cœur* of the late King of Sweden', and a conspicuous figure at the Tuscan Court of the period. His contributions all concerned Catherine the Great and Potemkin. It was curious, he observed, that the lovers of so beautiful and so mighty a princess should always have abandoned her, but greatly to her credit that she married one of them to the woman he loved. It is true that she sent another into exile, but that was because he made a scandalous scene in her presence.

D'Armfeldt's account of the rise and career of Potemkin was well worth transcribing. According to him, he was actually the husband of the Empress.

Potemkin began the comedy by shutting himself up in a monastery and writing to the Empress that he had done this out of despair. Actually he did it in order to educate himself — which he managed to achieve. When war broke out with Turkey he wrote to his sovereign declaring that he desired nothing more than to die in her service. She gave him an introduction to General Romanzov, who wrote to her that her *recommandé* fought '*like a man who wished for death*'. They sent him to give her an account of a recently-won battle — and after this his fortune was made. A tall man, he was handsome when seen from one side, but he had lost an eye.

From this time forth he wore nothing but a dressing-gown and ceased to appear on the battlefield.

When he heard that complaints were being made about this, he was carried in a sedan-chair, still wearing his dressing-gown, right up to the trenches. He emerged from the chair and talked very serenely, in the midst of a fierce artillery fire which laid many low. Seeing that the officers about him were getting uneasy,[76] he said, 'But, gentlemen, you complained earlier that I kept too much away from the firing. Now you say that I draw too near. You are never satisfied.'

His style of dress was very singular, and he used to enter the Empress's room *en robe de chambre sans troisième*.[77]

Continuing news of massacres in Paris afflicted the whole English colony, but it is pleasing to learn that early in July some sailors from the English ships lying off Leghorn seized a French naval officer, tore the tricolour cockade off his hat, tied his hands behind him, and sent him back to his ship.

It is curious that Bess has nothing to say in her Journal of that friction between her brother, Lord Hervey, and Manfredini, the Prime Minister of Tuscany, which ultimately led to Hervey's dismissal from the post she had with so much earnestness laboured to obtain for him. On June 30th Lady Holland found him 'much agitated' at the prospect; but he had certainly brought it upon himself if she is correct in stating that 'in those letters which he wrote remonstrating against the exportation of grain from Tuscany to France he calls the Grand Duke a fool and Manfredini a knave'. Later, by insisting in what Horace Walpole called 'a violent note' upon the expulsion of La Flotte, the French Minister, from Florence, he sealed his own fate. It must have been most disappointing for Bess.

Early in July the English ladies left Florence for Bagni di Lucca. 'Miss Hervey', Bess's godchild, the only daughter of the bellicose Ambassador, went with them, and on July 14[th78] the children helped to celebrate the birthday of Lady Bessborough, who was still very far from well.

> The Duchess wrote some charming verses in Italian, which Miss Hervey, Caro and Caroline sang, while presenting a bouquet to Lady Bessborough — but nothing was so effective as the heart-piercing air of *Senti Mia Vita* sung to words specially composed for the occasion. Lady Bessborough sat in a temporary bower of branches festooned with flowers. She was affected even to tears ... Caro's voice trembled and finally neither of the children could continue the song.[D]

Later in the month they were all back in Florence, where they were visited by Prince Charlie's lively widow, the Countess d'Albany, and her poetical lover, Alfieri, an old friend of the Earl-Bishop's. When the news came that Marat had been murdered by Charlotte Corday, Alfieri commented that she was *'the only man in France'*.[D]

At the University of Pavia, Bess visited the University Museum, and noted that the Scale of Mammals begins with Man and ends — by way of monkey, dog, hyena, wolf, cat — with *quelques sortes de poisson*. She also copied a table of semi-precious stones in a manner worthy of the Misses Bertram of Mansfield Park. The human skeletons and the wax models of anatomical specimens she found upsetting.[D]

At Mogadino, on the Swiss frontier, they went out into the woods to wait for a relay of post-horses from Bellinzona because they could not bear the heat and stench of the inn and were afraid to sit in the carriage, fall asleep, and so contract malaria. At last they heard the welcome sound of the post-boy's horn, but he came only to tell them that they had another hour to wait. Caroline was 'dying of sleep' and her mother was forced reluctantly to keep her awake. Finally, when the coach did appear it was so high that it carried away half the grapes as it passed beneath the trellis spanning the road. *'We wrought a general havoc,'* says Bess.[D]

On August 19th the travellers, now homeward bound, dined on excellent milk and cheese at the Hospice on the summit of St Gothard, 'all very proud of themselves that they had crossed the highest of the Alps'. The Duchess was moved to compose a poem of thirty four-lined stanzas, each more like a coloured lithograph than the last. She was longing to see her children; and Bess, one surmises was longing to see the Duke.

In October 1793 they were all reunited at the Duke of Bedford's house, Oakley, in Rutlandshire. Clifford was at Clewer with a family named Marshall, who must surely have been akin to the Marshalls of Dunleer, if, indeed, they were not the same excellent people.

The existing Journals are sparse and laconic between the end of 1793 and the autumn of 1799, but the gaps can be partially filled from the Chatsworth Papers and from published sources. When she returned to Chatsworth with the Devonshires in June 1794, Bess wrote sentimentally of the recollections brought back by that beautiful place, and added:

> Whether fortune good or ill awaits me I know not, but amidst the various trials I have known of it is a blessing and fills my heart with gratitude to find in the owners of Chatsworth the same warm and tender friendship as united us ten years ago.[D]

When news reached London of Admiral Howe's victory off Ushant on the 'Glorious First of June', Bess happened to be at Devonshire House, and she immediately wrote to Georgiana a letter instinct with the excitement of the time.

June 10, 1794

... I went this morning with dear Louisa to see Mrs. Howe — crowds of people — heaps of notes were coming to her — she was quite nervous with the happiness, and poor Lady Howe received the account at two this morning — heard the sound of horses — the messenger called out 'Glorious news, my lady.' She, quite out of breath with agitation, called to the servant to open the door and bring her the letter. 'I can't, my lady, I am naked.' 'Well' says Lady Howe, 'I will get into bed again. Don't stay to dress but lay the letter on the table and get away.' Lord Howe has allowed her to come to Portsmouth and they set out today.[C]

Celebrations of the victory, both domestic and public, were oddly associated with *déshabille*. On June 15th she records,

The Opera was very full last night. Banti sang like an angel from Heaven — after the opera they called for her to sing *God Save the King*. She was gone home. In vain did the people tell the house so. No ballet would be heard of, and she was obliged to come on in her nightgown and sing it twice.[C]

The Duchess of Gordon's[79] characteristic comment 'when the poor wounded Admirals were named' was 'What signifies a few old legs and arms knocked off?' Three days later Bess wrote,

Never was there a more brilliant victory — Lord Howe's orders to the pilot was to lay him within half a pistol shot of the enemy's Admiral and he is said to have carried away a great part of his ship ... the general orders he gave were to break the French line wherever it was possible and then for every ship to engage its antagonist as seemed to them most advantageous.[C]

Reading this triumphant passage one remembers the strong strain of naval tradition in the Hervey family — Bess was, after all, the great-niece and sister of sailors, and she would shortly be the mother of yet one more. When in the ensuing year she visited Lord Howe aboard the *Royal Charlotte* at Torbay she enriched her journal with a delightful little water-colour of the fleet lying at anchor in the bay.

The year 1796 opened sadly with the death of Lord Hervey, which occurred aboard the *Zealous* man-of-war in the Mediterranean. Bess was not blind to his faults; she deeply pitied his wronged and unhappy wife; but there was a bond between them known only to themselves, and when it was broken she felt a sharp pang.

Three months later 'Brother Fred', now Lord Hervey, wrote to announce the marriage of their youngest sister Louisa to Mr Jenkinson — Robert Banks

Jenkinson, later Lord Hawkesbury and ultimately Earl of Liverpool and Prime Minister.

In the same month of March, Lady Elizabeth suffered 'a violent inflammation of the chest and lung', and was assiduously attended by Sir Walter Farquhar, ex-naval surgeon and now royal physician-in-ordinary, who refused to accept a fee from her.

One day when she was able to receive visitors the Duke of Devonshire brought Lord William Gordon to her room to give her an account of the disastrous Quiberon[80] expedition. 'Never', she writes, 'was there a more melancholy catalogue of bitter suffering, of unavailing proofs of heroic courage.'[D]

Her consequent agitation may have caused the relapse which alarmed her friends so much. The Duchess had to beg the Dowager to keep the children with her a little longer, as Bess had been seized with a violent fever. A few days later she still dared not leave her poor friend, even for the birthday of her adored elder daughter.[C]

Sea air was ordered for the invalid, and the journey to Bognor was broken at Goodwood. The Earl-Bishop, with whom his second daughter was corresponding again, wrote from Naples clamouring for a plan and elevation of the house. 'I am certain', he says, meaningly, 'on your speaking to the Duke of Richmond he will order it immediately.' Five months later he was plying his pen at Naples to enlist her aid in a wonderful plan, 'the beautiful, elegant, important and interesting object', which he had proposed to her second brother, now Lord Hervey. This was nothing less than that Hervey should marry the Comtesse de la Marche, illegitimate daughter of King Frederick William II of Prussia. 'She would bring into our family', he writes, '£5000 a year besides a Principality in Germany, an English Dukedom for Frederick or me — a perpetual relationship with both the Princess of Wales and her children as also with the Duchess of York and her progeny.' He entreats the assistance of his 'sweet Elizabeth' to persuade her brother to accept the 'real Cornucopia' he offers; but when he finds her unenthusiastic, and inclined to sympathize with Lord Hervey's attachment to Lord Templeton's daughter, Elizabeth Albinia Upton, his 'sweet Elizabeth' changes into 'a nasty little imp of Silence'.[81]

In the event Lord Hervey married Miss Upton, whereby their descendants became Founder's Kin of All Souls College, Oxford — a privilege which could certainly not have accrued from a union with the well-dowered and irregularly royal Comtesse de la Marche.

As the year moved on its way the matrimonial troubles of the Prince of Wales provided a little distraction. At the time of his marriage Bess had written of his bride, 'the Princess is pretty and he thought her so, but she disgusted him by the freedom of her manners'.[D] She now wrote:

The Prince of Wales's marked neglect of the Princess gave such offence to the public that some members of the House of Commons hint at a Bill of Exclusion should anything happen to the King. Lady Jersey has been insulted. Mr. Hare observed that her appearances in public were 'more to the credit of her personal courage than to the delicacy of her feelings'. The Princess was applauded at the Opera. The Duke of Bedford, though he 'thought the applause was wrong', felt himself irresistibly carried on rejoin in, and stood in the corridor as she passed, applauding with the rest.[D]

Up to this point the conduct of Caroline, Princess of Wales, was circumspect enough. The King was known to have represented to the Prince the risk he ran of never becoming King. He promised 'change of conduct', but soon forgot his promises.

As she melts into the Devonshire House background Bess becomes more politically minded, and her journals more infiltrated by politics. She had noted early in 1796 that the terms 'Tory' and 'Whig' were merged in 'aristocrats' or 'democrats', 'Pittites' or 'Foxites', and she was amused by another sign of the times.

Even a fashion accidentally begun last year at Woburn Abbey by a set of young men who for a bet cut off their hair and left off powder, even this, though begun by Lord Paget and Lord Villiers, yet, from its taking place at Woburn and the fashion soon being adopted by the opposition, the word 'crop' is almost become analogous to Democrat.[D]

Ten years later she wrote:

When D.D. was first cropped he said to Blake 'Don't leave the ears bare as the fashion is, I don't like it.' 'No, my lord, I did not intend to cut Your Grace's hair so. I cut the hair of the gentlemen of the Army in that manner because it gives them a bolder look.'[D]

Blake, who was the most fashionable barber of the period, did not apparently approve of the wholesale cropping of his patrons' carefully cultivated queues, for, after reassuring the Duke about his ears, he went on,

—— There is Lord John Townshend — the ladies at Roehampton[82] have persuaded him to cut off his tail and I met him in St. James's Street. I never saw a man look so ashamed of himself.'[D]

CHAPTER VI

First Widowhood — Bonaparte on the Horizon — 'The Rebellion of '98'
— Sheridan — Lord St Vincent — Nelson — 1796–1801

Unloved and unlamented John Thomas Foster departed this life at the end of the year 1796. Bess was at Chiswick when a letter from the Bishop of Kilmore informed her that she was now a widow. The Duke and Duchess advised her in what she had to do, and were as eager almost as herself for the arrival of her 'children'. They all seem to have forgotten that the small boys they last saw at Bath in 1782 were now respectively nineteen and sixteen years of age. Bess's agitation brought on a 'hemicrania', but this yielded to extract of bark in pills with ginger. When at last her sons arrived she received them dressed in black velvet with a miniature of the elder youth round her neck. It was an ecstatic reunion. And the Duchess hastened to tell the Dowager that Mr Foster was a plain but most interesting and sensible young man and Augustus a very fine boy. Their Irish accent was only slight. A few weeks later the Duchess was making arrangements to obviate the awkwardness caused by 'crowding a house full'[83] She informs Mama that on the next visit of these remarkably well-disposed and well-behaved young men their mother intended to take lodgings for them, but she herself strongly advised her not to let them out of her sight while everything was so new to them. She is puzzled because they seem to enjoy sitting quietly at home with her and Bess. It did not occur to her that such a home as Devonshire House and such a mother as Bess must have dazzled and delighted them both.

No dread lest these long-lost sons should fail to respond to her affection ever chilled the happiness of Lady Elizabeth; nor need she have felt any. They were from the first as dutiful and devoted as even she could have desired. Except that Fred ('F.F.') was a rather too-persevering humorist, there was not much amiss with either of the brothers. The younger, a future pro-consul, was not so constantly at Devonshire House as the elder, but Bess wrote fondly that they were both accepted there 'as *enfants de famille*'. The Ladies Cavendish might not have agreed, at least as far as they and Miss Trimmer were concerned.

Mr Hare, ever kindly, took the young Fosters to the House of Commons to hear Mr Pitt immediately after their arrival from Ireland.

Nearly a year had elapsed since the first mention of a name destined to clang through the later pages of the journal like the sound of a great bronze bell — the name of Bonaparte. New players were enacting a new play upon the stage of Europe, and in October 1797, the Treaty of Campo Formio, showed how vain were Pitt's endeavours to come to terms with the French Directory.

Associated with Lord Malmesbury in those endeavours was the spectacularly handsome Lord Granville Leveson-Gower,[84] youngest son of the Marquis of Stafford. This 'shadow like an angel with bright hair' had first fallen upon Lady Bessborough's path at Naples in 1794; they became lovers and two children are believed to have been born of their liaison. It was surely an ironic stroke of fate which caused both the Dowager's daughters to stray so far from the path she had so earnestly marked out for them.

Malmesbury and Lord Granville visited Devonshire House between their first and second missions, and amused the ladies there by their accounts of the splendour of the Parisian theatres and the magnificence of Madame Tallien's balls. But 'no half-dozen people could meet to talk in the clubs or in the streets without hussars with drawn swords dispersing them'. Lord Granville considered the dress of the women 'very extraordinary'. It was, he explained, 'in imitation of statues of the antique — sandals on their feet — and flesh-coloured stockings and gloves — crop wigs imitating antique busts'.[D]

French pounces on Wales and Ireland had sharpened fears of a large-scale landing, and Bess and her sister Louisa, who were at Bath together in the early spring, expected at any moment to be carried off by invaders. The mind of Bess naturally gravitated to Devonshire House; she begged her dear friends there to send for her at once if there should be an invasion, so that she might 'share all perils with them'.[C]

Edmund Burke was also at Bath, desperately ill, and 'so convinced that the French are coming that he has contrived hiding-places in the cellar'.[C] Bess wrote to her dear love that they had seen 'poor Burke', but so unlike his former self it had made her melancholy all day. She went up to him and spoke to him, and he put out his hand, which she took, and asked him how he did, and he said 'Very weak.'[C]

Comic relief was afforded by Mrs Crewe, the proposer of the well-known toast of 'Buff and blue and all of you' at a party held to celebrate Fox's victory over the King's candidate in the Westminster election of 1784. 'Mrs Crewe's terrors about the French', writes Bess, 'are rather amusing'; and she continues:

> She came from home piping hot with Burke's detestation of peace — then she collects by the way some story that terrifies her and she thinks herself ruined and the French at the door. She talks and questions and mixes up everything so that she no longer knows what she says or what she hears. Today she met and joined me out walking — then she saw Lord Bradford — she called to

him to hear all the news she could collect, then she sent him running after Sir
G. Colebrook. Poor Lord B. is in no state for running, but away she sent him
— then he brought back the report of a large army having landed in Norfolk;
however this evening she sent me a note to contradict this.[D]

With Lord Spencer, the Duchess's red-haired bibliophile brother at the
Admiralty, an admirable though reluctant First Lord, the Devonshire House
ladies were constantly in touch with naval matters, whether mutinies, victories,
or measures taken to protect the shores of Sussex and Kent from invasion. The
year 1797 was a glorious one at sea, and the names of St Vincent, Collingwood,
Troubridge, Nelson, and Duncan, passing from lip to lip, silenced any efforts to
harass Lord Spencer in the Commons.

As usual, the common danger drew the clashing political parties closer
together, with the exception of a few Foxites of the extreme Left. Sheridan spoke
eloquently in favour of a united front, but voted against that suspension of the
Habeas Corpus Act which Pitt considered necessary for national security. When
the suspension was carded he said bitterly to the Duchess and Bess, 'It were better
now to recruit for Bonaparte, for England is not worth preserving.'[D]

Bess opined anxiously that after Bonaparte's conquests in Italy one might
'expect anything'.[D]

With some consternation many of the great Whig lords were now finding
themselves 'out of step with Mr. Fox', whose speech advising 'those who had
arms to turn them against the interior foe whenever peace should be made' had
caused his name to be erased from the Privy Council. 'It is surely', writes Bess,

> to be lamented that so great and able a man should be hurried away by passion
> and heat of temper so as to excite that sort of apprehension in the public mind
> which lessens the weight which his advice and opinion might have had at so
> important a crisis.[D]

She personally would like to see 'D.D.' — now her usual name for the Duke
— taking a more active part in politics: and with her wonted flair for an apposite
Shakespearean quotation she adds,

> And it is very much lamented, Brutus,
> That you have no such mirrors as will turn
> Your hidden worthiness into your eye
> That you might see your shadow.[85]

And did not Mr Hare say that the Duke had the best sense and judgement of
anybody he knew?[D]

Sheridan and Lord Lauderdale, the uncouth but able Scottish Jacobin, were constantly sparring when they met at Devonshire House about this time.

> Lord L. denies Sheridan having any wit, and Sheridan says Lord L. thinks wit consists in a perversion of truth. Lord L. is also very coarse in his jokes, particularly against Sheridan, who said, 'a joke in Lauderdale's hands is no laughing matter'.[D]

A touch of comedy was provided by 'Fish' Crawford's description of Sir Sydney Smith as he looked after his escape from French captivity. So altered was that rather flashy paladin, Mr Crawford said he would not have known him. His dress was 'a long great coat, pointed shoes turned up at the end, and his hair long'. Sir Sydney considered that Bonaparte was 'losing ground in Paris'; he also described the French gun-boats as 'on a good construction though the guns were rather too high above the water'. 'The report now is', wrote Bess, 'that Bonaparte is steering towards the Levant but that the English Fleet is gaining upon them, Nelson urgent and sanguine in his pursuit'[D] Where could she have found two epithets more appropriate to Nelson?

In the meanwhile rebellion — the famous ''98' — had broken out in Ireland, with all the inevitable accompaniments of violence, cruelty, and destruction.

As the party pledged to Catholic Emancipation, the Whigs were naturally opposed to repressive measures against a population preponderantly Catholic. They had deprecated the recall of Lord FitzWilliam, a deservedly popular Viceroy whose support of Grattan outraged King George. They were convinced that if the United Irishmen had been differently handled they would never have lost their originally law-abiding character; and they had considerable sentimental sympathy with that picturesque will-o'-the-wisp, Lord Edward FitzGerald.

One person only in the opinion of Dearest Bess could do anything to set things right: D.D. On June 13th, 1798, the Duke of Bedford[86] arrived at Devonshire House when Bess was 'hardly dressed', and asked to see her. 'Go', said he, 'and find out what the Duke of Devonshire will do.' He also brought a message from Lord FitzWilliam urging the Duke to attend the King's levee that day.[D]

Bess obediently went to the ducal bedchamber:

> —— but neither being yet up I could only tell the D.D. what the Duke of Bedford had been urging, and that he was below, waiting to see him. D.D. said Lord FitzWilliam understood perfectly that he was against going to the levee that day, and that even if he had not [sic] it was now too late. I conjured him however to get up — he promised me to get up, and soon after he came to my room — he had a letter from Lord Thurlow saying that he had written his full sentiments to the Duke of Norfolk and that he agreed with the D.D. that

to ask an audience was not the right measure — the question was, however, as something ought to be done, what that something should be. When Lord Fitz[87] came I left the room and came to the Dss and we walked up and down in great anxiety, sometimes in the great saloon next to my room, sometimes in hers, waiting for D.D.'s decision. Soon the D. of Bed. came to us and said if the present moment was lost it was over with Ireland — perhaps even now that it was too late — it might be saved by showing the Irish that there was a feeling in this country that they had been improperly governed. In about an hour D.D. and Lord Fitz came out of my room — it was decided by D.D. that he would not go to the levee, but that he would speak after the Duke of Leinster's motion in the House of Lords on Friday. This has satisfied us all, but the Dss and I, though confident of his speaking well, as he did twice before, yet feel nervous about it.[D]

They need not have felt nervous. When Friday came the Duke of Devonshire supported the Duke of Leinster's motion for an inquiry into the state of Ireland in an excellent speech, of which the substance was to recommend 'conciliatory measures united to energy and vigour in the war'. The Duke of Richmond, however, failed at this juncture to satisfy Lady Elizabeth. She dismissed him as a shabby politician who often had so perverted a way of saying things that it was difficult for anybody to act with him.[D] This did not mean that she ceased altogether to flirt with His Grace.[88]

Rebellion continued to spread in Ireland, and Lord Edward FitzGerald's brilliant, erratic life was soon blotted out. Writing to Bess on June 16th, Lord Castlereagh declared that 'had Lord Edward lived the trial would not have been pushed forward', and he added, 'it is a deep tragedy of which the details are better avoided'.[D] His own ancestral home, Mount Stewart, was in possession of the rebels, and his father, Lord Londonderry, was marching at the head of his yeomanry to recapture, if possible, their town house in Dublin. 'It is hard', writes Castlereagh, 'on the father of 12 children, and who has never oppressed his tenantry, to be warred against by them.'[D]

The tone of the letter shows that the recipient was sympathetically inclined towards the ill-starred and ill-guided Lord Edward. She does not seem to have recorded any opinion, condemnatory or compassionate, of her first cousin, George Robert, otherwise 'Fighting' FitzGerald, son of the pious Lady Mary, who had been hanged for murder at Castlebar one summer evening eight years before.

Other Irish leaders appear in the Journal: Grattan, who is dismissed as 'coxcombical' though eloquent; Arthur Connor,[89] who 'on every occasion showed a cowardly disposition'. 'He is', wrote the diarist,

about 28, a dark, sallow complexion, his hair grey in different spots on his head
— his countenance, when I first saw him in 1794, appeared to me gloomy and
designing. He supped at D. House and I have seen him in our box at the Opera
— but I disliked a vulgar familiarity in his manner and a want of openness in his
countenance, and I begged of my dear G. not to see him often.[D]

Bess's recollections of Ireland must have been rather parti-coloured: quiet days
at Dunhill, gay days at Dublin, miserable days at Dunleer; but she never lost her
liking for an Irish story, and her friends, remembering this, sent her an example
from time to time: this, for example,

> There were two Irishmen who when they heard of the Act forbidding the
> eating of new bread held this conversation.
> 'Did you hear of the Act? But I'll be too cunning for them, for I shall lay in a
> stock of new bread the day before.'
> 'You fool,' said the other, 'You can't; and you don't understand the Act, I see. It
> is to prevent the Bakers from making new bread.'[D]

She transcribed the two following absurdities on one page in the year 1802:

> Two Irishmen disputed about Anchovies. One said, 'I passed by the finest
> field of Anchovies I ever saw.' The other laughed at him and said, 'Don't you
> know Anchovies are a fish?' The other, however, persisted. They fought and the
> first killed the other; when recollecting himself he said, 'O, Christ Jesus, what
> have I done? I meant all the time capers.'
> Two men met on a bridge. One thinking he knew the other, hastened up, but
> finding his mistake said, 'By G—— it's neither of us!'[D]

The Earl-Bishop, watching the Rebellion from afar, wrote to Thomas Pelham,
then Secretary for Ireland, warning him of the explosive state of his adopted
country and suggesting two remedies, namely, that parsons should exchange their
tithes for land of the same value and that every minister of religion should preach
'under the Great Seal of Ireland', whereby the Crown could control any subversive
activities on their part. It was unfortunate that he should have planned to explore
Egypt as an archaeologist at the time when Bonaparte was arranging to invade
it as a soldier; but worse things than disappointments were in store for him. His
immense collection of art treasures was seized by the French, and he himself was
arrested and imprisoned in the Citadel of Milan, where he was held for nine
months. Bess did not take to her bed from anxiety on this occasion. She feels some
concern; her father 'hates the French and ridicules Bonaparte'; but she records
quite tranquilly that after his attempted escape he was 'recaptured and confined

more rigorously than before', and owing to the sparseness of her Journal for the year 1799 she leaves his liberation unchronicled. The truth appears to be that her sympathy with her mother was too strong for her to concede any to her father.

When news of Bonaparte's landing at Alexandria reached London, the Duke of Devonshire observed in his calm way that the expedition would probably fail; but Sheridan, with that susceptibility to the glamour of foreign dictators so often shown by Left-wing politicians, said, 'No, Bonaparte would never have risked his gigantic fame upon light grounds. The project is an immense one; but his mind is immense.'[D]

In August 1798 the villages of Derbyshire, like the towns and villages all over England, broke out into twinkling lights and flaring bonfires to honour Nelson's victory at Aboukir, known in history as the Battle of the Nile. The Duchess wrote a triumphal poem. Bess recorded that 'it was impossible to describe the effect of the news'; but as her Nelson-mania was still only at the incubation stage she confined herself to prose.

Her notes for this eventful summer form a very mixed bag. First she is shocked by the duplicity of Lord Lansdowne.[90]

The very night that he was closeted with the King he sat down to the Pharo table at D.H. saying to the Dss of D. 'As I am to be an idle man I may amuse myself' The next day — or a very few days after — he was appointed Minister.[D]

She is then amused by Colonel Wormser's anecdotes of the Russian General, Suvarov,[91] who in the ensuing year so very nearly succeeded in sweeping the French out of Switzerland.

If you are talking to him on business he listens to you with attention and talks with judgment and discrimination — if a third person comes in he begins changing the subject to every nonsense that comes into his head; if three or four people come, he begins jumping about the room, playing strange tricks and does all in his power to pass for mad. It was said that he slept on straw, plunged into cold water during the night, and walked about the room naked to dry himself.[D]

During this same year the letters of Hary-O begin, and in them we get the too-well-known portrait of 'Lady Liz' drawn by a consistently hostile hand. We see an affected creature twisting her shawl about, and gushing over actors and Admirals; we hear her lisping in mock baby-language; we find her monopolizing the Duke's franks for her own extensive correspondence; we even detect what seems to be a hint that she had been known to administer a 'spinkum-spankum' across her knee. She had a knack of pervading the scene which both the Duke's daughters found it very hard to bear; but those little tricks of speech and manner which her friends found vastly amusing were to the forthright Hary-O the outward signs of a character fundamentally false and dangerous. Hart, who saw less of her, was more friendly. In a letter from Harrow to Miss Trimmer about this time he sent a playful message to 'Lizzy'; and later, when her woe over Nelson's death broke all bounds, he gave her a print of West's well-known painting. It is true, however, that she took some trouble to cultivate his good will. With his sisters — particularly the younger one — she probably realized that she was losing so much ground there would soon be none left for her to lose.

Jealousy in this instance brought forth its wonted fruits of suspicion and dislike; but in condemning 'Lady Liz's' little ways Hary-O was incidentally condemning the little ways of her mother and her aunt. All three ladies fostered the same facile enthusiasms, lapsed into the same foolish jargon, cultivated the same divinity whom George Saintsbury loved to call Divine Nonsensia; but only one of the three was therefore damned beyond hope of pardon.

Bess's Journal is missing for the first half of 1799, and it is thus from the Dowager's letter to Miss Trimmer, written in May of that year, that we learn that the two Carolines and Hary-O were confirmed together in Westminster Abbey, wearing plain white gowns and headbands, and that she never saw anything more impressed than they all seemed with calm seriousness and an earnest wish to perform their parts[92] with proper sentiments.[C]

Devonshire House enthusiasm for John Philip Kemble and his sister, Mrs Siddons, was kindled into a blaze by the production of Sheridan's *Pizarro* in the summer of 1799. Sheridan himself informed his friends there that the play was 'the finest ever known, though the plan was German'. He begged the ladies to applaud at 'something of a simile about a vulture'[93] and also when Mrs Siddons as Elvira said, 'It is fitting I should be rebuked, and by Pizarro.'[94D]

The King and the Royal Family were present at Drury Lane on June 5th. It had been reported that His Majesty's not having gone there for so long was 'owing to Sheridan's not having "lighted him" as was the custom' — by escorting him to and from the royal box with a candle in either hand: but on this occasion the playwright 'went through all the proper ceremony'. King George

applauded very much, with taste and judgment. The Duchess of York congratulated S. for the honour he had done her country, adding that she had read Kotzebue[95] and knew how much better Pizarro was, and the huge audience huzzaed at every speech or allusion to which a loyal or patriotic colour might be given.[D]

The extreme Whigs naturally fell foul of Sheridan for the 'excessive loyalty' evinced in *Pizarro*. Always sensitive as to the feelings of the inveterate enemies of their country, they were particularly affronted by the 'vulture' passage, with its ringing declaration:

> The throne we honour is the people's choice; the laws we reverence are our brave fathers' legacy — tell your invaders this, and tell them, too, we seek, no change, and least of all such change as they would bring us.

Sheridan dined at Devonshire House on his return from a visit to the Duke of Bedford at Woburn, where the company had been 'adversely criticizing *Pizarro*'.

> To Lady Melbourne, who was also critical, he said, 'You are an admirable *prose* woman, but God denied you a poetic mind. You are fit only to pick out the eyes of potatoes by the dozen: and as for Fox, he has a certain talent for speaking, and Hare has a namby-pamby wit with a dextrous arrangement of words, and FitzPatrick a pompous kind of decorum and propriety of speech; but as to judgment of the theatre I had as lief talk to my shoemaker.' Then he turned to me. 'Was not the dedication well done? You could not misunderstand it.' Then he added in a whisper, 'Tell me anything *you* wish altered in it, and it shall be done. Oh, that you would come, O, *Peruvienne*, with me!' He then renewed his protestations, and was very tender but very entertaining.[D]

Bess was not likely to take his protestations too seriously; she must have known that he had already begun that passionate pursuit of Lady Bessborough which later caused its object so much distress. Though his general conduct, his unreliability, his intemperance, his mischief-making propensities, often incur her private rebuke he seems never to have said or done anything to arouse in her that sense of sickly repugnance felt on occasion by Lady Bessborough. Nor does she associate him with the anonymous letters which afflicted the Devonshire House ladies in 1805.[96]

Lady Spencer's two daughters were now respectively forty-two and thirty-eight years of age. They had left behind them those enchanting graces of form and expression which so many artists, amateur and professional, the greater and the lesser, had vied with each other to transmit to posterity. Neither the passing of years nor the ravages of constant ill health had dealt as harshly with the younger as they had with the elder sister. Already in 1783 Horace Walpole had written to Lord Hervey's immediate predecessor at Florence, Sir Horace Mann, that the Duchess verged fast on coarseness. Her colour had always been a little too high, and the light auburn tints in her hair clashed with the deeper red in her cheeks when hair-powder went out of fashion. In April 1799, Lady Holland wrote that the change in her was painful to see. 'Scarcely has she a vestige of those charms that once attracted all hearts. Her figure is corpulent, her complexion coarse, one eye gone, and her neck immense.'

The unfortunate eye was probably a victim of the drastic remedies employed by the physicians to reduce the recurrent inflammation which showed itself in 1796.[97] At first these remedies seemed to have some effect, but the trouble returned with greater severity at ever shorter intervals, and when she died ten years after the initial attack she could distinguish objects only dimly and at short range.

It may have been yet another item in the score of Bess's transgressions (as seen by the Duchess's daughters) that she, the same age as their mother, had kept her figure, her complexion, and her effective brown-hazel eyes. Even her various illnesses merely left her looking prettily fragile, not distended or disfigured like her unfortunate friend.

However little some of his Devonshire House admirers may have liked his views upon regicide and revolution, they all rejoiced when in the late summer of 1799 Fox had two escapes, one from fire and one from water.

'His gun', writes Bess, on September 4th,

> burst in his hand — he was two miles from home. He sent for a surgeon and bid him bring opium pills with him. He suffered much, but the surgeon and Mrs. Armistead[98] brought him to town and he is doing well. He had a narrow escape[99] a little before this, for he was rowing Mrs. Armistead and the oar struck against him and he fell into a very deep part of the Thames — he swam to a part of the river in which he knew he would be able to stand and not be out of his depth, and he then called out to Mrs. Armistead, who was in agonies, 'You see, I am safe!' What good nature and presence of mind![D]

Devonshire House sympathy with the Royalist cause in France was soon heightened by social contacts with the exiled French princes, the brothers of Louis XVI. Monsieur[100] and his entourage were entertained at Chiswick in July 1800 to a great breakfast at which the Prince of Wales was present. Bess records that D.D., with 'dignified grace', attended Monsieur to his carriage hat in hand, 'and marked his civility to the exiled Prince beyond what he had done to the Prince of Wales'. She remembered Monsieur in his earlier years, when she found him pleasing but dissipated. For some time previous to the Revolution he had, however, lived entirely in the society of the Duchesse de Polignac, and was very much attached, it was said, to her sister-in-law, Madame de Polastron. 'Such was the decorum of manner observed, it would have been impossible to find it out'[D]

Marie Antoinette's death is not recorded in the Journal, which breaks off in August 1793, but Bess never ceased to remember her with sorrow and affection, and the sight of the exiled Bourbons now moved her to write:

> As I was a great deal at Versailles, where the Queen had given me an apartment, and, passing, over all etiquette, had invited me to the *Bals de Cour*, I can really speak of things from my own knowledge.[D]

It was from her own knowledge that she acquitted both the Queen and Madame de Polignac of every transgression and folly imputed to them except the folly of having listened to evil counsellors.

A month later the Duchesse de Grammont and her daughter Corisande,[101] daughter and granddaughter of Madame de Polignac, escaped to England, and Bess was at once invited to bring them with her to Chatsworth. The visit was duly paid, but not until the abnormally cold November of the same year, when this note appears in the Journal:

> With what delight I entered the Park gates and through the snow frozen on our windows showed the garden and then the home, with its cheerful lights and blazing fires to the dear little Duchesse Guiche [*sic*]. And then the Duchess came flying down to the library to see us.[D]

In July, Lally-Tollendal called on her, and repeated a conversation between La Fayette and Mirabeau which she rightly thought worth recording. La Fayette had turned down firmly the plans and measures proposed by Mirabeau, who said, '*Ah, ah, Monsieur is playing the Cromwell-Grandison! Very well. You will see what will be the result of trying to unite these two rôles.*'

In October 1800, Bess noted that the French had 'recommenced hostilities in Egypt', and quoted a letter from Sir Sydney Smith to Dr Blanc saying that it was 'hard to begin, all over again', but adding:

> 'Exterminate', which is the favourite word of those who fight the enemy from their writing-desks, is not the object; that to eradicate he had done all that could be done with the means that they had.[D]

The years 1800–01 were, however, sailors' years. Clifford left Harrow to join the Navy as a midshipman; Bess made the acquaintance of Lord Nelson; and Lord St Vincent at Devonshire House spoke his mind upon various subjects — including Lord Nelson.

On November 12th, 1800, Bess wrote a little incoherently:

> I went with Caro and Clifford to call on Lady Hamilton, whom I had known both at Bath as Mrs. Hart and at Naples as Sir William Hamilton's wife. Whilst we were there, Lord Nelson came in. She made us acquainted, and I was delighted with this opportunity of knowing him and making my dear Clifford known to him.
>
> His countenance is interesting and animated, his manner simple and unaffected. He is covered with wounds, has lost the sight of one eye and his right arm, is of a slight, rather delicate make, but his countenance is full of fire and animation, and

it was delightful for us to see and converse with the Hero of the Nile. — Clifford and I on going into the City on Lord Mayor's Day had seen him surrounded by an immense populace, his horses taken off, shouts and huzzas rent the air and the people drew his carriage in triumph. Clifford, who wanted to see him nearer, got out of the carriage and the good-natured mob, seeing the eagerness of this dear boy, lifted him up, saying, 'There he is! Nelson for ever!'

He had just come from the levee and said to Lady Hamilton in a loud whisper, 'I found St. James's as cold as the atmosphere.'[D]

Difficulties soon arose over the question of Lady Hamilton's presentation at Court. As the wife of an Ambassador she was clearly entitled to be received by the Queen, but as the once-notorious Emma Hart she was hardly the sort of person to whom the iron-clad virtue of Charlotte would make concessions.

Lady Hamilton did not mind not being presented, but Sir William was distressed. She said 'It is hard, because the examples of Lady Wellesley, Lady Yarmouth and Lady Ferrers[102] are quoted, which are cases quite different from mine, for I never lived with Sir William as his mistress. I was under the protection of his roof, my mother with me, and we were married in private two years before he married me openly in England.'

I told her that if this could be proved I thought that she ought to have it made known to the Queen, who certainly could not be expected to know more than public report and appearance made to be believed.[D]

Emma's assurances that she had been the means of saving the lives of many people at Naples were received by Bess with the dry comment, 'I trust that this is so', followed by the confession that the prejudice in Mr Fox's mind against her was very strong, 'from a different supposition'.[103]

It is supposed that Nelson was not so well received by the King as was expected, that H.M. disapproved of his having interfered with politics at Naples and that he was influenced to it by Lady Hamilton. Fox and many think that she did not exert that influence on the side of mercy — but I am unwilling to believe this. The Hero of the Nile is as humane as brave and she is a good-natured woman.[D]

On February 14th, 1801, the entry in the Journal is of such interest that it deserves to be given in full:

Lord St. Vincent called on the Duchess and me this morning. I was confined by the hurt on my ankle to my bedroom and he came to me there. He had but an instant to stay, but he would, he said, give me the satisfaction of hearing from himself how highly satisfied he was with Clifford, whom he said he really thought the finest boy he had ever seen or known. 'He has', he continued, 'considerable abilities, a heavenly temper and the most generous disposition I ever met with ... his attention to and his love of his profession are remarkable — in short in body and mind he is a glorious Boy.'

St. Vincent praised Mr. Ponsonby[104] also very much. He then told us he had appointed a man to be his successor who would unite the suffrages of all people — that he was the best and bravest of men. 'For myself', he said, 'I am only popular with my Mediterranean people — the others do not approve of my strict discipline.' 'Oh, yes,' I said, 'perhaps at first they were alarmed, but I believe full justice is done to you now and that your absence will be sincerely regretted.' 'Yes, perhaps,' he said, 'They are come round now. But I must go. And do you and the Duchess make my peace with Lady Spencer, whom I have not yet called upon.' We rang for his carriage. 'Oh, I have no carriage,' said Lord St. Vincent, 'I always go on foot, and I am going to the King, who expressed a wish to see me particularly on this day——^{D}

The anniversary of his great victory off Cape St Vincent,

> Lord St. Vincent, who loves Nelson as his son yet said to us 'That foolish little fellow Nelson has sat to every painter in London. His head is turned by Lady Hamilton, who sometimes writes him four letters a day. I conceal some of them when I can.' He said, 'Nelson is a brave man but a partizan. Troubridge is the best officer we have.'^{D}

St Vincent's praise of her dear Clifford must have been peculiarly comforting to Bess at that time, for she was still under the shadow of the great sorrow which had befallen her at the end of 1800 — the death of her mother, Lady Bristol. 'It was', she wrote on New Year's Day, 1801, 'quite sudden, and sudden was my hearing of it. A letter from my sister Louisa said. "our sad loss" — I knew not what it was — turned the page — saw, "our Mother" — I could no more. I lost my reason — almost my life.'^{D}

Two days earlier the Duchess of Devonshire had written to the apparently-still-hopeful Duke of Richmond to assure him of 'Dearest Bess' being better, though still kept under the influence of laudanum. The dreadful shock had very nearly deprived the Duchess of her dearest friend. They were all rejoicing over Lord Carlisle's letter giving his consent to Georgiana's marriage with his son, Lord Morpeth,[105] when Bess, who did not even know that her mother was ill, opened the shattering letter.^{C}

To the Duke Bess herself wrote later that her irreparable loss had left her 'a mere creature of feeling and affection'; she would try to do what her mother would approve; that would be her aim. 'May she be allowed to support and assist me!'[C]

Lady Bristol left a letter for her errant husband of which Bess was anxious to be the bearer. 'I should like', she writes, 'to be with him when he reads it.' In a little time, she adds, she will probably leave 'this dear country' for ever.

> Caroline will find abler protection from the Duchess and Georgiana than I could give her, and if I can recall my father to any feeling I shall know the little of good I ever can know.[D]

She does not mention either of the Fosters, both of whom had gone up to Oxford in 1797. In 1799 Augustus entered the Horse Guards (Blue) only to abandon the Army for diplomacy two years later. Frederick subsequently became MP for the Hervey borough of Bury St Edmunds. As for Clifford, he could obviously be trusted to make his way in the Navy, the profession of his choice.

On the evening of Lord Morpeth's formal betrothal to Lady Georgiana Cavendish three members of the Devonshire House circle were unable to be present; the Duke, because he was laid up (probably with an attack of gout), Hary-O because she was suffering from a sore throat, and Lady Elizabeth because she elected to stay and keep His Grace company. She dined with him in his room and read aloud to him till very late at night — apparently not an unusual procedure.

> Pope's *Dunciad*, and some of Churchill's poems have been our lecture, and delightful and improving it is to read with him — to him, to his unerring taste, Mr. Fox, Hare, Sheridan, all refer when they have any doubts themselves about any work or passage.[D]

Lady Elizabeth accompanied the Duke and Duchess and Hary-O when they visited Georgiana Morpeth in her new home at Castle Howard. They found her well and happy, and her father-in-law, Lord Carlisle, paid Bess the compliment of telling her what she rightly described as 'a curious anecdote'.

> Many years ago he went with George Selwyn and the late Lord Orford[106] to see a person at Twickenham. Lord Orford sat down in an arm-chair that was there and said 'I must tell you what Lady FitzWilliam (the Irish one) told me in this very chair. Sir Mathew Decker was her father, and Mr. Germain, husband to Lady Betty Germain, having read the Gospel of St Mathew, was so struck, he said, with the beauties of it that he bequeathed her an annuity as a homage to the memory of her father, whom he called, and believed to be, St Mathew, and she actually enjoyed the annuity in consequence of his belief of this.'[D]

The opening pages of the Journal for 1801 are packed with political items. Fox's 'imprudent praise of the Revolution' had alarmed the 'true patriots' at the head of whom Bess ranked 'D.D.'. Lady Bessborough, who had 'fifty thousand anecdotes' to relate when the two ladies should meet, avowed that she was 'growing quite a Pittite'.*D* Sheridan remarked that the cause of our war with Russia was that the Emperor wanted Willis[107] and King George dared not part with him.

The poor King did indeed want Dr Willis at this time. He was discussing affairs of State with his footman and had only a short while previously read aloud a highly confidential dispatch from Lord Spencer at a garden fete held in honour of Pitt.*D*

Apparently Bess never enjoyed the possibly painful experience of delivering her dead mother's letter to 'that cruel man', her father, and watching to see its effect upon him. He died at Albano, near Rome, on August 8th, 1803, and his purple-edged white hat, his crimson coat, silver-spangled black sash and purple stockings appeared no more beneath the warm Italian sky which he loved so well.

The Comic Muse, faithful to him in his lifetime, did not desert him after death.

He desired to be buried with his ancestors in the little church at Ickworth but nine months elapsed before his desire could be fulfilled. Even when his coffin was once hoisted aboard the *Monmouth* man-of-war at Naples, all difficulties were not at an end. The superstitious dread with which seamen always resent the presence of a corpse on board obliged Mr Elliot, the British Minister at Naples, and Captain George Hart, the commander of the vessel, to pack and ship the mortal remains of the Earl-Bishop in the guise of a piece of antique sculpture on its way to a collector in England.

CHAPTER VII

The Peace of Amiens — Paris Again — The First Consul — Junot —
1801–1803

The King's condition deteriorated in the early spring of 1801, and the Devonshire House ladies, while sympathizing with the pallor and agitation of the Prince of Wales, were anxious that he should observe all the correct forms, including attendance at the last Drawing Room in March. He was reluctant to go, and pleaded that he had 'no black coat'. Next day he wrote to Lady Carlisle and said that he had 'found a black coat and would go'.[D]

Once more, as in 1788–89, a Regency seemed imminent. At secret interviews between the Prince and Mr Pitt the Minister showed an inclination to 'soften down' the restrictions[108] he had wished to impose twelve years before and the Prince a reciprocal inclination to accept what he offered. Lord Egremont counselled acceptance 'on any condition'.[D]

Meanwhile Mr Fox was at St Anne's, 'more eager about the blossom in his garden or a literary dispute than about politics'.[D]

On April 13th the Tower and Hyde Park guns fired in honour of the Battle of the Baltic; but to a nation distressfully digesting the results of Bonaparte's second Italian campaign and the grim implications of the Peace of Lunéville the discomfiture of his Russian, Swedish, and Danish puppets brought little cheer. Even the alleged Peace negotiated at the end of the year and signed at Amiens in March 1802 was recognized by most people for what it was — an armed, uneasy, and precarious truce.

Lord Hervey seems to have been less sceptical. He brought the news to Devonshire House with 'so triumphant a look' that the ladies at once guessed his errand: but in the Commons, as Mr Hare wrote to Bess,

C. Fox, in one sentence as ill expressed and as ill delivered as it is possible to conceive, and quite like a person who was frightened at the sound of his own voice, declared that he received the Peace 'with joy and *exultation*', a strange word for which he hesitated some time and might as well not have found at last.[D]

'It was', as Addington said, 'a Peace everyone was glad of and no one was proud of.' The funds fell, instead of rising. And even when ratification followed in March 1802 only a few squibs were let off.

But it was 'in consequence of the Peace' that, as Bess wrote, 'our two dear little midshipmen'[109] had leave from Lord St Vincent to go with the Bessboroughs to Hardwick at the end of 1801.

The party at Hardwick amused themselves and each other very well. Of Lord Cornwallis's appointment as Minister Plenipotentiary to Amiens, General FitzPatrick said that he was 'like the gaudy gowns at Oxford — brought out on all occasions': and Bess demonstrated her erudition by pointing out that, though La Harpe had declared that the absence of the word *chien* from French drama demonstrated the superior dignity of the French language, the word actually occurs in *Athalie.*[D]

Mr Hare departed at the end of February, after a visit of two months all but a few days. 'No character,' writes Bess, 'not even Shakespeare's Biron, can give an idea of Mr. Hare ... wit, taste, judgment, sensibility.' In the notes which Clifford added many years later to those parts of his mother's journal which he believed to have been 'written for Memoirs', he gives this account of her admired friend:

> Mr. Hare was a college acquaintance and intimate friend of the Duke of Devonshire who brought him into Parliament for the Borough of Knares-borough. He was celebrated for his wit. It is related of him and his colleague, Lord John Townshend, that during the horrors of the French Revolution the Duke having given some Vote *contra* the opposition of that day and in favour of the Government, they both waited on the Duke next morning and tendered their resignation of the seals of the Borough. — The reply of the Duke was so characteristical that they both burst out laughing. His only remark was — 'I never interfere with your Votes — I don't see why you should interfere with mine.' The only question on which he put any restriction was that they should vote in favour of the Bill for the suppression of cruelty to animals.

It is hardly necessary to add that Hary-O disliked and ridiculed her father's old friend, whose habit of 'sitting with his taper legs crossed like a tailor's' she found particularly annoying.

Presently there was once more a French envoy in London from whom the Devonshire House ladies could ask for news from Paris. Monsieur Otto assured them that it was in reality Danton who ordered the September massacres and that Robespierre was merely his instrument. He also pleased them by praising the gaiety and courage of 'women of the first fashion' as they waited for the summons to the guillotine:

When the jailer came to open the door all turned to see whose turn it was, and those who remained would often exclaim to those who went, 'You are very lucky to go first but if the jailer said he had only come to prepare them and they had yet some hours, they would, with the most unaffected ease and cheerfulness, say '*Come, let us dine — or sup — together once more.*'

Poor Monsieur Otto was much disappointed at the lack of public enthusiasm over the Peace. It is true that when Lord Hervey sent the news to the Lord Mayor, who lived at Clapham, that worthy flung himself into the messenger's chaise and proclaimed the glad tidings with a loud voice all the way back to London; but there was 'lethargy among all ranks' except in the city itself, and even there uneasiness prevailed on 'change.[D]

Monsieur Otto seems to have been in a constant state of agitation during his stay in London. A variety of small incidents ruffled his anti-Royalist feathers. For example, the three guiltless sons of Philippe Egalité, having been released after four years of rigorous imprisonment, were naturally received in English society, both Whig and Tory, with every sign of sympathy. 'I think', wrote Bess,

> the offence which Otto took at the three young Orleans Princes being at the Mansion House banquet in their *cordons bleus*[110] was beneath a triumphant Republic to notice. 'Your friend the Prince of Wales was the cause of this,' said my brother, 'He invited them, and when Lord Moira saw them come in he took the names out of the three plates next to the Prince's and put theirs in.'[D]

Though Mr Fox and Lady Elizabeth Foster may not have agreed about the Peace of Amiens, they were at one in their immediate personal reaction, which was a resolve to cross the Channel at the earliest possible opportunity. On July 17th he paid a morning call at Devonshire House and was 'quite delightful'. He talked of his forthcoming visit to France. 'Bonaparte', he said, 'had very foolishly made a regulation about people being presented to him.' The rule was that they should be presented on the 4th of one month and if they were there on the 4th of the next month they were asked to dinner. The ladies suggested that Bonaparte would not adhere strictly to this rule, but would have what Lally-Tollendal called '*a little streak of vanity*'. But Fox was resolved to be home by September 4th, 'on account of his farm'.[D]

> 'I don't read as many novels as I did,' said Fox. 'Oh, fie!' said the Duchess. Fox then confessed he read them only when Mrs. Armistead was ill, or when he was in town; but he was far from thinking, as most people did, that there was no good in modern novels. He complained of his eyes, and said he needed more magnifying glasses than three years ago.

The Duchess confessed she did not talk about politics at night as it prevented her sleeping. Fox found that if he wrote his History[111] at night it agitated him, and when he went to bed he thought over what he had written, and thought one word wanted changing, and another would be better elsewhere, and it kept him awake.

They had the last print brought in from Smith's picture. C.F. thought it good, but also said it looked as if some disagreeable proposition had been made to him. They examined the brow. 'When Charles,[112] Lord Holland's son, was born,' said Fox, 'who has no more eye-brows than my hand, Lady Holland said she did not know who he was like, but it was evident that he had the Fox eye-brows.'[D]

They were Stuart eyebrows, a heritage passed down from Charles II to his remotest posterity.

Bess noted with pleasure that when Sir Francis Burdett topped the poll at Brentford on July 28th and a long procession carrying blue flags and laurel boughs escorted him to his house in Piccadilly, there were 'no democratic cries — only against Bastilles and unjust imprisonments'.[D] Clearly England was sound at the core.

On August 9th there occurs an entry which demonstrates the almost Boswellian skill of Dearest Bess in recording conversations.

A few days ago, whilst Mr. Hare was sitting with me, the Dss came in and asked him if there was any news. 'I know such news,' he said, 'But I'll give you to guess. You, who guess well, now guess.' 'Is it a marriage? Your son, your daughter?' 'No, but you are nearer. The deed is done — I will tell you both. I know that you and Lady E. are full of a very right feeling——' 'Oh, it is Charles Fox,' I said. 'He is married,' continued Mr. Hare, 'To Mrs. Armistead.' We were silent a moment. I don't know rightly what was the feel — it was something of surprise — of regret——

Mr. Hare had been told at Brooks, where Lord Robert had received a letter from C.J.F. mentioning their arrival at Calais —— 'as I thought it would be more agreeable to Mrs. Armistead to travel under my name than hers I think our marriage need not be a secret any longer.'[D]

They had been secretly married for more than six years. Apparently Fox was brought to the point by Mrs Armistead's distress over the efforts of Thomas Coutts to arrange a marriage between him and his daughter Fanny.

Robert Adair[113] fed the Duchess and Bess with gossip about Fox's visit to the First Consul. He doubted whether the Whig leader had actually called the First Consul the 'greatest man of the greatest nation', but he confirmed the report that he had vigorously combated Bonaparte's conviction that Georges Cadoudal[114] had been directed and financed from England. As an instance of the imperturbability of Mr Fox, Adair related that after his first audience Mrs Fox wanted to know all about it. He answered only in general terms that the Consul had been very civil, and immediately asked her where was the place they had left off at in the novel they were reading. He did, however, confirm later to Bess that Bonaparte had said, *à propos* of the Tuileries, '*At least they cannot say that I have inherited this from my ancestors.*'[D]

Sir Thomas Troubridge was good enough to call on Lady Elizabeth towards the end of September 1802 to inform her that Clifford's ship, the *Argo*, commanded by Captain Hallowell, had been commissioned 'for a 3 years' station on the coast of Africa'. She was able to visit the ship, a 74, as she lay off Woolwich; and on October 27th she herself set off for France, with her daughter as her companion.

Immediately after her departure the Duchess wrote to her that she had been battling with herself all day not to make her head ache or to make 'Ca' uncomfortable. He was very sorry, too, for their 'dear Racky', and as she herself was not in spirits she felt gloomy as to her powers of keeping up his 'oldacrity'. This, like 'whops' and other misspelt or mispronounced words, was Devonshire House jargon. She promises to watch for dear Clifford on the morrow: a glimpse would make her as happy as it would make him.

'From Boulogne', wrote Bess to the Duchess,

> we had a view of the English Coast — when it appeared so near and distinct I almost jumped out of the carriage. The postillion laughing said, '*Yes, yes that's England — that's Dover Castle.*' Other English families reached the Inn first, occupied the best rooms and eat up all that was in the house.[C]

She found the officials civil but not respectful, the people friendly enough but inclined to be insolent.

> The postillions and people would look into the chaise and then say, '*What the devil, they are pretty, anyhow,*' — very good to hear, but odd.[C]

In Paris, where Frederick Foster was with them, they put up at the Hotel de l'Empire, formerly the home of a banker named Laborde. It still contained silk-covered furniture, fine glasses and ormolu clocks.

Bess was anxious to catch a glimpse of Bonaparte at a parade.[115] The streets were full of soldiers; and then 'a faint acclamation and several horses in motion showed them that Bonaparte had got on his horse'. Although the already-celebrated smile was not on this occasion visible it is clear that she quickly came under the spell of that extraordinary personality.

Our eyes were rivetted on Him who, in a plain uniform, attended and surrounded by his generals richly dressed, his faithful mameluke in the most splendid apparel, rode along the lines, he alone bowing when the colours were lowered and stopping to speak to the soldiers whom he called out of the line... then receiving the Petitions which we saw men and women eagerly pressing forward to offer him.

I could see the animation of his countenance though not the sweetness of his smile.

It seemed to me to be the most worth seeing of any sight I ever had beheld — this extraordinary Man in all the simplicity of acknowledged greatness, the creator — the commander — the head of this and innumerable other armies ready to act whatever he commanded, who had acted and executed whatever he had planned, riding from line to line, certain that at a word of his these men would march to the extremity of Europe, and then returning to his Palace, the Palace of 14 centuries of Kings, himself a foreigner, and of such limited fortune that the day that he commanded the Army of the Convention against the sections he had not money to buy a General's uniform.[D]

Sheridan had offered to 'bet anything that she would faint seven times running when she first saw Bonaparte if nothing else would attract his attention'.[116] She did not faint even once, but, as will be seen hereafter, she did find a means of attracting the attention of the First Consul.

Her letters to the Duchess do not reflect these ardours. She writes of dining 'comfily' alone with Caroline, who afterwards plays on the harp; she urges her friend to bring Hary-O to Paris. Even the being in a new place arouses the attention of a young person, she remarks; and one hopes that Hary-O never saw the next sentence; 'the corsets here are very advantageous to the shape'.[C] It would appear that Lady Harriet's outward apathy as well as her awkward figure had been discussed by her mother and 'Lady Liz'.

The Duke, in a short note beginning and ending with 'Dearest Bess', asks to be remembered to 'Caroline and Mr. Foster'. Although he was cautious in his attitude towards their daughter, there can be little doubt that she was nearer to his heart than either G. or Hary-O. He was making a quarterly allowance to Caroline, and Bess begs that this may be sent in guineas. Money, she explains, melts like sugar; but she laid some out on a handkerchief and a lace cap for her 'angelic friend', adding an elaborate drawing to show exactly how the cap should be arranged.[C]

Concern about the Duchess's failing health and drooping spirits constantly peeps out, often expressed in the baby-talk so abhorrent to Hary-O. 'My dearest, why are oo gloomy? Why are oo vexed?' writes Bess; and the Duchess answered pitifully, 'My dear Bess, do you hear the voice of my heart crying to you?'[C]

Lady Bessborough was among the English ladies of fashion who felt the magnetic pull of a Paris now purged of its revolutionary taint and glittering with the rather tinselly splendours of a new régime. At several points her letters to her lover, Lord Granville Leveson-Gower, overlap with Bess's to the Duchess, and with the entries in the Journal about this time. Some of the same figures cross the scene: Narbonne,[117] Camille Jordan,[118] Berthier,[119] Madame Récamier.[120]

The Earl-Bishop's daughter cared for other things than lace caps and corsets and other people than dictators, politicians, 'aristos', and fashionable beauties. She made friends with Canova,[121] whose munificent patroness she was destined to be during her last years in Rome, and she heard from his own lips his retort to Bonaparte when the First Consul asked him if he had seen the four horses he had brought from Venice and placed on the Carrousel: '*I saw them only too well.*'[D] The sculptor deeply resented the treatment meted out to Italy by the victor of Marengo, and desired only to make his way back to Rome; but for the moment he was busy upon a statue of Bonaparte.[122] His model, as he told Lady Elizabeth,

> gave him sittings while at breakfast, but when he grew weary he would ring the bell and tell the servant to ask Madame Bonaparte to come. He would talk and joke with her, leaning on her shoulder and patting her cheek, and had every appearance of loving her very much. Canova praised Bonaparte's brow and eyes but said there was no expression of sweetness or feeling except when he smiled.[D]

Nor was literature neglected. Bess went to call upon La Harpe,[123] a little old man dressed *à la* Voltaire, who after some persuasion recited his latest poem, *La Révolution*; but when the English lady asked him some questions about Voltaire himself she was, to her great annoyance, interrupted and headed off by another pilgrim — none other than Mr Edgeworth[124] Maria's father, who in the worst possible French, would ask the aged poet again and again to repeat what he called '*ces bels vers*'.[D]

Keenly alive to everything she saw and heard, Bess was shocked at the sight of the Tricolour flying over the Tuileries and the wooden frame still marking that spot in the Place de la Concorde where the guillotine had been set up. She listened attentively when Marshal Berthier and others declared that 'all might have been saved' as late as August 10th, 1789, had Louis XVI placed himself at the head of his troops and appealed to the people; and when the Marshal told her that Marie Antoinette could never be persuaded to cry '*Long live the Nation*' even in response to a cry of '*Long live the Queen*', she answered warmly, 'She was wrong there; but she had a great and generous heart, incapable of hatred or revenge.'[D]

In her old acquaintance La Fayette she marked a great change.

Eliza Ellis *née* Hervey.

He has grown very fat and looks much healthier, but quite a different man. Instead of fair hair powdered and a pale face, he has a brown wig and a good deal of colour. He told us that nothing that was told of his captivity was exaggerated. Prussian and Hungarian officers showed great interest in him, but the Austrians were 'immovable'.[D]

The pleasure of Dearest Bess in all these sights and scenes was clouded by her anxiety about her favourite niece, the charming, fair-haired Eliza, only child of the unforgotten Lord Hervey. She had been married[125] in 1796 to Charles Rose Ellis, the son of a wealthy West Indian planter, and their home had been at Claremont, the house of which Jane Austen would write in 1813 that it seemed 'never to have prospered'. This was like a touch of second sight in Miss Austen, for two more happy young wives associated with that place were destined to die untimely: Princess Charlotte in 1817, and the Duchesse de Nemours in 1857. Writing to her sister, Lady Erne, in January 1803, Bess said, 'Were I more at ease about our dearest Eliza, I should amuse myself excessively at Paris'; and in her Journal she wrote, 'Oh, my heart — and yet I hope — she is so young.' She also consoles herself with the reflection that Vaughan[126] says her lungs are sound.

Eliza Ellis died at Nice on January 21st, leaving three small children, two sons and a daughter. Even Hary-O had not found it possible to be ill-natured about this gentle young creature, but after a visit to Claremont in August 1802 she animadverted on the ugliness of her 'frightful child', the baby girl who if she did not inherit her mother's beauty did inherit her tendency to consumption, of which she died in 1822.

Bess was heart-broken. 'It is', she wrote to the Duchess, 'losing my dear brother all over again';[C] and it must have been for that brother's sake that she loved his child better than she did the charming little daughter of her sister Lady Erne.[127] Bess was ready to rush to Nice, to her sister-in-law, Lady Hervey, who always used to turn to her for comfort; and she spares a compassionate thought to the 'poor Baby, so wished for, received with so much joy, and never to know its mother'.[C] Miss Mary Berry had written a letter so unsympathetic that the recipient had to remind herself that it was 'not her fault if her heart and mind are made of coarse materials'.[C]

It was before this bitterly felt loss that she dined with Narbonne and La Fayette, and noted their comments upon the state with which Madame Bonaparte had been received at the Ministère de la Marine and also upon her 'scarcely speaking' on that occasion.

La Fayette said, '*It is really a little too much. When the Queen went into Society no particular distinctions were made — she spoke to everyone.*' 'Oh,' said M. de Narbonne, '*Apprentice Queens do not know their job. They are like tight-rope-dancers — it takes time to learn not to go too high or too low, and to acquire aplomb.*'

The First Consul was certainly irritable and uneasy about this time. When the French Minister in Stockholm wrote to complain that Mr Arbuthnot[128] had dined with the Swedish Royal Family 'on account of Prince William of Gloucester living at his house' and that he himself had not been invited, Bonaparte said it was beneath his dignity to interfere in such things, but he scolded the unfortunate Swedish Minister in Paris without giving him any reason, and reminded him sharply that his country was a *third-class Power.*[D]

He was apprehensive, too, still haunted perhaps by memories of the Chouan conspiracy, and afraid even to go and see the pupils of Madame Campan act *Esther.* In conversation with that excellent woman, to whose seminary for young ladies he had consigned his sisters, Caroline and Pauline, he talked of marriages of convenience and *amourette* marriages. '*Eh, mon Général,*' said Madame de Campan, '*That is garrison language! One must not say "amourette".*' '*Oh, I beg your pardon,*' said Bonaparte, '*I know one ought to say "marriages of inclination". I am not very well up in the language of high sentiment.*'

Always avid of new impressions, Bess obtained permission through Lally-Tollendal to visit the library of the *Corps Législatif.* She was shown over by 'an elderly man of melancholy countenance'.

When he heard from Lally-Tollendal that I was English he came up to me and with his eyes full of tears expressed his gratitude to the English nation for their humanity to the French *émigrés.* On hearing that I had been in France before, he said, 'Perhaps you may have known my unfortunate Master?'

He spoke of the King and Queen with regret and attachment, but looked round as if afraid of being heard. I said to him, 'But at least you can breathe freely now Bonaparte has restored order?' 'Yes, one can breathe. But will it last?'

A visit to the *Corps Législatif* followed. The members were wearing blue coats embroidered in gold and tricolour sashes. When one rose to speak two *huissiers* solemnly conducted him to the tribune immediately below the President's chair.

Among the British visitors to Paris was the Duchess of Gordon, concerning whom Bess wrote to the Duchess of Devonshire, 'elle s'est surpassée'

> At Lady Cunningham's[129] where she dined she chose to say that no English-men were 'men of honour', and at Duroc's apartment, where she went to see the Parade, on Lady C. coming in, she said, 'Nobody has a right to come in here but those who know General Duroc. Do you know him?' Lady C. said, 'No.' The Duchess said, 'You had better then go out.' Lady C. was ready to cry at the coarseness of this when Lord C. stopped her, and the servant who opened the door said, '*Miladi, you have as much right as anyone else, since General permits us to receive people who are willing to give us something for their places.*' I think it is too good that the Dss. of Gordon was giving out as a favour to her what was a perquisite of the servant.[C]

This redoubtable termagant was, for some reason of her own, inclined to conciliate Bess, whose portrait she vowed that she always carried in her pocket. Political lines of cleavage seemed to have been washed out by the waters of the English Channel, for it was at a great ball given by the Duchess of Gordon that Caro Ponsonby made her debut. Caroline St Jules was there, too, and her half-brother, F.F. Bess attracted attention by walking up and down with Madame Récamier, 'which', she remarks, 'occasioned some people to come up very soon and ask me to present them to her'.[C]

Between these rival beauties there was none of that reciprocal jealousy which cynical persons would regard as inevitable. They remained good friends all their lives, each perhaps feeling that she had little to lose by comparison with the other. When Bess dined with Juliette a few days after the Duchess of Gordon's ball, she found the lovely creature as depicted by David, reclining gracefully on her bed:

> ——she continued so till dinner — people went up to her and grouped round her. I sat down on the bed. She was very coaxing. After dinner she called me to her and said in a very pretty voice, 'My dear, I love you.' The gentlemen were kneeling, standing by, and leaning over the bed.[C]

One might have wished that she had written a description of Talleyrand instead of an account of the dress which she wore to receive him: a black velvet gown trimmed with point lace with a gold tissue handkerchief on her head, 'arranged like a diadem':[C] but no doubt she endorsed the verdict of her son Augustus Foster that he was 'a shocking ugly fellow with both his feet turned inwards'[130]

The English newspapers published reports that Lady Elizabeth Foster had been presented to the First Consul, but neither she nor Lady Bessborough was willing. Their friendship with Marie Antoinette was a sufficient excuse, even though the existing régime bore no direct responsibility for the horrors of 1793. When Marshal Berthier suggested to Bess that she might like to go (apparently with him) to Versailles, she shirked the thought of seeing again a place 'where she had been so kindly treated by the Queen'. The Marshal ended by saying that she should go, 'but not with company, and alone — to think of her perhaps'.[D]

It may have been a touch of what a modern psychologist would call masochism which prompted Bess to go on that sorrowful, sentimental pilgrimage. Her way was made smooth by Dominique de Denon,[131] whom she had known some years before he accompanied Bonaparte to Egypt in his character of archaeologist and who was now Director-General of Museums. She had not at first recognized him in the 'little man in a dressed coat, his hair out of powder, his eyes full of fire and genius', who had come up to her saying, *'I am afraid Milady has forgotten me?'* They were soon bending together over his great book, *Voyage dans la Haute et Basse Egypte*, while he 'explained things' and expatiated on the terrible silence of the desert, *'beyond all description'*.[C]

Denon remembered things even more terrible than the silence of the desert. He told Bess that on the day that Robespierre was arrested

> a figure of an old man, lean, wan and pale, followed him everywhere, saying, *'It is all over with you — you shall commit no more crimes — your hour is come'*: and never could they then or since find out who he was. Nothing could be more awful and solemn.
>
> Denon said that to go to the *Comité du Salut Publique* you were conducted at night. They sat in the apartments which Bonaparte now occupies — six of these men of blood were there, sitting round — the person brought before them [was] preceded by torches. All around was silent.
>
> When Robespierre was arrested he was sitting in the very room where he had signed the death of thousands, and he begged for a glass of water. A woman came up to him and said, *'You are thirsty? Drink blood, then.'* And a man came up to him and said, *'You are thirsty for blood. Drink your own.'*[D]

When Bess went to Versailles her son F.F. and her daughter Caroline went with her. She was painfully impressed by the silence, desolation, and decay on every side, the grass growing in the courts, the many windows boarded up, the passage which had led to Madame de Polignac's apartments, once encumbered by gay if incongruous little stalls, now 'silent and dark as the cloisters in a convent'. The Petit Trianon was in ruins and much of the fine timber had been felled. She was glad, however, to observe that here and there the emblems of the crown and the fleurs-de-lis had been blotted out but not destroyed.[D]

The guide told her that Bonaparte had visited only the gardens at Versailles, not the Palace, and she was surprised at the frankness with which he uttered his royalist sentiments. Denon's permit gave her access to whatever apartments she wished to enter, and even her desire to look once more on Madame Vigée Le Brun's portrait of Marie Antoinette and her three children was not denied.

> We were conducted along a long and melancholy deserted passage ... all was dark and closed up — not a creature did we meet. A small staircase led to a kind of lumber-room — the very key was lost, so little was it in use — they broke open the door for me and here were the pictures of the Royal Family, and in particular that one of the Queen, the Dauphin, Madame and the Duke of Normandy, finely painted by Madame Le Brun.
>
> M. Denon 'thought it better that it should not be shown to the public. There had been imprudent remarks. *People had made comparisons.*'[D]

Overwhelmed by memories, Bess sent F.F. and Caroline to explore the English Garden at Trianon without her, while she sat where she could see one of the finest views of the Palace. 'No words', she wrote,

> can express what I felt; for I had known the Queen intimately enough to have witnessed how she united the comforts of private life to the brilliancy of the first situation in the world.[D]

Yet neither sorrow for her dear Eliza nor melancholy memories of Marie Antoinette could long obscure her interest in the figure which dominated the whole scene.

'At last', exclaimed Bess on March 24th,

> I have seen Bonaparte near, where I could examine his countenance and observe its changes and expression. I am not disappointed. I never saw a face it would be more impossible to overlook. I never saw one which bore a stronger stamp of thought, penetration, and a daring mind.
>
> He came in about the fourth Act of *Phèdre*, and it had the appearance certainly of his going to overawe the cabal[132] party at the Theatre who had expressed a disapprobation of Madlle George[133] the two preceding nights for her acting.[D]

Mademoiselle Duchesnois had previously acted the part of Phèdre with great success, and there had been a riot in the theatre when, at the end of the play *Tancrède*, 'a murmur was heard in the pit of '*Phèdre*, Duchesnois'. An actor came forward and said, '*Phèdre is in our repertoire.*' This 'equivocating answer', says Bess, 'angered the pit, who sent an ambassador on to the stage to ask for *Phèdre* by their favourite actress'. He was seized by the guards. A riot ensued. People surged on to the stage. Arrests followed. And when two days later *Phèdre* was acted again with George in the title role the entrance was full of soldiers. It was on this occasion that Bess and her party were present.[D]

When the First Consul arrived during the scene between Theseus and Hippolytus he was received with great applause which Bess and her friends imagined to be intended for the actors. Lally-Tollendal 'with great *bonhomie*' called out, '*It is a fine scene — bravo, bravo!*' and clapped with all his might. Then Bess saw that Bonaparte was bowing. At the end of the performance he went away while the audience were still applauding Mademoiselle George. 'Nothing', she writes emphatically, 'can be a stronger proof of the subjection the people are in than this submissive reception of an actress whose acting in this part they and everybody disapprove of.'[D]

Talma, Bess reveals, once told Kemble that Bonaparte who loved to meddle in theatrical affairs, blamed him for acting the part of Caesar as if Caesar really felt what he said. '*People like that never feel anything.*'[D]

Kemble was in Paris at this time. He presented Lady Bessborough and Lady Elizabeth with necklaces made from 'the famous salt rock in Spain',[134] but these, said Lord Duncannon in a letter to his mother, were 'only for show, as the least damp melts them immediately'.

Madame de Montesquiou[135] threw further light upon the ostensible hard-heartedness of the First Consul in an anecdote thus set down in the Journal.

Madame de Montesquiou said that Bonaparte though rough with his wife was very much attached to her and said that there was nobody who understood him so well as she. She related how one day she had called on Josephine early and found her not yet dressed. Bonaparte came storming in, reproaching her with never being ready, and Madame de M. offered to withdraw. B. said '*Come on, get dressed, and I will talk to Madame Montesquiou.*' Madame de M. was, she confessed, both flattered and fatigued; the First Consul walked up and down the whole time and she came near fainting. However, she had a favour to ask him on behalf of someone in whom she was interested, and she spoke with warmth. Presently she thought she saw signs of relenting in his eyes, and exclaimed, '*I have won the day.*' He took her by the arm and said '*No, Madame — one must govern by the mind and not by the heart.*'[D]

The Peace was wearing very thin, and Lord Whitworth,[136] the English Ambassador, had need of all his good humour, tact, discretion, and forbearance to stave off the clash which the First Consul was obviously determined to provoke. As Narbonne remarked to Talleyrand, it was impossible to correct Bonaparte's misapprehensions. 'If', said Narbonne, 'I were falsely accused of poisoning Lady Elizabeth nobody would dare produce her in good health. Bonaparte could still believe me guilty if he wanted to.'[D]

Before the inevitable happened that lady had two more opportunities of contemplating the now brooding and ominous Bonaparte at short range. One night in Lord Whitworth's box at the opera she remarked that she had never been so well placed to see the First Consul. 'Yes,' said the Ambassador, laughing, 'it is a good place for me to take aim; it is a *batterie de commande*.'[D]   On April 2nd she and her friends occupied windows with a fine view of the Place du Carrousel when Bonaparte inspected the troops, walking this time instead of riding on the favourite dun charger of Louis XVI.

> After the infantry and dismounted cavalry had formed squares he went round each square on foot to talk to the soldiers. When he came to the square opposite our windows we not only saw him distinctly as if we had been in a room but heard him speak to the soldiers. To one he said '*Have you seen active service?*' '*No!*' '*You're lucky.*' To another, '*You will have good Generals.*' The moment he had done speaking to one particular square the soldiers began smoking, talking and joking to one another, or repeating what *le petit bonhomme* had said to them. Quin[137] heard Bonaparte say to a soldier, '*You are a jolly fellow. You will fight well.*' '*Place yourself near me, mon Général, and you'll see!*'
>
> I felt the greatest eagerness to see Bonaparte, I own, and the moment that he came up to where I was I only thought of him as a conqueror amid his troops and forgot the Tyrant.[D]

Caro and she saw him perfectly, and she herself caught his eye and his smile. She had asked Berthier to make him turn towards where they stood, and the Marshal had 'evidently' mentioned her to him. Sheridan ought to have known that Dearest Bess would find an easier and more elegant way of attracting the great man's attention than by fainting even once.

Bonaparte was, she observed, taller than Berthier. He walked well 'but generally with his arms across'.

Little more than a fortnight had passed since the famous interview with Lord Whitworth, but the First Consul was not likely to deny a glance and a smile to a pretty Englishwoman who had through Berthier solicited that grace. As for Berthier himself, he confessed, '*this woman fascinates me*'.

Bess's account of the interview, though corresponding at many points with others already well known, seems worth inserting here.

The First Consul began by remarking to the English Ambassador that it appeared as if there would be '*a storm of some sort*'; that French armaments were intended only for their colonies; and that after fifteen years of war it would be a sad thing for Europe if it had to begin again. Whitworth replied that if it depended on England there would be no war. Bonaparte then went to the other end of the room and said abruptly to Mrs. Greatheed,[139] '*Are you English, Madame? I took you for German.*' Then to the American Minister, asking what news there was from his country, and whilst poor Livingston[140] was lifting up his hair [or wig] to hear, B. was off to the other end of the room. Then returning to Lord Whitworth, he exclaimed with an animated countenance that if war must come the fault would rest before God and men upon those who would not carry out the Treaty of Amiens. After which he strode so rapidly out of the room that there was not time to open the double doors for him.[D]

One person at least was in no doubt either as to the imminence of hostilities or the site of the decisive battle. This was Marshal Junot? There was present on that embarrassing occasion an English M.P. named Green who had not long before been much confounded when Berthier mistook him for Charles Grey. To him Junot now went up, saying genially, 'Come and dine with me once more before we fight each other.'[D]

The Marshal was obsessed by the idea of 'St. James's Street'. In a pessimistic moment he prophesied that it would be his fate to 'fall in St. James's Street amid cannons'. Could he have seen official English 'documents headed 'From our Court of St. James's'? He had also heard of another famous London district, for in a more hopeful humour he declared that he would one day be called 'Junot of Westminster'.[D]

The atmosphere grew daily more ominous. The Bessboroughs had returned to England at the end of February 1803, and as the weeks passed the cross-Channel packets became more and more encumbered with the travelling carriages of those sanguine Britons who had hurried over to France during the preceding year. Bess and her daughter, reluctant to leave Paris with the Bois de Boulogne in full leaf, lingered on, and did not disembark at Dover till the end of April, only three weeks before the outbreak of war.

The reluctance of Dearest Bess was augmented by the fact that her son Frederick Foster, young Lord Duncannon and Mr Hare remained behind. She made desperate, and in the end successful, efforts to obtain passports for them through Berthier. Writing[141] to a cautiously unnamed French correspondent on July 12th she pours forth '*thousands upon thousands of thanks*' for the '*good news*' which was beyond anything she had hoped for. She is writing also to thank General Berthier for all that he has done.

All the travellers were back in England by the middle of July, but Berthier was so 'shockingly scolded' by the First Consul that he dared issue no more passports. [D]

By way of epilogue we overhear this fragment of conversation:

Lord Hertford stopped the Duke of Devonshire in the street and asked if it was true that they were come. D.D. said, 'Yes.' 'But how', said Lord Hertford, 'did they get here?' 'Lady Elizabeth Foster obtained it.' said the Duke, 'but I don't know how.' [D]

Napoleon as First Consul, by Gerard.

CHAPTER VIII

The Invasion Scare — The Young Roscius — Prelude to Trafalgar
1803–1805

On July 28th, 1803, the Prince of Wales called at Devonshire House, much agitated by the riots in Dublin and 'the cruel murder of the Lord Chief Justice'.[142] Was Tom Moore right when he said later of the Prince that 'he loved the Green Isle'?

It was foolish as well as harsh of George III to bar his eldest son from any share in the defence of the country against the danger which began to loom on the French coast from the teeming camp at Boulogne. To the Devonshire House ladies the Prince confided his eagerness that the public should know that he was not less anxious than his brothers to serve. He told them that a friend of Addington's had said he (Addington) was deterred from making the Prince's offer[143] known to the King by his (the King's) situation.

> The Prince answered, 'What situation? I know of but two in which at such a crisis the King can be. Either he is well, and able to decide on subjects submitted to him, or he is ill, and ought not to govern at such a moment.'[D]

We are not told what Mr Addington's friend said to this.

News came on July 30th of the capture of Santa Lucia, and Bess recorded with a fluttering hand, 'My dear Clifford then has been in actual war, and only 13 years old!' A week later came news of another complexion — the death of the Earl-Bishop. An express was sent to his only surviving son, who was at Eastbourne and returned to London next day. 'It was', wrote his second sister, 'an affecting moment to us all,' but her tears flowed rather for the kindness of her brother than for the demise of her father. The new Earl promised to obtain a Secretary-ship of Legation for Augustus Foster; he said that if he had not been hampered by some prior engagement 'he would have brought Fred F. in' for the family borough of Bury — a thing he was ultimately able to do. He himself was at that time the sitting member; he had also been Under-Secretary of State since February 1801 and would hold that office until November 1803. A man of serious tastes, a Fellow both of the Royal Society and the Society of Antiquaries, he was better equipped than his elder brother had been to share the interests of their second sister; but it may be doubted whether he could have dealt as competently with her distressful problem in 1785.

Even in her scarcely abated grief for Eliza Ellis and her constant concern about the Duchess's still mounting financial harassments, Bess had consolations over and above the affectionate attentions of the new Lord Bristol. Just before leaving France she had received a letter from the Duke declaring that he was convinced he would approve of whatever conduct her own judgement led her to pursue, and ending:'You may depend on it that the love and friendship I have so long had for you are firmly fixed and unalterable.'[C]

That extraordinary person Lord John Townshend[144] amused the ladies with an original *jeu d'esprit* one evening later in that same month of August 1803. It was a parody of what Lady Bessborough dismisses as a 'stupid Vaudeville song', namely 'Comin' through the Rye'; and Bess must have obtained a copy from the parodist, for she quotes from it at greater length than her friend cared to do, and her version is slightly different. Three stanzas may be given as typical of the whole absurdity.

Mr. Addington

If a body put a body in the Speaker's chair
Need a body keep a body fixed forever there?
My gown and wig so long and big they pleased the royal eye;
Both King and Queen admired my mien, and Minister am I.

Mr. Tierney

If a body join a body called a party Whig
Need a body for that body care a single fig?
Like an ass retired Dundas[145] from Bench of Treasury;
So in his barge I sail at large, triumphant — G. Tierney.

Mr. Sheridan

If a body everybody seeks to please and court
Must a body from no body find the least support?
Not a man trusts Sheridan with half a halfpenny;
Yet all the day I'm blithe and gay, and drunk at night am I.[D]

Intense physical pain was added to the other tribulations of the Duchess in the middle of September, but on the 15th her devoted friend recorded with thankfulness that 'a stone of most extraordinary size and substance passed, and gave her instant ease'.[D] A month later she was well enough to present the colours to the Marylebone Volunteers, among whom Frederick Foster was numbered.

'For my part, I cried', writes Bess, 'and so did most of us.'[D]

Invasion was now the major topic of the hour. When would Bonaparte[146] strike? In what strength? And where?

On October 18th, 1803, Bess wrote in her Journal:

The Prince came tonight to Devonshire House. He appeared nervous and agitated. Lord Moira is appointed to the command of the troops in Scotland. The Duke of York got the King's consent almost before the Ministers knew of it, so that when the Prince told Tierney of it today he had not heard of it from Addington and was indignant. 'How,' he said, 'after all the sacrifices I have made, not even to treat me with confidence!' I said to the Prince unthinkingly, 'Pray, Sir, if it is not wrong to ask Your Royal Highness, where is it thought best that the King should be? 'By G——' said the Prince, 'I don't know — I know nothing — they say he means to head the Army.' 'But then,' I said, 'where will the Queen and the Princesses be?' 'Faith, I know nothing,' said the Prince.

I was struck with his manner. When he had gone I went to the Duke's room and he told me that the Prince had told the Dss that Captain McMahon had come to him from Sir George Shee whom Addington had sent with a sort of message to the Prince — and telling him that they had a sort of scheme for sending the King to Scotland and that in that case the Prince would be called to take the supreme command: but the Prince seemed to disapprove of this idea, refused listening to anything that did not come from the King, and said also that as to command of an Army he could only collect the best Generals round him and that they might in fact command and direct him. The Duke thought the whole a blind sort of story, but gave the Prince credit for acknowledging that he did not know how to command an army — for the danger of the Duke of York is his thinking that he is equal to the command of it all.[D]

Captain McMahon told the Duchess just over a week later that the Ministers had received information that the French were 'expected in 48 hours'. The Prince of Wales was dining with Fox and Sheridan at General Fitzpatrick's house when the question arose of 'some situation' in which His Royal Highness could be useful to his country. Sheridan implied that the Ministers intended to make offers to him, and wanted to know what answer he should make if he were approached. 'Bring them to the point first,' said Fox. There was, observed Bess, 'perfect agreement between the Prince and Mr. Fox except when Fox said he was disgusted with politics and wanted to leave them. "That", said the Prince "can't be. They won't leave you — and you are of too great consequence to leave affairs in such times as these."'[D]

The next excitement was a message from Mr Addington hoping that His Royal Highness did not intend to go out of town, and that if he returned to Brighton would he double his guard? There were persistent rumours to the effect that Sussex smugglers had been offered large sums by Bonaparte to kidnap him. The

Prince replied that

> he had intended going the next day, but that if Mr. A. had reason to expect the invasion immediately he would set out, that very night if necessary, and join his Regiment, which was the situation the King had pointed out to him.[D]

No summons came; but he and Moira sat up at Carlton House until seven on the following morning, waiting for it. The Duchess and Bess went to see the King reviewing the Westminster Volunteers on October 27th. He was attended by all his sons except the first-born, and by the Bourbon Princes. Bess, who always had a quick ear for the comments of the crowd, noted that great admiration was expressed for Monsieur, but that the Duc de Berri was considered to be 'like a pug'.[D]

And then Mr Green, whom she had left behind in Paris, escaped with the aid of an American passport and arrived in London full of the French plans for invasion, probably during the winter months, when the long nights would favour their transports eluding the English fleets.[D]

Bonaparte, said Mr Green, was to issue a proclamation promising quarter to all who should surrender immediately but threatening to shoot all Volunteers who did not return quietly to their homes. One hundred and eighty-seven English-speaking guides were to accompany the Army. Junot was to command the *Avant-Garde*. When informed by his friend Mr Green that England had a million men under arms, the Marshal replied, '*With thirty thousand I would sweep them all away*.'[D] The scare grew. An unnamed lady of fashion went to Mr Reeve of the Alien Office to ask if he had yet sent away Lady Elizabeth Foster's French housemaids; whereupon Mr Reeve summoned Bess to 'give all necessary information' about Laure and Rosa, the maids in question. He interviewed her in a locked room, was perfectly civil, but explained that Devonshire House was considered 'an asylum for all foreigners'. Bess replied that it was — for those whom they had known in prosperity and now found in adversity. Mr Reeve observed 'It is, however, for ladies of high rank and fashion, like you, Madam, not to protect foreigners who may be hostile to this country.' She replied with spirit that it also belonged to women of birth and education to protect those who were wronged, and she 'hoped that by his present conduct he would set an example of justice to show that authority was to protect and not to oppress'.[D]

After a second interview on the following day, she came off; as she proudly records, 'with flying colours'. He promised to protect not only Laure and Rosa, but also the crowd of 'poor, expecting foreigners' through whom he handed her on her way out.[D]

At the end of 1803 and the beginning of 1804 the Devonshires and Bess were in Bath, where we find her almost anticipating Queen Victoria's cult for anniversaries. On January 10th she writes

Georgiana, Duchess of Devonshire, in 1805.

Giorne semprè amare — te perdri caro amato fratello.[147D]

As the date of 'dear, dear Eliza's' death drew near, there was another sprig of rue to gather; and then came the note:

It is now 22 years since the dear friends I am with were at Bath — together almost daily — and when began our strong and unalterable friendship.[D]

Even Sir Sydney Smith's announcement, transmitted by Augustus Foster, that the French troops were actually embarking did not dim Lady Elizabeth's pleasure in 'fashionable fax and polite annygoats'. She recorded a little story of George Selwyn which, for once, detaches his figure from its usual environment of gibbets and graveyards.

One May Day early in the morning when walking in the Street, which was full of little chimney-sweepers, he met Lord Winchelsea, a very dark, swarthy man. After the first salutations were over, Selwyn turned to the chimney-sweepers and said, 'The Master Finches,[148] I suppose? I hope they are all well .'[D]

In February a Regency seemed imminent, and all the Whigs were at once in motion, like a set of puppets jerked upon hastily pulled strings. The Prince wanted the Duchess to return to London. Mr Fox wanted her to incline His Royal Highness 'more towards Grey'.[149] The Morpeths were afraid that Sheridan was pouring poison into the royal ear. And what did Sheridan want? Power and office no doubt, but Lord Cowper told Bess that

> S. said he never went to Brooks' because he only saw there a set of scoundrels following suit — that he went to Miles's, where there was a group of honest fellows who had been in all parts of the world, and could drink all night, which was all he wanted.[D]

'A bright star', wrote Bess in March, 'is about to be extinguished.' It was Mr Hare. His death at Bath chilled for the moment all the political excitements which were heating to fever-heat the blood of his friends in London. No wit ever had a kinder epitaph than that pronounced on him by Bess: 'he was not always on the watch to utter something witty'.[D] The piece of rhymed grandiloquence[150] in which she and Georgiana collaborated looks poor beside it.

Regret for Mr Hare was both personal and political; but when on April 3rd news reached London of the arrest and execution of the young Duc d'Enghien a sort of incredulous horror descended upon all persons and all parties in England. 'Barnave's words', wrote Bess, 'have come true. "Once make war upon us and we shall be savages again."'[D]

It was reported that when Lucien Bonaparte pleaded with his brother for the Duc's life, the First Consul answered 'with a sort of savage determination', that nothing could save him, as he was the only one of the Bourbons from whom he had anything to fear. Another report declared that Josephine had interceded for the unfortunate young Prince 'on her knees'.[D]

The night before the news came Hertford, Cholmondeley, and others were laying bets that Bonaparte would not put him to death. Bess's comments upon the dictator whom she had so recently contemplated with admiring awe sound strangely apposite in modern ears:

> This is the man whose power they persisted in believing to be shaken, this is the War of which I have heard the most enlightened amongst the Ministers say, 'We shall be better friends after it — the war will be a short one, and we shall have learned to esteem one another and all will go on the better.' Fatal, fatal way of seeing and reasoning on such an event as war.[D]

There are times when it almost seems as if Dearest Bess were something of a crypto-Tory; but she melted very prettily into the political as well as the social and sentimental background of Devonshire House.

Here flowered the feminine aspect of Whiggism ... Here in the flesh was the exquisite eighteenth century of Gainsborough, all flowing elegance and melting glances and shifting silken colour.

So writes Lord David Cecil, in pages[151] which seem to call the portraits of Georgiana and Harriet and Bess down from their frames and set them before us in three dimensions, living women who cast moving shadows on the ground.

After sitting up with Mr Fox till 3 a.m. on April 30th — May 1st, 1804, the Prince of Wales came and 'sat for a time' with Bess. She told him that she had heard that he had said that the result of recent events could but be good for him, since he was restored to his original friends. He laughed and said, 'How did you hear that? It is very true, and, by God, now I have got him again they shan't part us!'[D]

Dinners and breakfasts succeeded each other at Devonshire House; the clubs and the drawing-rooms buzzed with rumours and conjectures; the names of Mr Pitt and Mr Fox echoed on every side; yet into a Journal where the pages are congested with politics the following light-hearted anecdote is slipped.

Miss Byng related that a servant of her father's announced one night a visitor to them — 'the late Mr. Timms'. They could hardly command their countenances, but when the company were gone asked him what he could mean. He insisted he was right, and to prove it brought the gentleman's card. It was 'Lt. Timms'.[D]

The news that Bonaparte had proclaimed himself Emperor of France did not cast a shadow on the great concert given at Devonshire House in honour of 'dear Hart's' birthday on May 19th; and they all went to the Speech Day at Harrow three weeks later. Then the *Argo* anchored off the Isle of Wight; and after a breathless interval of three days 'dearest Clifford' was in their midst.

Supping at Devonshire House early in July, Prince Pignatelle Egmont reported that 150,000 men were encamped between Havre and Ostende. Before he left Paris, Madame Bonaparte said to him, '*You are going to a country where hard things will be said of us — but send us peace — speak of peace to two people there.*' He thought she meant by that the Duchess and Bess.[D]

Then, as usual, cheerfulness breaks in, this time in the form of the latest pun current in Paris *à propos* of the newly created empire. *Une belle comédie dont il faut ôter vingt scènes* —Vincennes, the place of the Due d'Enghien's execution.

The King was now in high spirits, thought himself capable of riding a hundred miles in a day, and was determined to 'erect the Royal Standard in case of invasion' [D] At the opening of Parliament on August 7th Bess notes that he was observed chatting, and even joking, with Lord Melville during the Speaker's remarks. He began by saying, 'I don't like that phrase Great Britain and Ireland. I never did.' Then he said, 'Did I keep up my voice well?' 'Very well, Sir. I never heard Your Majesty read better.' 'That is,' said the King, 'Because I liked what I had to read. It was a speech a gentleman might speak with pleasure. I always speak well when it is not milk and water.'[D]

None the less his parlous mental plight was becoming every day more apparent, and the reluctance of the Cabinet to acknowledge the fact placed the Prince of Wales in a painful position. This reluctance persisted even when the King took to locking himself in a room with a favourite housemaid; directed scarlet breeches to be worn with the Windsor uniform; and then gave orders that in the case of the Generals in attendance upon him at the castle the uniform should be made 'strait before like the French general's uniform'. General Grenville begged for a little to be cut off; he said he could not walk. 'The tailor said it was as much as his place was worth. He had the King's orders.'[D]

On August 21st Bess writes that they all went to see Clifford set out for Plymouth to rejoin his ship, the *Argo*. She adds proudly,

> Lord Spencer came to D.H. His high opinion of Clifford and all that he told him of Captain Hallowell[152] has determined him to send his second son[153] to serve under him.

She records with less emotion the departure of Augustus Foster to take up the Secretary-ship of the English Legation at Washington. They corresponded regularly, and he made no attempt to conceal his dislike both for his environment and his company. Washington he unkindly described as an 'absolute sepulchre'; and he exclaimed with conviction,

> Even you, with all your resources and powers of self-amusement, would absolutely be puzzled here. You can bear many things, but you cannot bear vulgarity.[154]

It is hardly surprising that he was unsuccessful as Secretary of Legation, and when, after an interval of service at Stockholm, he went back to America as Minister, he was more unsuccessful still.

In the autumn of that year the Bessboroughs, undaunted by the massing of French battalions just across the Channel, paid a visit to Hastings. Lady Elizabeth with Caro St Jules proposed to join them there, and 'Hartington not being quite well, the Duchess begged that I would take him with me'.[D]

The coast was dotted with fortifications and encampments. At Bexhill they went to hear three thousand Hanoverian soldiers singing hymns. Then Hart was seized with a desire to see Dover, where he had not been since he was four months old. Bess bestirred herself to grant his desire and they were nearly blown away as they stood on Shakespeare's Cliff — which, however, 'answered his expectations' [C]

It is interesting to compare Bess's account of this Sussex sojourn with Lady Bessborough's.[155] They both describe the Northern Lights which, to the alarm of the inhabitants, gave a magnificent display one night in October; but it was Bess only who, with her artist's eye, saw that at the same time the moon appeared behind the hill, shedding that silver light which contrasted so admirably with the bloody streaks in the sky.[C]

A letter from the Duchess was anxiously awaited, for yet another financial crisis had developed, and once more she was twisting and turning like an unhappy creature in a trap. Bess wrote shortly before she joined her friend at Chiswick:

> No letter from you, but one from dear Ca, which surprised dear Hart. 'What does Papa write you? He hardly does to any lady.' It seemed to raise me very much in his opinion.[C]

The Prince of Wales, as familiar a figure at Chiswick as at Devonshire House, enriched the Journal with one or two interesting confidences. The Duke of Kent, he said, had remarked to him after a visit to Windsor, 'Brother, I do assure you that whatever resentment you may have felt against the King it will all give way when you see him, and compassion alone will fill your heart for the degradation of the Man and the Sovereign.' He also told Bess and the Duchess that

> the Duke of York had said to the King, 'Mount your horse, Sir, and let me attend you through the City to your Parliament — throw yourself on their affection,' and if so, added the Prince, 'perhaps Pitt, Fox and myself may be in the Tower and our heads not very steady on our shoulders. It would be a comical thing to have Pitt, Fox and myself in the Tower at the same time and for the same thing.'[D]

The Prince added that nothing would induce him to remove the Duke of York or do anything to mortify him. 'Quite, quite right, sir,' said the Duchess.[D]

Other worries were agitating the Prince at this time, notably the Chancery suit over the custody of Minney Seymour, the orphan child of Lord Hugh Seymour and his wife, one of the three lovely Ladies Waldegrave painted in a group by Reynolds for their great-uncle, Horace Walpole. Lord Hertford, as her eldest uncle, could 'settle everything', remarks Bess, 'but he is shabby, and dare not'. Both the Prince and Mrs Fitzherbert were anxious that the little girl should remain in that lady's care, and they were both distressed when 'the law decided that she must be given up'. Mrs Fitzherbert, according to Bess,

> once told Lord Thurlow that she had a mind to run away with the child. 'If you do,' he said, 'it will be a felony, and by G—— you will be hanged for it.'[D]

In the end Lord Hertford, persuaded by Lady Hertford who was persuaded by the Prince, ceased to be shabby and apprehensive, whereby Mrs Fitzherbert had the satisfaction of retaining Minney chequered by the mortification of seeing her unofficial husband abandon her house in Tilney Street for the Hertfords' house in Manchester Square. Bess never drops any hint of any suspicion that Minney was not Lord Hugh's daughter.

At the end of 1804 a bombshell struck London in the shape of Master Betty,[156] the Young Roscius. Hysteria mounted. People were carried fainting out of the theatre. Others kept on shouting, 'The Boy, the Boy!' and would not allow the rest of the caste to proceed with their parts. Even the Dowager compared him to Garrick; and the Duke, after seeing him in *Lovers' Vows*, called him a 'deuced good actor'.[D]

The enthusiasm of Dearest Bess is fully depicted in her letters to Augustus Foster,[157] which need not be quoted here; but her Journals contain some vivid little touches which it would be a pity to leave in oblivion. 'His form and face', she writes, 'are irresistibly attractive, and his voice, though sometimes hoarse,[158] has tones in it that penetrate to the heart.'

> Kemble presented him with a handsome edition of Shakespeare which delighted him, and still more some Spanish dolls to make a puppet show with. 'Another boy of 13,' said Kemble, 'would have thrown such things in my face.'[D]

Two months later she gives a fresh instance of Master Betty's boyishness.

> One day at rehearsals he found an old drum, hung it round his neck and kept beating it to the great annoyance of the other actors: another time he recited, 'My name is Norval' while kneeling down and playing marbles.
> 'Where,' said General FitzPatrick, 'does the little urchin get all his intelligence?'[D]

The Devonshire House ladies were shocked when Thomas Lawrence reported that a cabal was forming against The Boy, and that Kemble was said to be jealous of him.

One evening towards the end of February 1805, Master Betty was received at Devonshire House. 'Hart', writes Bess,

> tried in vain to make him laugh, but he said he would smile twice 'to show

that he saw him'. Mrs. Opie[159] after tormenting him with questions, asked how tall he was. 'Seven feet, seven inches, ma'am.' 'Then I wonder,' she said, 'They don't show you for a wonder.' 'So I think they do, Ma'am.'[D]

Rumours that Lord Melville[160] was 'in a great scrape' now fluttered the hearts of the fair politicians, but long before he stood his trial in Westminster Hall another figure had blotted out all others from their minds — the figure of Nelson.

At this time (1804–5) acrimonious negotiations were in progress between the King and the Prince of Wales concerning the establishment and the education of the Heiress Presumptive, Princess Charlotte. The Prince was constantly in and out of Devonshire House, confidential, agitated, and affectionate. On December 25th, 1804, Bess wrote:

> The Princess Charlotte is at Carlton House but the Prince said that after the child had been with him Lady Elgin came up to him and said 'Sir, I think it right to tell your R.H. that a great change has taken place in the Pss Charlotte, and that the Pss has told her things she ought not have an idea of.'[D]

Whatever Hary-O may have thought of 'Lady Liz's' sincerity, there were those who turned towards her for help in times of family sorrow. William Lamb, for example, who sent an express on January 23rd, 1805, asking her to break to his sister in Whitehall the news of the death of their eldest brother, Peniston Lamb.[161] She went at once, and found Emily Lamb and Caroline Ponsonby together, 'full of hope' since Emily had left Peniston 'feeling better'. Both Carolines, Ponsonby and St Jules, were becoming interested in the younger Lambs, one in the brilliant William, the other in the amusing though rather unsatisfactory George. A few weeks later William proposed to his Caroline and was accepted. Bess's desire for her young friend's happiness was so intense that it had to be uttered in Italian *felice sia quella cara ragazza!*[162D]

Hart and F.F. were both present at the Garter ceremony at Easter, 1805, when the King again sported the enormous wig with which he had startled his lieges at the opening of Parliament in January — 'very large, very white, and square behind'.[D]

> The King's responses were very loud but appeared perhaps more so from being the only person who made any. He looked at the Duke and held up his hands with an earnest action as if he thought he really was going mad, but the Duke soon found out that it was to make him take off his hat while the service was being read. As the Duke was returning to his stall the King called him to him and asked if he remembered officiating in the same ceremony in the same character as Lord Worcester, train-bearer to the King.[D]

Shortly afterwards the unfortunate King lost the sight of one eye entirely, to his great distress. The Duchess too, was in the hands of the royal oculist, Mr Phipps, 'an excellent little man, but in constant motion — he says of himself, "Wherever the King goes, I pop in before him — I am the torment of his life."'[D]

Always eager to oblige his friends, the Prince of Wales lent his special 'easy carriage' to take the Duchess down to Chiswick. He lent it to Princess Amelia to bring her home from Weymouth in 1809; and in 1818 it — or one like it — was hastily sent to Hammersmith for the benefit of his nephew, George FitzClarence,[163] who had been thrown out of his gig and rather badly injured.

Private advices from the Admiralty grew ever more exciting as the memorable summer moved on its way. On June 3rd word came from Nelson that he was 'under sail to go to the West Indies'. 'I will', he declared, 'pursue the French to the Antipodes.'

Then Lady Hamilton informed her friends that she had had a letter from Nelson, dated 'June 12th', saying that the French fleet was heading again for Europe, and adding triumphantly that the West Indies had been 'liberated from all the projects of the enemy'.

Sir Robert Calder's 'poor conduct'[164] in letting Villeneuve elude him off Cape Finisterre on July 22nd was forgotten in the excitement aroused on August 18th by the news that Nelson was at Portsmouth and coming to town.

Only one incident deflected the attention of Dearest Bess from the great sailor for whom her enthusiasm was now steadily mounting — the sudden death of Lord Jersey[165] while walking beside the donkey of his youngest daughter, Lady Harriet Villiers. She noted rather dryly that his widow,

> with hands as cold as death, sometimes screams, sometimes laments the loss of a man who for 35 years had protected her against every unkindness.

That best-natured of men, 'Fish' Crawford, brought to Chiswick the news of Nelson's approach. After he had seen and talked with the Admiral he told Bess that Nelson had spoken to him of Clifford, saying that he was 'a most delightful and very clever Boy', and also spoke generous words about Sir Robert Calder. He hoped, said Nelson, that 'it would all be forgot in success and rejoicings', but when urged to speak his opinion, he said, 'Oh, he is a good officer, but he ought to have continued fighting. The French fight well, but not as long as we can.' Bess was later struck by Nelson's 'great unwillingness to condemn' on an occasion when she heard Mr Fawkner questioning him about Calder. It was, he remarked, 'really so scrambling an action that I can form no judgment'.

Augustus Clifford in Naval Uniform.

He said the enemy had 100 sail of the line to oppose us. We asked how many we had to oppose to them. 'Oh,' he said, 'I don't *count* our ships.' However, he said, 'I could soon run up to a hundred.' 'Frigates,' he said again, 'frigates are what we want.'[D]

One evening at the end of August, Nelson agreed to dine with Mr Crawford 'if no person of party of either side would be there', but Lady Hamilton 'very good-naturedly' proposed that Bess should be an exception.

Crawford asked if the King has seen or written to him.[166] He said, 'No, nothing.' Why, when he returned from Copenhagen the King on seeing him at court had said, 'Lord Nelson, do you get out?' And, said Nelson, 'I was tempted to say, "Sir, I have been out and am come in again. Your Majesty perhaps has not heard of the battle of Copenhagen."'[D]

'I own', remarked Mr Crawford, 'that I wish he had.' 'This truly great Hero', continues Bess,

has his weaknesses, but his love of praise has led to such glorious actions to obtain it that one must forgive him, and his love for Lady Hamilton I feel inclined to excuse also. She was beautiful when he first saw her, and he thought that she had contributed to his glory by influencing the Court of Naples to give him those supplies that enabled him to go and attack the French at Aboukir — from that moment Lady Hamilton was associated with all his ideas of Victory

and triumph. She fed his vanity by every art that could gratify it. Crawford
described how she sat by him and said, 'I would wish with all my heart to die in
two hours, so I might be your wife for one.' Nelson, delighted, kissed her hand;
and it is by this enthusiasm that she keeps up his love and his vanity.[D]

Popular excitement kept pace with the ardours of Lady Elizabeth.

Wherever he appears he electrifies the cold English character, and rapture
and applause follow all his steps. Sometimes a poor woman asks to touch his
coat. The very children learn to bless him as he passes, and doors and windows
are crowded.[D]

It was heady wine for a man always thirsty for such refreshment. On September
7th Bess went to Lady Hamilton's house, at her invitation, to meet their common
idol. There were many people waiting to see him, including his brother, Dr
Nelson[167] and his wife, 'very strange-looking people'. Clifford's mother was eager
to hear from Nelson's own lips the praises which, repeated by Lady Hamilton,
had been 'so delightful' to her. She waited breathlessly for his arrival; every knock
made her nervous. At last

somebody looked out of the window and said, 'This must be him, for nobody
else would the people in the street stop to look at.' It was him.
I went up to thank him for the happiness his letter[168] had afforded me.
'I cannot,' he answered 'say too much, I cannot praise him beyond what he
deserves.'[D]

He spoke of the general popularity of Clifford with officers and men:

'but he is not a boy now, he is a fine young man, and he will be an honour to
the country.' — I asked if he were 'much grown'. He said 'Yes', and added 'That
beautiful delicate face of his is now formed into a handsome, manly countenance.'
He then asked me if I had sent the parcel, for that he would take care of it. I was
delighted and affected to the greatest degree and could have stayed on much
longer but that I felt it was time to go: he had been four hours with Mr. Pitt. So I
got up and took leave of him saying only 'God bless you' in a faltering voice.
He took my hand and Lady Hamilton told him to embrace me. I consented
with great pleasure and hurried away. Lady H. told him also to embrace Lady
Percival. When we were in the carriage my son[169] a who had not seen Nelson
embrace me, said, 'Are you not jealous?' 'No,' I said, 'for he embraced me also.'
'Do you think', said Lady Percival, with some humour, 'that I should otherwise
have ventured to have got into the same carriage?'[D]

CHAPTER IX

Laurel and Willow — Nelson — Lady Hamilton — Pitt — Fox
1805–1806

The hospitable Mr Crawford seemed never to weary of inviting his friends to meet Nelson at dinner. On September 9th — with Trafalgar only some six weeks away — the Duke of Devonshire, Bess, and F.F. were the guests. D.D. was 'much pleased' with the hero; but Bess's pleasure broke all bounds when Nelson asked her to drink a glass of wine with him,

> 'so that he might tell Clifford I had done so,' and after dinner, when I asked to
> put into his own hand the letter I gave him for Clifford, he said 'Kiss it then, and
> I will take that kiss to him.'[D]

This soft streak in Nelson goes far towards explaining not only his happy love for Lady Hamilton but also his essential unhappiness with his hard and frigid if estimable spouse.

Presently Lady Hamilton announced that 'he had a new plan which he intended to call "the Nelson touch"'. Any other Admiral would have been acutely embarrassed at having his ideas revealed and expounded over the dinner-table by a woman, even if she were the wife of his bosom; but Nelson seems to have made no demur. It was otherwise, however, when she was urging him to talk of his having been mobbed that day in the City.

> 'Pray don't,' he said to her, in a low voice, and as she persevered, he said 'I own
> I have been very much gratified and touched with the kindness shown me now,
> because this time I have done nothing. It is all kindness to me personally.'
>
> They all drank to his return at Christmas; 'I hope', he said, turning to his brother,
> 'to eat my Christmas dinner with you.' 'You'll promote Clifford before,' said Lady
> Hamilton. 'How will you settle this matter' said Nelson, good humouredly. 'For I
> will promote Clifford as soon as I can, but that won't be till May, when his time is
> out.' 'Oh, bring him back with you,' I said. 'I will do what is best for him I promise
> you,' he said. 'I will be satisfied with this,' was my answer.[D]

Not until November 6th did the news of Trafalgar reach London. Bess then wrote:

> This day will be ever memorable for the greatest victory, and the greatest loss this country ever knew. Nelson, dear, dear Nelson is no more. Great gallant and generous Nelson — no, no words, no expressions can give any idea of the effect of this beloved hero's death.[D]

She was reading Herodotus with Caroline in the gallery at Chiswick when the Duchess came to her, looking so pale that she thought she was ill, and asked, 'Will you come with me to London?' 'Certainly,' Bess answered, 'but what has happened?' 'A great victory, but —' 'From Cadiz?' 'Yes — it is great news, but poor Nelson——' Her voice faltered. 'Oh, good God!' cried Bess. 'Yes,' said the Duchess, 'he is killed, I am afraid.'

> I flew upstairs. My heart bled for Nelson, but sickened at the thought of the *Tigre*[170] having been in action.
>
> We soon set out. Hartington went with us. There was a look of gloom in the streets. At the Admiralty there was a crowd, but exultation was lost in sorrow. We got out and in extreme agitation asked where we might enquire. A man came up with the utmost civility and said he would show us; then looking at us he said to the Duchess, 'Your Grace, Mr. Spencer[171] was not in the action.' These few words took loads off our minds. We went to Marsden's room. He soon came in, looking quite wretched. The *Tigre* he said was sent with Admiral Louis on other service. 'The victory is great, but' — 'Then is Nelson killed' we said. 'He is indeed, ma'am, a midshipman from the mainmast of the *Rédoubtable*[172] took aim and shot him.' 'Did he say anything?' 'Yes, he lived two hours, sent his congratulations to Admiral Collingwood on the victory, and died.' Mr. Marsden seemed quite overcome, for Nelson was his friend.
>
> As we came down a rush of people came into the Hall, but no sound of joy or triumph was heard. — When F.F. told the news to the D. he hardly believed him, and when the Dss and I came back he could talk of nothing else — first anxiously asked about the *Tigre* — the papers came after, and the Dss read them to us at Dinner.... A public mourning is recommended and in a way to allow of all people wearing it — by a black scarf or rosette, so that all may with case procure it to themselves. [D]

Bess urged the Duke to 'write something upon this sad event'; and after a sleepless night in the throes of an attack of gout he handed her the 'following noble lines':

Oft had Britannia sought midst dire alarms
Divine protection for her sons in arms.
Generous and brave, though not from Vices free,
Britons from Heaven received a mixed decree,
To crown their merits but to check their pride
God gave them Victory but Nelson died.[D]

When Vere Foster, the son of Sir Augustus Foster, inserted the 'noble lines' in his book, *The Two Duchesses*, he expunged the third, thereby sacrificing both the symmetry of the little elegy and its impartial character.

On November 3rd, Bess came up to town and called on Lady Hamilton at her little house in Clarges Street.

I found her in bed. She had the appearance of a person stunned and scarcely as yet able to comprehend the certainty of her loss. 'What shall I do?' and 'How can I exist?' were her first words. She then showed me some letters which were lying on the bed — they were from Lord Nelson of the 1st and 7th — and I think the 13th day of October. The greater part of them had appeared in the *Morning Chronicle* of today.

In a letter not given to the press he wrote that he thought a battle was inevitable, but if he returned to be smiled upon by her he should be thrice a victor.[D]

At several points Bess's narrative corresponds to the well-known accounts in the standard biographies both of Nelson and of Emma; but it also contains certain vivid touches, personal and poignant, which seem to justify its inclusion practically verbatim in these pages.

Lady H. said she had heard nothing, knew no particulars. I told her as nothing could increase her suffering now, I would tell her what I had heard and read, for she kept repeating she was sure there must be some message to her, some later letters on board the *Victory*. I asked her if she knew when the *Victory* came. She said, 'Oh, no — I know nothing.' I then told her different circumstances. She cried and it seemed to relieve her. I asked her if she thought he had any presentiment of his fate. She said No, not till their parting. That he had come back four different times, and the last time he had kneeled down and holding up his hand had prayed God to bless her. She also told me he had requested her to take the sacrament with him at Merton, 'for', he said, 'we both stand before our God with pure hearts and affection'.

I asked her how she had heard the dreadful news. 'I had come to Merton,' she said, 'my house not being ready, and feeling rather unwell I said I would stay in bed, on account of a rash. Mrs. Bolton was sitting by my bedside, when all of a sudden I said, "I think I hear the Tower guns. Some victory perhaps in Germany, to retrieve the credit lost by Mack."[173] "Perhaps," said Mrs. Bolton, "It may be news from my brother." "Impossible, surely. There is not time." In five minutes a carriage drove up to the door. I sent to enquire who was arrived. They brought me word, Mr. Whitby, from the Admiralty. "Show him in directly," I said. He came in, and with a pale countenance and faint voice said, "We have gained a great Victory." "Never mind your victory," I said, "My letters — give me my letters" — Capt. Whitby was unable to speak — tears in his eyes and a deathly paleness over his face made me comprehend him. I believe I gave one scream and fell back, and for ten hours after I could neither speak nor shed a tear — days have passed on, and I know not how they end or begin — nor how I am to bear my future existence.'

I asked her if his family were kind to her. She said 'No words could say how much so, and how affectionate, and most particularly that dear Boy, Lt. Marten.[174] He scarcely leaves me, but tries to make me take some food, or medicine — something to do me good — and with the greatest affection — the present Lord is a strange original, but he'll cry one moment and sing the next.'[D]

She said she understood he [Nelson] had left her Merton, that at first she would have given it up to this Lord Nelson but then she thought not. I advised her not by my means.[D]

Bess was quite favourably impressed by those members of Nelson's family whom she met on this occasion, 'but', she added, 'they have no likeness to their Uncle'.

He was certainly not what was called handsome, but he had a most interesting countenance — a cast of melancholy was very remarkable in it. When conversing he had great animation and fire — a very agreeable-toned voice, the mildest, most unaffected and unassuming manners I ever saw in anybody. D.D. thought so too.[D]

One member at least of the younger set at Devonshire House shared Bess's undoubtedly febrile enthusiasm for

The greatest sailor since our world began.

This was Hart, who set out for Portsmouth on November 28th 'to be there for the arrival of the *Victory*'.

Hary-O raged at the outward and visible (and audible) signs of what she called 'Lady Elizabeth's despair', her sobs, her grunts, her groans, her black cockades, the name of Nelson embroidered on every drapery she wore.

She is all day displaying franks to Captains and Admirals and heaven knows what, and whilst she is regretting that she could not have 'died in his defence' her peevish hearers almost wish she had.[175]

Four days after this atrabilious letter was penned the Duchess went to call on Lady Hamilton, and incidentally gathered up a curious and touching circumstance which does not appear to have been recorded elsewhere. It will be remembered that Captain Hallowell had presented to Nelson a coffin made from the mainmast of *l'Orient*, the French Admiral's flagship at the Battle of the Nile. Bess does not seem to have known either the name of the donor or the exact source of the timber from which the funereal object was made, but she must have known that her hero took a macabre and active interest in his own obsequies.

From the Duchess's narrative, as repeated to Bess and written down by her, it is clear that he also sought to associate the last scene of all with the first scene in his overmastering passion — even to the point of having a 'Popish' chant sung at his funeral.

Lady Hamilton:

> told the Duchess that there was a wish of his which, though trifling, was now distressing them all.
>
> There was a dirge he had heard at Naples and he had told her when he died he should like to have that sung — he got it and it was put into his coffin — that one made out of the planks[176] of *l'Orient* — he spoke about it before he went away — and since that it has disappeared — every enquiry has been made, and no tidings can be had of it. 'He had told me', said Lady Hamilton, 'he wished I should sing it. But how could that be? For unless I sung it in madness, if I lost him I should be unable to sing."Yes, yes, I suppose you would," he said.'[D]

A week later it was Bess's turn to go and offer consolation. She found Emma still in bed, her looks 'expressive of the greatest anguish, her pulse indicating high fever'. Mr Davison, Nelson's banker and agent, was with her. 'When I was announced', writes Bess,

> Mr. D. said that he had known Lord Hervey. 'She is his sister' said Lady Hamilton. 'Oh, yes,' he said, 'the eyes, nose, manner, are all like. I should have guessed it was Lady Elizabeth. I first introduced Lord Hervey to Lady Hervey, then at Quebec.' After he went Lady Hamilton repeated the account of Nelson's death quoted from his servant Chevalier, in whose arms he died. It differs little from the well-known accounts of Beattie, Scott, etc.

Near the end he said, 'Now I feel it is almost over; and, pointing to his finger, he said, 'let her have that' — it was a ring she had given him and he had given her the same.——

In telling me these details, which made me cry[177] she seemed stunned and distracted. All the time that the account was being given to her, she said that she screamed, and that it had done her good. 'I have promised', she said, 'that if they will let me kiss his lips once I would neither cry nor speak. He is preserved in spirits, and looks just the same as if asleep.'[D]

'I, too,' confesses Bess, 'feel as if I should wish to see him'; and she adds, in a revealing parenthesis, 'but oh, what it must be to lose one whom one so dearly loves — oh, what should I do — what could I do — oh, friend of my life — beloved——'[D]

She was apparently sunk too deep in woe to accompany the Duchess, Hary-O, and Caroline St Jules to the Priory, the Abercorns' house, at Stanmore on December 20th to see performances of *The Rivals* and George Lamb's comic opera, *Who's the Dupe?* by a company of amateur players which included Lord Aberdeen, Lady Cahir, Thomas Lawrence, Lady Charlotte Lindsay, Tom Sheridan, and William and George Lamb. The Priory had been the scene of many such lighthearted productions, for one of which poor Peniston Lamb once wrote and spoke an epilogue. Bess might have bestirred herself to go also if she had foreseen that George Lamb would four years later become the husband of her daughter. The uncouth manners of the Lamb brothers, their snorts and guffaws, their habit of rolling themselves about in their chairs, must always have affronted the fastidiousness of a woman who, as her son wrote, could not 'bear vulgarity'. Still hovering round Lady Hamilton, Bess was told by her of Nelson's codicil 'bequeathing her to the nation'; and there follows a passage which reminds one irresistibly of the late Clennell Wilkinson's remark that there was always something of the fishwife about Emma.

'And now', said Lady Hamilton, 'ought I not to be proud? Let them refuse me all reward. I will go with this paper fixed to my breast and beg through the streets of London, and every barrow-woman shall say, "Nelson bequeathed her to us."'[D]

Bess denied herself only one emotional orgy: the actual funeral ceremony in St Paul's: but she went to see the preparations and was much impressed by the pyramid covered with the flags which had struck to Nelson at Trafalgar. And with the Duchess she dared the Lying-in-State in the Painted Hall at Greenwich, and did not give way till passing the coffin, when she was 'quite overcome'. On their way out they overheard the comments of some of the women in the crowd. One said,

'Well, after all, he is no more than a bit of clay, as I shall be, so God be peaceful to his soul, that is all I care for.' Another who stood near her said, 'Oh, it was for us poor souls he died and he deserves every halfpenny that has [been] spent for him.'[D]

Still not sated with melancholy sensations, they went to the Admiralty to witness 'the Arrival of the Body'. Mr Mander and Admiral Gambier received them:

——soon we heard distant music and distinguished the Dead March in Saul — all besides was profound silence — the music sounded louder and louder — at last a murmur was heard of 'Hats off!' 'Hats off' was repeated on all sides — the procession entered the great gates — the trumpets drew up and continued playing — and the attendants, the Admirals and officers bearing his flags, in solemn slow pace, scarcely heard on the sand which had been everywhere spread, advanced to the Admiralty doors through the great columns.[D]

On January 12th, 1806, Bess had the mournful pleasure of receiving Lady Charlotte Nelson, Lady Hamilton, and Mr Davison in her own apartment at Devonshire House, and of seeing Lady Hamilton burst into tears 'when she looked round the room and saw everywhere Nelson's prints and busts'. Lady Charlotte, too, seemed 'much affected' at the print of Nelson's death, a gift from Lord Hartington. An entry in the Journal for June 7th provides a curious comment on this passage. The Duchess of Devonshire had been dead for not quite two months when Bess wrote:

What happiness was mine when I could give the servants' room a framed engraving of Lord Nelson with Her verses written at the bottom![D]

'Her' verses, which are very bad, will be found in *The Two Duchesses*.

The first three weeks of the New Year are almost entirely filled with notes about Nelson. We find the Prince of Wales desiring Bess to say to Lady Hamilton that 'all he could do or say without endangering her interests he was ready to do'; and 'never man showed more real feeling than the Prince has done', she comments approvingly. She writes, reverting again to the fatal walk on the quarter-deck with Hardy:

His life by a few steps might have been saved. He was walking on the quarter-deck with Capn Hardy when something caught his eye — he stopped — Hardy walked on to where they usually turned — he heard him fall — ran up to him — 'Hardy,' the Hero said, 'they have winged me at last':[D]

And she mentions for the first time his 'adopted child Horatia Nelson Thompson', now to be called 'Horatia Nelson' only.

The account of Nelson at breakfast with his officers on the morning of Trafalgar Day recalls once more his preoccupation with 'glory' and his anxiety that his funeral should be carried out in a way worthy of the country, the Royal Navy and, it must be added, of the central figure in the ceremony — himself.

> 'Some of us will not meet again,' he said, 'For myself I think that I shall lose a leg — that would be a victory cheaply gained.' Then again he said, 'They will bury me with honour, I know. Once I wished for Westminster Abbey, but it will be in St. Paul's, I think, and that will be better. Westminster Abbey will be washed away, but St. Paul's will stand for ever. Let them do it well — heap honours and magnificence — they cannot do too much, for on that day every naval officer who sees it will aspire to the same.'

All these propositions sound undeniably strange in modern ears: but the last is the most characteristic of Nelson, who was never a typical English naval officer of his own or any other age.

On January 15th, Bess dined with her brother to meet Nelson's chaplain, the Reverend Alexander John Scott,[178] who had been at college with Lord Bristol. Accident, she says, made her stand near him, and she was so struck with his countenance, and had been so the day they went to Greenwich, that she could not wait for her brother to introduce them to each other. Scott expressed himself as shocked at the coffin being shown to whoever would pay money to see it, and quoted Napoleon's dictum that the English were a nation of *boutiquiers*. He told Bess that when Nelson asked him, 'I have not been a great sinner, have I?' he could not say 'No', but he bent and kissed his forehead. When he died,

'I could not believe it;' said Mr. Scott, — 'His loss was one I could not think of. I continued rubbing his breast. At first — as he had always talked of the misfortune it would be to him to lose the other arm — when I saw he was wounded in the shoulder I lifted up his arm and spoke cheerfully to him — but he knew it was mortal, and Beattie on examining the wound, shook his head and his looks told me everything — but still I could not believe it.'

'Little Horatia', he says, 'is a lovely child.' 'Is she his?' I said, 'For I should love her more.' 'I don't know,' answered Mr. Scott, 'But she is a most interesting little creature.' I cannot help thinking that she is, and that motives of prudence, for the mother made him call her his adopted daughter in his Will. He must have had good motives for what he did.[179D]

Bess later consigned to Coutt's Bank a small packet entrusted to her by Lady Hamilton and confidently believed to contain proofs of the 'interesting little creature's' parentage on both sides; but when opened it yielded up only 'two letters from Lord N., the last dated October 29th, 1805, to Horatia, to whom he calls himself Father'.

Nelson's womankind, among whom one may regard Bess as being co-opted, held a sort of indignation meeting two days after her encounter with Scott. She, Lady Hamilton, Countess Nelson, and Lady Charlotte Nelson met to hold forth upon the extraordinarily unenthusiastic demeanour of George III when the newly created Earl went formally to restore to him Nelson's ribbon of the Bath. At first the King merely looked at it, fumbled with it a little, and was walking away without a word when Lord Nelson stopped him, expressed his gratitude for the honours heaped on him and his family owing to his 'loved and honoured brother'. He then proceeded to speak of his brother's religion — 'the true religion that teaches to sacrifice one's life for one's King and country'. 'He died the death he wished', was His Majesty's uninspiring comment: and he then changed the subject by asking a question about the new Earl's son.[D]

It is a point of some interest to devotees of Nelson that in the opinion of Bess the portrait by Hoppner and the Westminster Abbey effigy were the best likenesses of her hero.

And now another figure moves to the centre of the London scene. On January 20th she wrote:

> D.H. looked tonight as it used to do in the Regency winter. Many people came to discuss Pitt's illness, the under ones rejoicing in it, while Fox, Grey and Fitzpatrick lamented.[D]

Earlier in the day the Duchess and Bess had called on Fox. They found a lady there who went out as they came in.

> After the usual enquiries, etc. Mrs. Fox said, 'That was a mild, gentle little creature who went out, yet she has been rejoicing at this good news — as she calls it — of Pitt being so ill.' 'Oh, no,' said Fox, 'shocking.' 'It is impossible', the Duchess and I said, 'to be glad.' 'Quite,' said Fox, 'How can one rejoice in the death of any man? Death is a thing without remedy. Besides, it is a poor way of getting rid of one's enemy. A fair, good discussion that turns him out is well — but death-no!'
>
> Fox then expressed the view that the news would 'render every debate flat and uninteresting. I hate going to the House. I think I shall pair off with Pitt.'[D]

Eight months later he 'paired off with Pitt' — surely one of the most remarkable instances of two great political adversaries dying within so short a time of each other.

Harriet, Countess of Bessborough.

On January 22nd the Duchess, 'cold and nervous', came before Bess was up to tell her that Pitt was dead. It was a fake rumour, so the ladies went that evening to see the Young Roscius, observing that Mr Fox was there, and that he 'applauded very much'.

Next day in truth

the beacon light was quenched in smoke.

The Duchess was ill with agitation; Lord Hawkesbury was in tears; Lord Grenville in 'violent convulsions of grief'; Lord Melville 'quite subdued'. Bess quotes Fox's well-known comment, 'one feels as if there were something missing in the world'. The Whigs were full of generous anxiety about the dead statesman's niece, Lady Hester Stanhope; 'she had been entirely dependent on the kindness of her uncle, to whom she fled from her father'.[D]

When Bess told Lord George Cavendish[180] that, according to Lady Hawkesbury, Angerstein and three other great City houses meant to pay Pitt's debts, he said, 'We must not let those monied fellows do it.'[D]

Encountering Sir Walter Farquhar at the Bessboroughs' house in Cavendish Square about a week after the death of Pitt, Bess asked him if it were true that the great statesman had exclaimed in his last moments, 'Oh, my country!' as Mr Rose had stated. 'No, ma'am,' said Sir Walter,

'He never for the last five days mentioned King, Lords or Commons, never enquired what was doing: but he might in the sort of fever and delirium which his weakness occasioned have said those words, for he spoke in a low voice often, and even attempted to write.'

Farquhar added that when Pitt had asked him how long he had to live, he had answered that he 'hoped he might long' and that if he had anything to say to the Bishop it would relieve his mind to do so. 'Then it was he took the Sacrament?' 'He did not take it. The Bishop[181] prayed by him. — I was in the room.' Finally he (Farquhar) said, 'It was the perpetual doing too much, going beyond his strength, and his anxiety, that killed him as much as if he had been shot.'[D]

Cabinet-making was soon in full swing, and Fox sent his wife round to Devonshire House with the request that the Duke might be persuaded to 'take something', as 'the thing that would lend most grace and sanction to their administration'. The Duke was given *carte blanche* to choose what he would have. He answered that 'nothing could ever make him accept anything — but that there was nothing he would not do to mark his approbation and esteem for them'.[D]

Mrs Fox good-naturedly asked Bess how her son liked America. 'Not much,' was the answer. 'His accounts are terrible.' 'Well then,' she said, 'we must get him back to a pleasant situation.' About a week later the Duchess conveyed a message to Bess from Fox himself:

'Do tell Lady Elizabeth to be quite at ease about her son. I shan't leave him in America. I can't promise anything to be sure, before I am in office, but tell her if I am, he shan't stay in America.' The Dss praised Augustus and said she believed he had been sent there to be trained under Merry. 'Merry,'[182] said Mr. Fox, 'Augustus was more fit to train *him*.'[D]

In the midst of all these excitements Lady Elizabeth found time to note 'a fair joke upon Thelluson's title', repeated to her by G.'s father-in-law and Byron's former guardian, Lord Carlisle. The banker[183] had hastily caused the new coronet to be painted on his sedan-chairs, carriage, etc., but difficulties had afterwards arisen.

Grey, in talking of the title, said it was the oldest in England. 'How so?' replied [*sic*] another. 'Yes, it is before the Creation.'[D]

The good-natured Mrs Fox informed the Duchess, who, of course, informed Bess, that Fox was 'miserable' because he could not, as he had always intended to do, make Robert Adair his private secretary. The impediment was Adair's French wife, suspected of being in the pay of the French Government.

Lady Holland had said that Sir F. Baring had remarked that Mrs. Adair received 'lumps of money'. A few days ago Adair came here in a great fuss and said she had not spoken to him for three days, and he meant to say 'Explanation or separation.' However we agreed all would now be made up — and if, as we have too much reason to believe, she is Talleyrand's spy, what can she do better than stay and get from Fox's Secretary all she wants to know?——

D.D., with that look of sense and animation which he has when a subject strongly strikes him, said 'Anything but the place of Secretary to Fox.' 'Certainly,' said the Dss, 'and he is determined against it, and Mr. Adair has come to me like a distracted man and said "If it is my accursed marriage that has done this I will blow out my brains. I have educated myself for the place — I knew he always intended me for it, and I care for nothing else. Money is no object to Me."'[D]

The Duchess urged that 'the chief thing' was to be of use to Fox in any way he pointed out. She also suggested, with characteristic kindliness, that Mrs Fox should ask Adair to go to her the next day, as Fox wanted to speak to him. 'That will at least soothe him,' she said.[D]

Next day Adair came in a state of agitation to Devonshire House, saying that he could 'bring the testimony of Monsieur' in Mrs Adair's favour and had himself written a kind of *pièce justificative* of her. 'As if', interjects Bess, 'that proved anything.'[D]

Later, he returned radiant from Fox's house. 'Oh, Mr Adair,' Mrs Fox had said to him. 'Why have you not been near us? You know how useful you are to Mr Fox — he wants to see you.' And she then told him from Fox that 'he knew he loved him and would act by him as if he was his brother'.

'This woman', comments Bess, 'shows good sense as well as good nature.'[D]

A few days later the Duchess, after an interview with Mrs Adair, came in much agitated and said, 'it felt terrible to her, being with "an avowed spy", for so in fact Mrs A. owned herself, saying, "*J'ai des oncles, des cousins, partout.*" His marriage', observed Bess, 'has been his Bane.'

In the end, Adair was sent on a mission to Vienna — without his wife. A year later she joined him uninvited, thereby filling him with alarm; but his career was not wrecked, and he was later sent by Canning to open up peace negotiations with Turkey.

The Ministry of All the Talents was certainly a strong team. Lord Grenville was Prime Minister, Fox went to the Foreign Office, Lord Spencer to the Home Office, Grey to the Admiralty. Sheridan was Treasurer to the Navy. But some surprise was occasioned at Devonshire House when it became known that Addington, newly created Lord Sidmouth but still nicknamed 'the Doctor', would be Lord President of the Council. Canning remarked that Sidmouth was like the measles — 'everybody must have him once'.[D]

Early in February, Grey related to the Duchess and she repeated to Bess a rather puckish trick he had just played on the Treasurer to the Navy. Sheridan had arranged to have a clandestine interview with Sidmouth at his house in Clifford Street, not far from Savile Row, where he himself lived.

Mr. Grey had seen Sheridan in his slouching way walking in the street and thought to make him see him — but not at all. Sheridan never looks off the ground, walked on, knocked at a door and walked into the house, Mr. Grey went on to his sister's.[184] In course of conversation she said how much she wanted Sheridan's Box at Drury Lane; but how to get it? where to find him? Mr. Grey, with a little malicious pleasure, said, 'He is at number 9 Clifford Street. Send there.'

Mrs. Whitbread, without enquiring if it was his house, or whose it was, sends her souffre-douleur,[185] F. Atkins, to ask for the Box. Mr. Atkins, who thinks Mrs. Whitbread must be obeyed, set off, knocks at the door, asks for Mr. Sheridan. He, supposing something of consequence, comes instantly, but in rather a guarded and mysterious manner, treading softly. 'Good God,' said Mr. Atkins, thinking Sheridan was at his own house, 'I hope I have done no harm — nobody is ill here?' 'No, no,' said Sheridan. 'What the d—— do you want!' 'Why, Mrs. Whitbread must have your Box at Drury Lane.' 'D—— the Box,' said Sheridan. 'Nay' said Mr. Atkins, 'she says she must have it.' Presently another knock is heard. They, thinking Atkins too slow, had sent Regnold the engraver, a stout, zealous man determined to carry his point. 'Is Mr. Sheridan here?' said he, in a loud voice. Sheridan, enraged at the intrusion, thinking the Doctor would suppose he had boasted of this projected interview, could have no patience at the second message. 'What do you want, Sir?' he said, impatient and angry. 'Sir, Mrs. Whitbread wants your Box at Drury Lane.' 'D—— take the Box!' said Sheridan again, and went away quite furious.[D]

One of the smaller fry who had been disappointed of office was that rather ridiculous, spluttering little person, Lord Ossulston, otherwise 'little O.', eldest son of Lord Tankerville and soon to be the husband of Corisande de Grammont, Madame de Polignac's granddaughter. 'Fox', says Bess, 'had only expressed a wish that he might have offered him some place, and little O.'s vanity made it into a promise.'[D]

Most of the new appointments caused resentment and gloom. When Bess returned from the theatre on February 3rd she was greeted by the Duchess with the news that 'they' — the Devonshire House group — were all 'as cross as possible' because the Addingtonians were more in number than they had expected.

I looked round. There was Lord Morpeth, silent and discontented; Lord Ossulston, pale and sulky; Mr. Robinson, loud and violent; and Mr. Cowper pensive and pale. Lord M. said to me, 'It would have been better to have had the

Pittites, if any other party was necessary, but thus it is offending the great men of property for mere nothing — the Duke of Rutland, Beaufort etc. Lord O. said 'it is abominable. One feels ashamed to sit on the same side of the House with such fellows. I have a horror of this administration already, and don't care how soon it is dissolved.' 'I am as sorry as you can be,' I said, 'at having them. But I think one owes Mr. Fox a little more confidence than to condemn at once without knowing his reasons or not concluding that he has good ones.' — I am afraid Lady Holland tries already to do mischief and make jealousies.[D]

General Walpole, who was now Fox's Secretary at the Foreign office, found his work at first 'very laborious' as he was ashamed to depart while his chief was still there, and 'whilst light remained Fox never seemed tired'.[D]

Grey, being at the Admiralty, became a sudden object of intense interest to Bess, who hastened to show him the letters she had received from Nelson and St Vincent about her 'darling Clifford' and also one from Captain Hallowell 'with the request to keep him in his ship when he is a Lieutenant'. She next invaded the Admiralty itself, armed with 'a little memorandum' about her son, admired the maps in Grey's room, and 'the very ingenious contrivance for seeing at once where all the fleets are stationed', and within an hour of her return received through the Minister a letter from Collingwood which she 'hoped would secure promotion for Clifford and his remaining aboard the *Tigre*'.[D]

Mrs Fox continued to be an object of friendly, if amused, interest to the Devonshire House ladies. Bess recorded an anecdote of Lady Buckingham, whom she had observed talking to the good-hearted 'Lizzy' though 'some years ago she would not have stayed by on the same side of the room'.

Being set down to cards at Frogmore with a Lady of known gallantry in the world, she[186] said, 'I have the luck of it — if there is one of them in the room, I am sure to be set down to cards with them.'[D]

Five months later anxiety was felt at the 'bold measure' Mrs Fox took in giving a ball. 'One can't bear', wrote Bess, 'to think of any mortifications to her, both for her own sake and Charles Fox's.' A surprised postscript records that the ball was crowded and a story was later circulated to the effect that when someone asked Fox who the guests were he answered by referring them to the 21st chapter of the Second Book of Samuel — where Rizpah, Saul's concubine, spreads sackcloth upon the graves of his seven sons slain by the Gibeonites 'in the beginning of the barley-harvest'.[D]

CHAPTER X

'Brightness falls from the Air'—*1806*

Dearly though the Duchess of Devonshire was loved, there seems sometimes to have been a certain lack of sympathy in the attitude of her friends and family when she was afflicted — as she so often was — 'in mind, body or estate'. Lady Melbourne's expressions of concern in 1802 drew from Bess the rather cool rejoinder that when the Duchess was well she was 'apt to forget all caution and eat and drink a great deal too much, and yet not take exercise enough'; and three years nearer to the end Hary-O, though conceding that Mama was not only unwell, but also in 'a very unpleasant, anxious situation', added a little harshly that she had 'a most unfortunate knack of making everything into a scene'. It may have been this propensity in his wife which made the Duke all the more responsive to the gentle equanimity of his mistress — for one feels sure that Bess confined her 'grunts and groans' to such public events as the death of Nelson and was careful constantly to practise in private her now perfected technique of 'soothing Canis'.

There was a rapid deterioration in the Duchess's condition early in March 1806. She was out of spirits, and had 'some jaundice', but Bess still felt cheerful enough to record that Fox had told Mr Rolleston when they met over the dinner table at Holland House that he 'wanted to recall Augustus Foster and had it at heart to place him'. She also noted that Mrs Adair was considered mad, but that her husband desired their pending separation[187] to be amicable. Then, from March 20th onwards the Journal tells the story of restless nights succeeding miserable days, of Baillie and Blane, Pitcairn and Farquhar, hovering assiduously round, prescribing 'the warm bath' and administering laudanum in ever larger doses.

It was Dr Blane who suggested to Bess that 'dear Hartington' should be sent for, and it was Bess who sent for him. 'Tonight', she wrote on March 23rd,

> The Dss had a return of paroxysm but not so violent and much shorter. Yet what anxiety and suffering! She wished me to read to her and Farquhar forbid. She always knows me.

March 25th.

——a better day — the attack of fever was slighter this morning though the interval was shorter — it was dreadful to see, but the rest of the day the Dss has been more collected, and on the whole I think she is better. She saw Hart yesterday without alarm about herself — yet at times she has. — We all try to keep up our spirits. If gall-stones, the passing will be painful but will surely relieve her. Lady Bessborough sleeps at D. House. The Duke hardly goes to bed. I am chiefly by her bedside — yet all will surely be well.——

Crowds come to enquire. Some we see, but I am mostly by the bedside. Oh, my G!

Wednesday, 26th. Early in the morning.

D.D. and us all have been up the whole of this miserable night — the fit began about ½ past 11 at night and about one was so alarming that Blane bid me send for Farquhar and Baillie — It was a moment of agony to me — the fit lasted with dreadful appearances till near 7 — her head has been shaved and a blister put on it. The lethargy was terrible. She has taken bark[188] twice at one-hour interval and she is to all appearances out of the fit at present. — but Oh, Good God, what is one to look to, or how bring oneself to think of her and danger!

Thursday March 27th, 2 in the morning.

The morning passed off well as to health, terrible as to expectation. The fit came on about 10 and lasted little more than an hour and a half it was succeeded by a sort of hysterical sigh which lasts now, but rather subsided.

D.D, is up night and day, but she told me she feared the pain and pleasure of seeing him.

They were a curiously contrasted group, the medical gentlemen gathered round the pathetic, half-sightless figure with the closely shorn red-golden curls. England was represented by Vaughan (Halford), diminutive and obsequious; Scotland by Dr David Pitcairn, tall and erect, a lover of outdoor sports, especially golf; Dr (afterwards Sir) Gilbert Blane, author of a pamphlet on *The Most Effectual Means of Reserving the Health of Seamen* and an authority on diseases of the liver; and finally by Dr Matthew Baillie, a homely, douce figure, who did not think it beneath the dignity of a court physician to don his tasselled nightcap when sitting up with a noble patient.[189]

Fear crept like a lengthening shadow through the long, low house, so dull and dwarfish without, so magnificent within. Tidans and Tintorettos, Van Dycks, and Rembrandts looked down from the walls upon the hushed figures moving wearily to and fro. A faint hope sometimes flickered up only to sink, and so leave the darkness deeper than before.

Bess made no entry in her Journal on March 30th, the actual day of the Duchess's death;[190] but on the 31st she resumes her chronicle, incoherently enough.

Saturday was a day of horror beyond any words to express — yesterday and today have passed, and we are alive — but stunned, not yet feeling or conceiving the fullness of our loss, scarce believing it true. Georgiana[191] is not ill — the Duke is rather calmer — but we are a family of sufferers and my heart feels broken.

My angel friend — angel I am sure she now is — but can I live without her who was the life of my existence! — friend, companion — farewell indeed — yet even the last day she knew me.

2nd April

We are all rather calmer and I want to retrace all my Angel friend's illness and the few things her poor disturbed head allowed her to pronounce — but it will not be.

There is a passage in Lady Bessborough's account of Fox's death which shows that she, too, had striven to interpret the wandering murmurs of the dying Duchess. Fox's friends, she writes, 'have not experienced the agony of seeing eager efforts to speak, of listening with agonizing attention to inarticulate sounds which it was impossible to understand and seeing the pain this gave'. Her letters to Lord Granville Leveson-Gower[192] tell the same story as Bess's Journal; they tell it as vividly, though less disconnectedly and with fewer pious interjections, but they do not suggest with the same almost startling clarity what was the atmosphere in the great hollow house after death

stole thence
The life o' the building.

At three o'clock in the morning on April 5th Bess wrote:

I stayed as late as I could in D. Devonshire's room and then came, sad and almost horror-struck, to my own room. The door opened and Lady Bessborough said, 'Don't be frightened — but I want to see and speak to a human creature' 'Oh, come,' I said, 'for I was wishing for you.' What is this horror that has seized us! We have been almost every day in her room — tonight again we knelt by the coffin, kissed it, prayed by it, and we were calm — prayed to be a comfort to each other — and I offered up prayers that my heart might be purified by the tears of agony I had shed. We returned to my room — talked of her — we were calm and soothed; yet now I am no longer calm, no longer soothed. I cannot describe my own feelings, but I traversed the Great Hall with horror — every noise makes me shudder. I feel cold and appalled.

The next paragraph shows that it was the closing of the coffin which had produced this nervous crisis; it breaks off unfinished.

It is now that Death, death in all its horror, seems to strike me — I had not lost her before — she was there, we could see her — even now we knew, tho' we could not see her, that she was still in that sad room where we had seen——

Two hours later, at five o'clock, Bess sought relief for her o'er-fraught heart by giving sorrow words:

We have seen the coffin pass — we have heard the deep sound of the hearse — we saw the long procession leave the Court and pass through the gates of Devonshire House — those gates that seemed to open but for kindness or to gaiety.

It is done. It is over. And we have scarcely wept. Involuntarily we kneeled as it passed.

Never shall I forget Hartington's look and figure first as I saw him in the Great Hall as if to attend on his poor Mother there and then on the steps — fixed — without his hat — his innocent, interesting countenance and looks bent to the last on the coffin as it was carried slowly down the steps, and on the Hearse as it was placed within. He did not appear to weep but his whole soul seemed absorbed by what was passing.

The morning just began to dawn — all was reviving to light and life but her — her who was our light and our life.

Lady Bessborough and I hurried back to my room — our maids brought us something and we parted for the night, but scarcely to sleep, but to think and wonder how we had borne what we have witnessed.

The mind of Bess then reverted to the events of the preceding night. Lady Morpeth had gone home about twelve, after their dead mother's friend had had some 'interesting conversation' with her and 'dear Harriet'. Caroline St Jules and Corise de Grammont had gone upstairs, to bed, Bess hoped; and suddenly, between twelve and one, Hartington came to her room 'for some ink', and said that he would sit up.

This gave me courage to ask at what hour it[193] was to be. He told me four. I felt then I could not go to bed — I hope those dear girls are sunk in sleep. — Dear, dear D.D. — he has not left his room.[D]

The mind of Bess now groped a little farther into the immediate past. 'One night', she writes of the Duke,

> he was hysterical. I stayed late, very late, with him. I then went feebly to my room — when I got there I saw in his anxiety he had followed me. Oh, God bless and support him!*D*

Interpolated between these narrative passages are fervent supplications which only a confirmed cynic would lightly dismiss as insincere. Bess did not ask, like Lady Bessborough, 'what can I hope from prayer?' Nor did she, in the manner of her admired Lord Nelson, boldly and blindly by-pass her own transgressions. 'To Thee', she exclaims,

> O gracious God, I repeat my prayer — look down on me, a miserable sinner, with pity and forgiveness. Receive that dear friend into Thy bosom, pardon her errors, reward her virtues — and O my God deign to purify my heart and make me a comfort to her husband and children. Through my Dear Saviour, Jesus Christ, do I beg for mercy — strength to do good, sorrow for what is evil. Amen — Amen.*D*

The day which broke upon the departure of the hearse was Easter Day. Before it ended she again commended the soul of the Duchess to God: and when she began the distressful task of going through her dead friend's papers she found 'prayers, prayers, everywhere'. This task had been assigned to her by the Duchess herself, but she did not attempt to carry it out unaided. Many packets of letters went to the Dowager Lady Spencer, many were sifted and sorted with the active help of Lady Bessborough, whom Bess accompanied back to Roehampton.

The two of them went up to Devonshire House every day, and saw there 'the sad escutcheon and the deep mourning' which reminded them so poignantly of what it was not likely that they would for one moment forget. They also went to Chiswick seeking letters and papers, disregarding the new beauty of leaf and bud around them, and a little daunted by the magnitude of their task.

When the violence of her grief ebbed a little Bess must have given some thought to her own future prospects and to the effect which the death of her 'beloved Angel' would have upon them. The Dowager, the Spencers, the three Cavendish children, cannot have been free from uneasiness about the next *démarche* of the outwardly shattered 'Lady E.'. And at this juncture Lady Melbourne decided to intervene.

Seven years had passed since Lady Bessborough had confided to Lord Granville Leveson-Gower her 'serious fears' that Bess might marry the Duke of Richmond. 'It seems', she then said, 'quite a separation from us all, and changing the habits of fifteen years standing is always a serious thing, especially at our age.'

Bess, as her Journals show, never intended at any time either to separate from them all or to change her habits: but this Lady Bessborough did not know in 1798, and in 1806 Lady Melbourne conceived the bright idea that the old flame might be fanned into life again.

If her ladyship had ever taken part in the amateur theatricals in which her sons excelled, and if *Measure for Measure* had been one of the plays produced, there was a part which would have suited her all too well — the part of Mistress Overdone. She was always ready to make amours easy. Had she not acted as a go-between when the Duchess of Devonshire and Charles Grey had been separated in 1791–93? And if her intervention of 1806 seems curiously insensitive, it may at least be pleaded on her behalf that it was lawful matrimony which she was then all agog to bring about.

The Duke of Richmond, who had long abandoned all thoughts of Bess as his Duchess, must have been much disconcerted to receive in his retirement at Goodwood a letter[194] from Lady Melbourne urging him to come to town and 'comfort Lady Elizabeth'.

Four years had passed since he had described himself to Bess as 'a helpless, wretched man', unable to disregard the machinations of Lady Charlotte Lennox, daughter of the redoubtable Duchess of Gordon and wife of his nephew and heir, Lord George Lennox. She and her husband, as Duke and Duchess of Richmond, were to be host and hostess at the famous ball in Brussels on the eve of Quatre Bras.

Lady Charlotte's anxiety that her widowed uncle should not take unto himself a second Duchess is comprehensible, if not much to her credit, but it must have ebbed considerably before the spring of 1806, and the Duke of Richmond's reply to Lady Melbourne's letter was tepid and evasive enough to have set her last lingering fears at rest.

He wrote that he longed to hear how Lady Elizabeth 'went on' and had written to Farquhar to let him know; he had also written to Lady Elizabeth herself, begging she would not take the trouble of answering him. He shared Lady Melbourne's fear that she 'might not be equal to all the trials she was put to'. If he could hope to do any good, he would readily go to town, but 'under all the circumstances he would fear the contrary'.

After that even Lady Melbourne must have lost heart.

Among the trials enumerated in the Duke's letter to Lady Melbourne was that Bess would have to 'keep up the Dowager Lady Spencer's spirits, who never was very kind to her'. One of the measures she adopted was, to say the least of it, curious. There is among the Chatsworth archives a tightly folded square of black-edged paper containing a lock of vivid red-gold hair, untouched by grey and curved in a natural curl — probably a curl shorn from the head of the dying Duchess and gathered up by Bess herself. The covering note, dated 'May 8th, 1806', is addressed to the Dowager, and runs:

Dear Madam,

The enclosed paper is the only thing that I *can* take the liberty of asking you to accept.

Your faithful, humble servant

Elizth Foster.[C]

If Bess was to be, as she had prayed to God that she might be, a comfort to the widowed Duke and his children, no other course seemed open to her but to remain firmly entrenched in their midst, whether at Devonshire House, Chatsworth, Chiswick, Hardwick, or Bolton Abbey. She continued to 'soothe Canis' in the old way, by listening to his anecdotes, by encouraging him to read aloud to her, and by discussing with him the events of the day. Even the Duchess's death had not removed all irritants from his mind. On June 7th she wrote:

Last night D.D. and I talked of the list of my poor G's debts which Mr. Adam[195] gave in. D.D. asked me what I should do, so circumstanced. I could only speak as my feelings prompted me. He said, with that angelic goodness and simplicity which characterize all his actions 'I should not feel comfortable if I did not pay these debts — and yet perhaps many may think that it is absurd in me to do so.'[D]

'Oh, my dear Augustus,' exclaimed Bess, in a letter to her second son, 'what a blank in my future life!' 'Oh, my poor Ma,' wrote Augustus, 'what a loss, what a dreadful loss!' He reminds her that she must bear up for the sake of her own and her 'adopted children', apparently Caroline St Jules and Clifford. Neither he nor any other member of the circle seems to have been aware of the implacable hatred masked by Harriet Cavendish's chubby face and small, observant eyes, and it probably did not occur to him that the presence of his 'poor Ma' would be unwelcome to anyone.

The Duke and Bess said to Farquhar that it all appeared to them like a dream; he told them, with truth, that 'it was always so'. Universal, too, is the distressful experience she describes in the same letter to Augustus Foster — 'She is so present to me and I am so constantly occupied for her that I feel as if she was absent on a journey and I catch myself saying, "I'll tell her this."'

It was not long before the colours and clamours of the great world began to break through the shadow and silence in Devonshire House. When Bess resumed her Journal the trial of Lord Melville was the main topic of interest. The Prince of Wales wrote to his 'Dearest Lady Elizabeth' to borrow the Duke of Devonshire's collar of the Garter for his brother, the Duke of Sussex, to wear at the trial. It was to her, too, that he later explained his own reasons for staying away. He 'thought himself too near the Crown to vote'; he also 'disliked Lord Melville and had been ill used by him'. When the trial ended in what was tantamount to an acquittal Lady Abercorn reported gleefully that she had offered her smelling-bottle to Samuel Whitbread, 'who slunk away'.[D]

This unedifying anecdote rather surprisingly inserts itself about this time:

> A shocking fire broke out yesterday or the day before and a Gentleman was burned who from having gone to the house drunk could not be waked. His friends are probably distressed what to do about owning the skeleton, for it is thought he was a clergyman and the house was one of bad fame. Poor, wretched man, how dearly he has paid for his errors![D]

In May, Bess had the consolation of seeing Clifford, who had come home to be 'examined for promotion'. Caroline brought him to their mother's bedside soon after 8 a.m., but the joyfulness of the reunion was chequered by sorrowful remembrance. 'Oh,' wrote Bess, 'how I want her to share my happiness in Clifford, how I want her, everywhere and every hour, dearly beloved G.!' And no doubt the Duchess would have shared her happiness in Clifford with all the ungrudging warmth of her nature.

On June 4th Bess, watching for her son's return from his examination at the Navy Office, saw him enter the court of Devonshire House and make an agreed sign that all was well. Later he went to the Duke, 'who was most happy and gratified'.

It was not until after the Duke's death that Clifford and his sister knew beyond any doubt that they were his children, but his obvious pride in his sailor son and his unconcealed affection for Caroline must have made the truth obvious to everyone else. He may have thought — if he thought about it at all — that they provided a reason, if hardly an excuse, for the continued presence of Lady Elizabeth under his roof.

The Dowager, who thought a great deal upon these things, took every opportunity of gathering up Hart and Hary-O at St Albans. On June 17th she brought her grandson back to London suffering from what seems to have been an attack of that hay fever which afflicted him during the early summer and may have been a contributory cause of the deafness which was his bane in later life.

Reassured by his hearty appetite during his stay with her, she does not seem to have been excessively uneasy. It was otherwise with Sir Walter Farquhar who came to Bess's bedside 'a little after 9' on the 18th, and said,

> 'This is a thunderbolt from Heaven. I can't sit under it alone. Who shall be sent for?' 'Pitcairn,' I said, 'I know the Duke likes him.' 'And Blane Lord Hart does,' said Farquhar— 'so let both come. The sad alternative that I can see,' he added, 'is that either this may be a decisive attack on the breast or if he is saved now it is to be a poor, nervous, asthmatic person through life.' What words![D]

Clifford's comment is that the Duke recovered from this illness and 'lived to be a remarkably strong, handsome man'.

The oddly mislabelled Delicate Investigation provided a rich fund of gossip as the summer moved on its way. Lady Hawkesbury imparted to her sister an anecdote not without its bearing upon the Princess of Wales's later attempts to harass her husband by reminders that she *had* slept under the same roof, if not under the same ceiling, at a date subsequent to their separation after the birth of Princess Charlotte. Some years before the investigation,

> the Princess of Wales on coming to Carlton Home had found her bed broken down.[196] She was very much distressed and mentioned it to Lord Gwydir who offered her R.H. to lodge her.[197] She said she must consult Lord Thurlow;[198] 'for,' said she, 'when I first came the Prince said to me in a letter "if ever you want any advice in any difficulty consult Lord Thurlow as your best and ablest adviser"'. She sent for him and he said to her, 'Sleep on a tent-bed, sleep on a couch, sleep on the floor, but sleep tonight under that roof.' She did so: and the advice, as D.D. said, does honour to Lord Thurlow.

Between July 26th, when the Duke first expressed alarm about Fox's health and September 13th, when the greatest of the Whigs died, the main part of the Journal is a record of the day-to-day struggles of a herculean constitution with the ravages of the disease and the only-tooenergetic measures of the doctors in attendance.

Bess was in the thick of it all, weeping with Lady Bessborough, endeavouring to cheer Mrs Fox, bringing reports to D.D., oscillating between Devonshire House and Arlington Street, and later, when the dying man was moved to Chiswick, wandering like a ghost through the gardens and galleries which were so full, as she wrote, of

> *Cento memorie e cento.*

Here again her account complements and at the same time expands the well-known pages in the Leveson-Gower Correspondence.[199] She shows us in greater detail and from closer range Fox's indomitable courage, wit, and patience; she makes us understand why — as well as how much — his friends loved this gentle — black-browed Vulcan.

The fatuous optimism of the doctors made the reaction all the more severe when at last they were forced to acknowledge that the castor-oil administered inside, the plasters of liver-wort applied outside, and the withdrawals of incredible amounts of dropsical fluid would not avail to prolong a life for which they had battled with all the resources that contemporary medical science made available to them.

As late as September 4th there was a deceptive rally. Mrs Fox came out with a smiling face — all was going on well — he had been in the drawing-room and 'hoped to eat a little landrail for his dinner'. D.D., however, was pessimistic from the first.

On the evening of September 10th Sheridan supped at Devonshire House and had a *tête-à-tête* conversation with Bess, beginning by 'things personal to herself' and saying 'how much he wished to see her married to D.D.'. Sheridan's own version, as related in a letter from Mrs Creevey to Miss Ord two days later, was that Lady Elizabeth 'had *cried* to him because she "felt it her severe duty to be Duchess of Devonshire"'. Bess declares that she 'stopped him, saying she was too unhappy yet to hear that language'. He then, she writes,

> went on talking of Fox, mentioned how eager he had been at his setting out in life to get introduced to him. 'It was, I believe, at Sir Joshua Reynolds, and never from that time have I had a difference with him.[200] But when people have abused me to Fox he — with that noble liberality of mind he has on all occasions — said, "I know Sheridan has his whim, but he will never leave me" — Nor will I ever. There is something soothing,' continued S, in the midst of this calamity to have him at Chiswick, there at the Duke of Devonshire's — a dignified attention to the last.' He cried so much I was obliged to make him drink Port Wine, and then he went on, 'But if this calamity must happen the only thing to keep us together is for the Duke to be allowed to consider himself as our head — to be the head of the Whig Party' — I own I agreed with him. Sheridan now got so intoxicated that I was glad to get him to go away.[D]

On the following evening he had a woeful fit of 'the dismals' at the Creevey's house. They also, on the principle of *similia similibus curantur*, plied him with wine and thus, strange as it may appear — 'composed his pulse'. He told them that he had received a letter from Lady Elizabeth Foster with a good account of Mr Fox. It ended with 'try to drink less and speak the truth'. 'He was very funny about it,' writes Mrs Creevey. 'He said, "By G-d I speak more truth than *she* does, however."'

At the actual moment of Fox's death Bess was in the covered walk from which she could see into the room where he lay. 'I still saw', she writes,

> the attendants around, and whilst they still seemed to give any medicine I felt as if the thing was yet possible — Presently I saw both windows thrown open. Mr. Hawkins and others walked up and down the room, their handkerchiefs pressed to their eyes. I knew then — I felt it must be so — that he was dead. I thought I saw poor Lord Holland fixed in a corner of the room — a servant seemed to go up to the bed as if to look at his master——

I left the place and went to the chestnut trees — Mr. Allen came to me very pale. 'Well?' I said. 'It is over,' he answered. I knew it must be so yet it came like a blow on my heart.[D]

Far down the Thames the guns at the Tower were firing a salute to celebrate the capture of Buenos Aires.

On her return to Devonshire House Bess found the Duke 'very pale and much affected'. She stayed up with him till three in the morning, answering his questions. She assured him that if he followed his inclination to cancel his engagements for that day no one would attribute it to affectation. 'He went', she says, 'to his great arm-chair and I could observe him wiping the tears away with his hand.'[D]

Two days later Lord John Townshend told Bess that he had seen Mr Fitzpatrick that morning 'who had expressed himself hurt at Sheridan's cold manner of discouraging a public funeral for C. Fox'.

When he[201] is very drunk he says he will be Minister — he'll show them what he can do, and boasts that he has the Prince behind him.

Less than a week later Bess went to call on Mrs Fox at Chiswick, and on her return she jotted down what she could remember of the poor woman's words.

'Never was there so beautiful a death, and his countenance expressed it. He held my hand as long as he could grasp it and when through feebleness he opened his hand, he left it for mine to rest on.'

Near the end he said to her, 'Liz, wipe my eyes, for I think they are growing dim.' He gently agreed that the Reverend John Bouverie should pray beside him, and joined his hands like a child while the prayers were said.

Even at the height of their grief for their irreplaceable leader the Whigs could not forget politics. Another election at Westminster would be the first sequel. Lord Spencer announced that he would not return to the Admiralty. And, inevitably, their thoughts veered to the great man with whom Fox had 'paired'. Lord John Townshend related how he remembered seeing the younger Pitt as a boy standing 'under the throne' to hear his father, Lord Chatham, speak, and often asked him his opinion. Fox used to say to Lord John, 'Depend upon it this young man will be the greatest speaker we have ever had — not his eloquence alone, but I have questioned him, and his observations on the speeches are all admirable.' The Duke later told Bess that 'it was the observations which Fox had heard Pitt make to others whilst standing under the throne that had convinced him how excellent a speaker he would make'. It was Lord John, who had known Pitt at Cambridge, by whom the young Tory was introduced to Fox. 'But there was no comparison, by

God,' said Mr Daly, 'between the two!' 'I think not in some things,' answered Lord John. 'One came home to your heart and feelings, he came directly to the point — but the other also, taking the whole together, was magnificent.'ᴰ

The Prince of Wales arrived at Knowsley on a visit to Lord and Lady Derby just after hearing the news of Fox's death. Lady Derby met him as he alighted, but he was so overcome that he could only take her by the hand,

> and he ran by her to his room where he threw himself on a couch and gave way to a passionate fit of tears. He wanted to shut himself up — he said he no longer cared about politics — that the only real interest he had ever felt was about Fox, and having lost him all was indifferent to him. They at last persuaded him to appear, but he never opened his lips, never eat or drank — this continued even to the day that he went to Liverpool — he would go in a closed carriage, refused to look out and bow, and gave great discontent.ᴰ

Later he was reported to be 'very low', not eating, drinking or sleeping. Sheridan, noted Bess a little uneasily, had promised Lord Grenville his most active support,

> and has begun his reform by limiting himself to a pint of Port Wine at dinner. He was to call on Lord Fitzpatrick by appointment, but finding him in bed at ½ past ten, he wrote on a piece of paper which he stuck on his roll [sic] 'In bed at ½ past ten! For shame!'

Another vanished figure from the happier past came to life again one evening when

> we were talking of accidents in curricles — D.D. said that I had been alarmed very much one day when he was driving me by the horses kicking very much and the traces getting between their legs; 'but' he said, 'I was in more danger once driving Hare. It was just by the Grosvenor Gate and the pin came out which held the pole, and the bar knocked against the horses' legs. Hare said to me "Jump out", which would have been very dangerous. I held the horses as fast as I could. People came up, and he jumped out but fell down and was covered with mud. I got out afterwards and rode home upon one of the groom's horses. Hare walked home. A great concourse of people had assembled, who laughed very much when they saw him make me a bow and say, "I am very much obliged to your Grace for this pleasant airing."'ᴰ

Bess, always sensitive to her own sensibility, declined to go with Lady Bessborough and 'the girls' to Fox's funeral in Westminster Abbey, but later, 'feeling a terror at being so alone in the house', she went, escorted by her servant, to Cleveland Row. Arrived there, she felt faint — conveniently near to the house of Dr Blane, who gave her up his study and let her remain there quite alone to watch the procession from the window. 'My object', she says, 'was not to see it as a pomp, but to satisfy my anxiety about D. of Devonshire' — who was among the Whig peers following the coffin.

Of the younger persons in the cortège she thought the two Lambs, William and George, 'seemed most to feel'.[D]

Anxiety about events on the Continent continued all through the close of the year to deepen and spread. Lord Morpeth, returning from a mission to Berlin, announced that Prussia had ceased to exist: Lord Lauderdale, newly arrived from Paris, showed Bess Bonaparte's own catechism, inserted with 'the other one', to teach children to love, honour, and serve him as the instrument chosen by Christ to restore the Church and Order upon Earth. Miss Trimmer gave it as her personal opinion that 'the prophecies are fulfilling'. The Sanhedrin, which Bonaparte had caused the Jews to assemble, was the first since the destruction of Jerusalem, and should have been held only at Jerusalem. She also believed that the end of the world was 'as near as a year and a half hence', but of this Bess could not persuade herself. The eldest Mr Trimmer was, however, so fully persuaded of it that he said if he were not afraid of being laughed at he would leave off trading and enjoy himself for the little time he had left.

Berthier after Pajou the Younger.

CHAPTER XI

Bridal Garlands — 1807–1809

According to Hary-O, 'Lady E.' meddled actively in the Westminster election made necessary by the death of Fox. She did not, as the Duchess had done in 1784, offer kisses for votes, but she seems to have been very free with 'Papa's anxiety and gratitude'.

Sheridan and Hood were duly elected, though not without a sharp tussle, and when the result was declared a procession set off up St James's Street, swerved westward to Devonshire House, and asked leave to enter the forecourt. The Duke was apparently indulging in a peaceful nap, but Bess took it upon herself to reply that she could not give permission till he woke up. About two o'clock she went to him, and he said he 'thought it would be impossible to refuse'.

> The procession was well conducted. Music, gentlemen on horseback, and the Members were in a barouche drawn by six horses — a vast quantity of laurels quite o'ershadowed them — The Duke stood on the steps, and with a dignity and grace peculiar to him bowed to the mob, who were huzzahing him, and to Mr: Sheridan and Sir S. Hood, who were returning him thanks.[D]

This incident, trivial enough in itself, was typical of those assumptions of authority which made Hary-O rage. And Bess's constant preoccupation with the fortunes of her sons must have been an added irritant. Lord Howick[202] found himself canvassed on behalf of Augustus Foster as well as Augustus Clifford. 'We must do what we can,' he said. 'But every day the difficulty increases. Soon I suppose we shall have no place to send anybody to.'[D]

A sore throat gave Hary-O a good excuse to stay in her room during the excitements of the Westminster election. 'Lady RE', she informed her sister, 'paid me the most unconscionable visits, but as that is one of the things that must be meant kindly, I will not complain of it.'[203]

William Lamb, now MP for Leominster and husband of Caroline Ponsonby, was chosen to move the Address when the new Parliament assembled on December

19th. Lord Ossulston, not usually prone to enthusiasm, reported that he had done it 'as well as possible', attempting a great deal and succeeding perfectly.

In the midst of this was a great anxiety. Caroline Lamb was missing! We guessed she had been to the House of Commons but she pretended she went to Holland House. She was not come back to Whitehall and Lady Melb. was angry; however, she said that if William Lamb did not disapprove she would say nothing more. It came out that W. Ponsonby had got her some of his clothes and with the help of Mr. Ross had gone with her to the House of Commons — her delight was extreme, as was her agitation — but gave no sign of it. She thinks she was known by Col. Stewart.[D]

There was all too much of Puck in the sprite whom Bess had called 'the delicate little Ariel'.

Sorrow for her mother had not in the least softened Hary-O's implacable young heart towards her mother's closest friend. She tells her sister with a sort of savage amusement that Lady Jones had told Miss Trimmer that Lady Mary Fitzgerald was saying, 'What noble sacrifices Elizabeth is making; she is an angelic creature, and it is 10 thousand pities that she should be in such a family among such people.'[204]

When Lady Mary died seven years later an obituary notice mentioned that 'as a proof of the delicate Attention of her Friends she was never made acquainted with the circumstances of the death of her son, George Robert Fitzgerald': the same delicate attention would appear to have shielded her from any perturbing rumours concerning the 'angelic creature'.

One fears that Bess sometimes betrayed by an arch look or an artfully planted question a familiarity with Hary-O's inmost thoughts which that young lady was very loath that she should possess. For example, one evening in November 1806, she came up smiling significantly with a letter in her hand saying, 'I suppose you know who is coming? — Lord Granville.' In the event, Lord Granville failed to materialize, which may have added to the exasperation of Hary-O, who was trying to conceal from her family, her friends, and, not least, herself, her increasing preoccupation with her aunt's one-time lover. No wonder that the kind-hearted Caroline St Jules was haunted by the heart-breaking look of Lady Bessborough; that look which seemed to say, 'I have lost everything.' Hary-O had no such compunctious visitings.

On Christmas Day, 1806, Bess was invoking divine protection upon her children and a threefold benediction upon her 'sole friend, D.D.'. Her future was still undetermined, and she had not yet found a way of bringing home to her 'sole friend' that this uncertainty was both damaging to her reputation and distressing to her feelings.

During the first weeks of 1807 the Journal is a little disjointed, but it contains a characteristic glimpse of Sheridan.

> When Lady Melbourne reproached Sheridan for being idle, 'No, faith,' said Sheridan, 'I get up at 7 every day, and am so regular, go by such clockwork, that were I ill I should not send for a physician or apothecary, but a watchmaker.' 'Why did you not come to Brocket?' said Lady Melbourne, 'We asked you over and over again.' 'Give me the allurement of prohibition,' said Sheridan. To which we could only answer, 'A true Sheridan that is!'[D]

Solicitous attentions to her 'sole friend' occupied much of Bess's time. When the Duke had an attack of ophthalmia she hovered over him constantly, and even put the ointment into his eye at the bleak hour of 3 a.m. He on his side came to her while she was in bed to tell her of that 'great event', the passing of the Bill abolishing the Slave Trade. Catholic Emancipation, another reform to which the Whigs were pledged, was much in the air; and Lord Spencer heard one dustman say to another, 'Aye, I told you so — I told you the old King would stand by us.' The old King was indeed digging his heels in to keep inviolate his own interpretation of the oath he had sworn at his Coronation more than forty years before.

The tawdry figure of the Princess of Wales obtrudes itself again. On April 29th, 1807, Bess wrote:

> How strange it seems now to recollect all that Canning said to Lady Bessborough of the Princess's encouragement of him, and of the King being hurt at having a letter telling him of Canning's intimacy with the Princess![D]

A fortnight later she records that when the Princess appeared at the opera and was greeted with cheers, 'God Save the King' and 'Rule, Britannia', Lord Stair said he 'supposed the latter was for Captain Manby and Sir Sydney Smith', both of whom had come badly out of the Delicate Investigation.[D]

The interest felt by Bess in the political pageant at Westminster grew keener as time passed. Presently her friends in Parliament took to sending her almost hour-to-hour reports of what was passing there. Upon narrow strips of paper they jotted down who was speaking, to what purpose, and with what result. They sent her the figures after the divisions. Sometimes they added brief comments, but in general this news service was confined to plain facts. She bound up the strips with her Journal, and there they still lurk, proving how willing these eminent politicians were to oblige 'dearest Lady Elizabeth'.

Politics provided a point of contact between her and Hart as well as between her and D.D. She followed eagerly all account of the Yorkshire election in June

1807 at which Hart canvassed actively for young Lord Milton,[205] son of that Lord FitzWilliam who had been so successful a Lord-Lieutenant of Ireland on the eve of 'the '98'. There was a blood relationship there to reinforce political affinities, for Lord Milton's mother had been a daughter of the second Earl of Bessborough by Lady Caroline Cavendish.

The youthful Whig candidate, being only 'a week past 21', was elected by a majority of 187, and Hartington returned from Chatsworth in triumph with a little cold, probably hay fever, and some hoarseness, no doubt the result of cheering vigorously for his friend and kinsman.

'At the Election', writes Bess, 'they called him [Lord Milton] "the Boy"', and

> 'let the Boy have his playthings', was the whole cry of Lascelles[206] people. At last one day they handed up a large box to Lord Milton which when he opened he found to be full of toys. He took it, and coming forward he with the greatest good humour thanked them for what they had sent him and said, 'Gentlemen, though I have no children yet,[207] yet I have one so near being born that I shall certainly keep these toys to give him the first moment that he can take notice of anything.' The populace were so pleased they huzza'd and cheered him as much as his own people did.

Always interested in natural curiosities, Bess went in July with Caroline and F.F. to see the Siboyan (?) serpents from 'near Brazil' — apparently some species of boa-constrictor. F.F. saw one of them 'writhe itself round a rabbit till the bones were crunched before sucking it down'. It is with surprise that we learn that in Bess's opinion the serpent had 'a very handsome countenance'.

Why 'Mr. Hume, the best surgeon in England' should suddenly appear on September 18th, 1807, is not clear, but one item at least in his conversation was thought worth recording.

> He mentioned a singular thing of a person, a Mr. Pattenson, 'Everybody remembers,' he said, 'the line in Pope,
>
> > If where I am going I could serve you, Sir,
>
> and many have thought perhaps that it was carrying it too far, but it really happened to me to have it said to me. One Mr. Pattenson I had attended ... thought himself obliged to me for the attentions I had shown him. He was sitting in his chair and very weak and feeble, when turning to me he said "I can do nothing for you here, but if where I am going——" his voice failed him and he spoke no more.'[D]

Bess, of course, was present at Melbourne House when the Prince of Wales, 'looking better but complaining of a pain in his head and eye', stood godfather to Augustus, the large, apathetic infant son of William and Caroline Lamb. 'He stayed', she says,

> from six till two in the morning — the fatigue was great to us all. — I am assured the Prince scarcely goes to bed, but sits up all night writing to Lady Hertford — it is really an infatuation — He talked of his reception at different places — the fête at Bristol he said was magnificent. I asked him if he had behaved well and shewn himself to the crowd. He said that he really had, but could not go in an open carriage as it rained — but that he had come on the balcony, though with a horrid pain in his head and face.[D]

The presence of Louis XVIII in England was causing a certain amount of embarrassment that summer. The Duke of Devonshire declined to lend the exiled Bourbon his riverside villa, having, he said, refused so many friends, and making an exception only for Fox when he was dying. In the state of his health and spirits, Bess adds, it was quite necessary for D.D. 'to have Chiswick to drive to'. The refusal of the Duke of Queensberry to yield up his house at Richmond was attributed to a belief that Bonaparte would come in triumph to England and might deal severely with any Bourbon partisans.

A pretty little historical argument blew up between Lady Elizabeth and her brother-in-law when Lord Hawkesbury announced that the King had offered Holyrood 'as the only unoccupied Palace he had'. She observed that Louis XIV had received and maintained James II. Hawkesbury remarked that this King had been banished from France by the Treaty of Utrecht. 'Oh, no,' said Bess, quite correctly. 'Not James II. He lived and died at St. Germain.'

Molly Lepell, her Jacobite grandmother, had been a partisan of that unhappy exile: it is possible that some tradition of pity for him had persisted even against the strong Whig tides running in the Hervey blood, and Bess may have found some of the Jacobite books which must have been tucked away somewhere at Ickworth.

The New Year, 1808, began with the inevitable regrets and the equally inevitable misgivings, but her children and D.D. are still sources of thankfulness to Providence. The Duke was pretty well again, dear Hart quite recovered, there were hopes of dear Clifford's return. As for Caroline, she was 'almost faultless'; yet what would be her fate in life?

This uncertainty seems curious, for Caroline was already tacitly, if not formally, betrothed to Caro's brother-in-law, the robustious, red-haired, red-faced George Lamb, and the two were so artlessly and openly in love with each other as to arouse the good-natured amusement of Hary-O. It was not a brilliant match, but George was a pleasant fellow, and his own birth had upon it a shadow not dissimilar to that which clouded Caroline's. It was no doubt for his sake that she had rejected the Reverend Mathew Marsh, a charming and devoted parson of the Castle Howard circle: and that pushful politician, Mr Brougham, whom Grey wanted D.D. to 'bring in' for the family borough of Dungarven, would have seemed to Bess a comparatively poor *parti*. By a curious twist of circumstance Brougham's affection for Caroline begot that savage *Edinburgh Review* critique of Byron's *Hours of Idleness* which in its turn begot *English Bards and Scotch Reviewers*.[208]

In spite of her constant awareness of Shakespeare, Bess perhaps did not perceive the affinity between Octavia in *Antony and Cleopatra* and the daughter whom she had once compared to Miranda in *The Tempest*; yet Octavia's 'modest eyes and still conclusion', her power of remaining poised between contending forces like

> the swan's-down feather
> That stands upon the swell at flood of tide
> And neither way inclines,

her demure sweetness in which there was no feeble element, all suggest Caroline St Jules. We can even picture the sister of Augustus Caesar singing *Hebrew Melodies* to her own accompaniment on the harp if such melodies and such an instrument had been known in the Rome of the first Caesars. Caroline would have made an admirable wife for a parson, especially if he were musical and had noble friends. She chose instead the third son of Lady — if not of Lord — Melbourne.

George Lamb's name begins to appear in the Journal of his future mother-in-law before the death of the Duchess. The date is recorded when he first became a contributor to the *Edinburgh Review*; the success of his comedy, *Whistle For It*, at Drury Lane, is set down with evident pleasure. Early in 1807 Hary-O, then on a visit to Althorp, received an eight-page letter from Lady Elizabeth, 'chiefly about Caroline', who was being tormented by her 'little thoughtless namesake', Caroline Lamb. Hary-O hastened to administer what she called 'contre-poison', and by the end of the same year she was 'quite in spirits' about Caro and George. He seemed 'to love her more than ever, if possible', and she, thought Hary-O, had it 'in her power to do him more good than ever one person did to another'.[209]

George Lamb had been educated at Eton and Trinity College, Cambridge. Though not normally prompt or energetic in action, he once knocked Byron's friend Scrope Davies down for casting aspersions on the virtue of his mother, Lady Melbourne. He was called to the Bar and went the Northern Circuit, but soon, as his obituarist in the *Annual Register* put it, 'ceased to practise in order to devote himself to literature'. Here his range was unexpectedly wide, extending from translations of Catullus to the *libretti* for the more light-hearted productions

Caroline St Jules
(Mrs George Lamb).

at Drury Lane and prologues to the revivals of Old English plays. For a time he sat with Byron and Douglas Kinnaird on the committee of management, and he was justifiably annoyed when Byron dubbed him the 'Mr Upton' of that theatre, the original Mr Upton being the lyric-monger at Astley's Circus over on the Surrey side.

After the tragic death of Sir Samuel Romilly in 1818, George Lamb was returned for Westminster only to be ousted by Byron's friend, John Cam Hobhouse a year later. Six more years passed before his unofficial brother-in-law, the sixth Duke of Devonshire, 'brought him in' for Dungarven, the very borough which Grey had sought to secure for Brougham. When his elder brother, Lord Melbourne, went to the Home Office in 1830, he became his secretary and is said to have delivered his speeches 'in a sensible and intrepid style'. An excellent amateur actor in the manner of the comedian John Emery,[210] he was also an amateur playwright of some competence, and two at least of his comic pieces, *Who's the Dupe?* and *Whistle For It* are remembered by their titles if for nothing else. His marriage with Caroline St Jules, though at one time it was in some jeopardy from his own inertia, was in the main a happy one, and they both did much to mitigate the blank loneliness of Lord Melbourne's last years.

Bess's Journal for 1808 is curiously patchy and impersonal; she may have kept a second, more intimate record which has not survived, for it was a year full of problems and perplexities. Augustus Foster had been appointed *Chargé d'Affaires* at Stockholm, only to be expelled by Napoleon two years later. In the last letter written to him by his mother in 1808 she observes anxiously that she 'hopes there is no danger to Sweden itself', and adds that 'they are a fine race of people' perhaps a final, unconscious evocation of the image of Count Fersen.

Caroline's engagement seemed for some reason to be hanging fire; Hart had not been well; and Bess herself had hardly recovered from the serious illness which laid her low at the end of the previous year and made her so meek that even Hary-O's granite heart was softened for a time towards her. One of the few literary events which she paused to notice was the publication of *Marmion*. Many of Fox's friends were indignant at the line,

> Record that Fox a Briton died,

and Lady Rosslyn was said to 'carry her resentment so far as to forbid Mr. Scott her house'. Other parts of the poem were admired by Bess, who, perhaps thinking of her recent ministrations to D.D., copied out the six famous lines beginning,

> O woman, in our hours of ease
> Uncertain, coy and hard to please.

When the New Year opened, the pages of the Journal began to fill up again. The Convention of Cintra[211] was a subject of frequent discussion, and Canning's opinion of Sir John Moore is set down:

'If I could depend on Moore I should expect good news, but he rests on his Egyptian laurels, hates the Spanish War, is not over anxious to do us good, will just save our credit instead of making a dash at Soult, will retreat the first step Bonaparte makes from Madrid' — While he was talking the despatches came. Canning flung them down, saying 'D—— my prognostics!'[D]

Anxiety continued to grow and when Bess went into the Duke's room on January 24th,

He said, 'Shocking news.' I anxiously asked what he had heard. 'General Moore is killed,' he answered. 'But the news is so far good that we have defeated the French.' I was so shocked that I Felt I had been unjust towards him — I was quite overcome.[D]

Canning, too, was conscience-stricken, and was reported next day to declare that he would be 'most eager to vote a public monument to Sir John Moore'.

The next excitement was Colonel Wardle's motion in the House of Commons that a committee be appointed to investigate the conduct of H.R.H, the Duke of York in his capacity of Commander-in-Chief. The Mary Anne Clarke scandal was 'on'.

When the final vote was taken there was a majority of eighty-two in favour of the Duke; but, as Bess recorded, the poor old King exclaimed, 'This is the severest blow to our family since they left Germany. The people will bear with me because I am old, but they [the family] will suffer for it': and indeed the damage to royal prestige was far deeper and wider than the circumstances would warrant.

I am indebted to Major Reginald Hargreaves, M.C., the well-known military historian, for the following note[212] on this deplorable episode:

> Both at the time and since far too scant attention has been given to the *modus operandi* by which promotions and appointments were put through. Such was the system at the Horse Guards — a system devised by the Duke himself — that it was impossible for any underhand work to come to fruition. — The whole suggestion is wildly out of character. Careless and casual about his private concerns to the point of criminality the Duke may well have been, but in anything affecting the Army, which was the very core of his being, he was, throughout a long life sedulously devoted to the Service, the very soul of probity.

Sir Arthur Wellesley, who had just personally received the thanks of Parliament for his victory at Vimeiro, would have told the same story. But at Devonshire House amusement and concern balanced each other. The 'middling class', according to Bess, said that the Duke 'did not take Mrs. Clarke's money but she saved his'. When assuring Wardle that she could make good her charge,[213] this notorious *fille de joie* was reported to have added that she would feel frightened at appearing before so many gentlemen, as she was 'the most bashfullest Woman in the world'.[D]

'Everybody agrees', writes Bess, 'that they don't know where another Commander-in-Chief could be found, — that he had the greatest merit in the regulations that he made, and in not attending to party in his promotions'. There is piquancy in her note that the name of Mr Wilberforce headed the subscription list when a purse was made up for Mrs Clarke's associate, Miss Taylor, 'a woman of the same description — only in a lower style'.

On March 12th, Grey called at Devonshire House and asked Bess what the Duke thought of 'all that was passing about the D. of Y.'. She answered that she did not think he had quite made up his mind, but that she wanted his (Grey's) opinion. He said,

'Were I in the Home of Commons and the motion was put that no corruption had been proved, I should vote for the Duke of York' — and he added that he disliked and disapproved of the whole business; he thought that the means of bringing it about were shabby and dirty, and the manner of conducting it indecorous and hurtful to the greatest degree.[D]

There was, unfortunately, 'a general disposition to find fault with the higher orders of society'.

Three days later Bess was pleased because D.D. told her that he had changed his mind and would vote for the Duke of York's acquittal on the charge of corruption. His Royal Highness was duly acquitted, but he resigned his post as Commander-in-Chief the same evening. Bets were soon laid that in six months he would be the most popular man in England .[D]

In the meantime George Lamb and Caroline St Jules had formally plighted their troth, and the Duke had announced his intention of giving her a marriage portion of £30,000.

Bess's future son-in-law wrote to her saying that the Duke's 'princely generosity' quite overcame him. 'I can only thank him', said George Lamb, 'by devoting my future life to Caroline's happiness.' The letter is endorsed by Bess, *I wish I had anybody I could talk to in my bliss.*[C]

The Prince of Wales promptly offered his congratulations

——there is not anyone I can most sincerely assure you that can or ever does participate more in the happiness of the young couple than I do myself. You may depend, dear Lady Elizabeth, on seeing me very soon——

Every your sincere friend and affectionate humble servant,

George P.[C]

The other Caroline, soon to be called 'Caro William' to distinguish her from 'Caro George', also congratulated 'dear, dear Liz'. Even the Dowager was pleased. 'Car: St J.', she wrote to Lady Bessborough, 'deserves everything that can be done for her.' She does not wish the sum a shilling less, but she almost wishes it had not been generally known, 'as it will become a subject of conversation which can never be a pleasant one to any of the party's concerned'.[214]

During the interval between the betrothal and the marriage George Lamb went on the Northern Circuit and brought back with him a gloomy conviction that the people were bent on Reform and had 'lost all affection for the Royal Family'. Then D.D. amused Bess early in May by telling her that Lord Erskine had said, *à propos* of Sir Francis Burdett's followers,

'I hear that I am out of favour with these gentlemen — rascals I ought to call them — and have lost my popularity with them. This is ungrateful. They ought not to forget how many of them I saved from the gallows.'[D]

On May 17th, when England lay under the shadow of the news that Bonaparte had captured Vienna for the second time, George and Caroline were married. For their honeymoon they went to Brocket, 'that perfect example of the smaller country house of the period, with its rosy, grey-pilastered façade, its urbane, sunny sitting-rooms, its charming park like a landscape by Wilson'.[215] Three days later Bess visited them, spent two nights at Brocket, and returned leaving them 'well and happy'.

During the years which divided the death of his first Duchess from his marriage to his second, the Duke made several efforts to break down the invisible *chevaux-de-frise* separating him from his daughter Harriet. These she perceived, recorded, even tried to meet; but she never thought of giving any credit to 'Lady E.'. If, on the other hand, he had remained stonily aloof, there can be little doubt as to the person on whom the blame would have been thrown.

The Duke's greatest effort was made in November 1807, when he earmarked for Hary-O one of a litter of puppies just produced by his favourite bitch, Lille — a namesake, perhaps a descendant, of the animal whose companionship had been so comforting to Bess during her banishment in 1788. It was an impulse which showed a kindly rather than a percipient nature, for neither of his daughters felt that love for dogs which both his mistress and his only lawful son shared with him.

Hary-O feigned delight; she even forced herself to interject sympathetic questions when the Duke and Bess sat laughing delightedly at the antics of the little squeaking, scrambling creatures: but she and Miss Trimmer must have performed prodigies of dissimulation to conceal their desperate boredom with the whole affair.[216]

It was not only Bess's excessive 'dogmanity' which irritated Hary-O. Everything that she did or tried to do was wrong. If she sought to persuade her young friend to accompany her to the opera, the young friend was deeply resentful. If she planned a visit to Brighton for herself and the Duke, it could only be because she desired to obtain favours from the Prince Regent for her daughter and her daughter's future husband, George Lamb.[217] if she charged Lord Granville Leveson-Gower with a message thanking the Boringdons for their kindness to Clifford, this brazen conduct covered Hary-O with vicarious shame and caused Lord Granville himself to give 'a loud and contemptuous laugh'[218] — which, all things considered, ill became him.

It is impossible not to feel sorry for Hary-O at this time. Writing from Chatsworth to Lord Granville Leveson-Gower in 1799, Lady Bessborough had said, 'Little Harrio — cries after you and wants a horse to ride after you, and fetch you back'; and this was very much the state of mind of the no-longer-little Hary-O in 1808–9. On his return from Russia it had seemed as if he would seek the hand in marriage of Miss Beckford, daughter and heiress of that opulent oddity, the author of *Vathek*; but both he and Hary-O must by now have been aware — if only dimly — what the end would be. The increasing exacerbation of her feelings towards Lady Bessborough is comprehensible, as to the fault of having been Lord Granville's mistress the poor lady now added that of remaining Lady Elizabeth's friend.

Bad news from the Continent darkened the summer of 1809. The surrender of Flushing, the loss of the Walcheren Forts, the advance of the French Fleet up the Scheldt towards Antwerp, all seemed to fill in the expanding outline of the Bonaparte domination of Europe.

On July 4th, 1809, Bess wrote in her Journal,

> 20 years this day since the taking of the Bastille, the murder of de Launay — in short, since the beginning of the Revolution. And what have they obtained now? The most dreadful despotism ever country was oppressed by, gilded to them by conquests and parades, shows and triumphs.

Talavera slightly relieved the general despondency, and Bess recorded on August 14th that

> during a performance of *High Life Below Stairs* one of the actors introduced into his part that he would propose a toast — 'Sir Arthur Wellesley' — on which the whole house applauded and for nearly ten minutes the acting was interrupted.[D]

It was only a flicker. The calculated British retreat after Talavera was completely misunderstood at home, and when Bess and the Duke went to Chiswick on August 11th they left London 'in rather gloomy opinions'.

There is then a two-months' gap in the Journal, a period full of alarm and despondency in the Spencer-Cavendish camp. Something was in the air; something was imminent; and Lady Bessborough alone of the dead Duchess's family had enough courage and enough compassion to accept, even if she could not approve, the event which they all saw to be inevitable. Even in her letters to Lord Granville she could not bear to put in plain words what 'it' was which was 'not to be told yet'; but she adds that Bess would offer, out of respect for the Dowager and apparently at the suggestion of the Duke, 'not to take the name' — the name borne so brilliantly and so unhappily by his first Duchess. Lady Bessborough liked this idea; but she realized that it might 'create more conversation'.

On September 3rd the Dowager announced[219] that she was coming up to town to take counsel with Lord Spencer, and with his aid to lay down 'some plan of behaviour'. Her own idea was 'to wish them happy', but to abstain thenceforth from visiting Devonshire House or Chiswick 'unless any severe illness of Harriet or Hartington should make this necessary'. Lady Bessborough at once realized that her brother, swayed by his wife and by Lady Morpeth, would wish that all connexion between Devonshire House and the Spencer family should cease. 'This', she wrote to her former lover, 'I thoroughly disapprove of'; but it pains her to take part against them and against the memory of what she 'loved best on earth' — her sister.

Yet she 'really loved Bess', too, and thought that she had 'many more good and generous qualities than were allowed her'. She was, however, beginning to think that she had 'more calcul and more power of concentrating her wishes and intentions' than she had ever before believed. Yet even so, she later declared, with a generosity worthy of Georgiana herself, that she would 'never be unjust to Bess'. She never was; and their friendship weathered even this storm, though not without being in some brief jeopardy.

The shuddering reluctance of the others to see the Duke do the obvious and honourable thing seems a little odd in a group of people themselves upright and honourable. There was no question now of a guilty passion. The Duke and Bess were growing elderly together, and the slowing rhythms of their lives kept time and measure as if they had been married for many years. If he now made her his wife she would be advanced at one step from an ambiguous position to one of great worldly splendour; but her presence would be as pervasive as before, neither more nor less. Only a formal banishment from the Duke's society would relieve his in-laws from the sound of her caressing voice, from the sight of her beguiling face, of her shawls, manipulated with something of Lady Hamilton's histrionic art, her lap-dog, her sketching materials, and all the other accessories which so exasperated Hary-O.

It is difficult to accept the theory that the Duke would have been 'ten thousand times a happier person' without her, though Hary-O was convinced of it. If it be true that he talked more, and more cheerfully to her when Bess was not in the room, that was probably the result of an automatic easing of the tension between him and his daughter when the cause of it was for the moment removed. But Hary-O had never accustomed him to look to her for companionship and affection, and in his own aloof way he needed both. Who, if Bess were eliminated, would listen to his old stories with pleasure, feed political gossip to him with intelligence, sit up with him into the small hours when 'pangs arthritic' kept him wakeful, or apply soothing drops to an inflamed eye? To whom would he be Sir Oracle?

Nobody imagined that he would eliminate her; but everybody would have preferred that if their long association must continue it should continue unsanctified. Yet she had an argument in her favour, and a powerful one, which they all seem to have forgotten: her children by him, his pride in them, and their devotion to her.

During the late summer of 1809 it was felt that the blossoming of 'her ladyship' into 'Her Grace' could not long be delayed. Caro Lamb wrote passionately[220] to her old flame, Hartington, on October 11th, 1809, saying that she detested such petty artifices as Bess employed, and accusing him of having told 'old Bess' that he would not disapprove of the marriage. 'Oh,' exclaims Caro. 'She is a deep one. She has flummeried up a certain young Marquis from his cradle.' But she had not flummeried him up on this particular question. In his answer he reveals that it was from Caro's own letter that he first learnt of what he calls 'this incredible marriage', and demands indignantly when she had ever seen him 'fawn upon that crocodile'. He is as furious as she could desire, and reading those choleric, intemperate phrases it is difficult to realize that fifteen years later he would kneel in tears at the bedside of his dying stepmother and deeply impress the English chaplain in Rome by his tender attentions to her.

The Dowager, the Spencers, the Ponsonbys, and the other members of the anti-Bess group, were kept in a state of maddening uncertainty as to whether the deed had been done or not: but when it became known that the ceremony had been performed at Chiswick by the Reverend James Preedy, one of the Dowager's own tame parsons, her feelings overflowed in a letter to her 'dear Harriet'.

'Let us', she says, 'forget as much as we can of what is past, and bear as well as we can the rest. Poor Preedy is an object of real compassion. He should not have gone to Chiswick, but he was persuaded as we have all been that the marriage was over, and when he was in the house I do not well see how he could have avoided doing what he did.' Her compassion for poor Preedy did not deter her from saying plainly how much she feared he would be blamed for it, how much it would be understood to be done with her consent and approbation 'from his being the person who officiated', and thereby making him 'quite wretched'.[221]

She expressed some surprise on October 18th at having received no letter from the Duke; but a letter had been drafted, if not copied and dispatched, on the 17th. The draft is at Chatsworth: and it is in Bess's unmistakable hand:

Chiswick, October 17th, 1809

Dear Lady Spencer,

As there is no person whose approbation or disapprobation can be more affecting to me than yours, I write to you upon a subject which I think it will be less troublesome to you to be informed by letter than by conversation; and the purpose of my letter is to let you know that it is my intention to marry Lady Elizabeth Foster, which I have for some time thought of doing, from having been informed that in the opinion of the world there is an impropriety (which I have not been aware of, and do not yet perceive) in her being in my house upon any other terms.

Lady Elizabeth is a person for whom I have the greatest friendship and regard and of whom I entertain the highest opinion possible, and I believe I should have come to my present determination sooner if I had not disliked the idea that came across my mind that in that case it might possibly have been supposed that I was not sufficiently grieved at the event which put it in my power to do so, which supposition God knows would have been so far from a true one that I am not able even now to write this letter without the greatest pain and anguish of mind.

I wish you, my dear Lady Spencer, not to answer this letter, as it must be disagreeable to you to do it, and I shall know by other means whether you approve or disapprove of my conduct. If I should hear the former, it would be a great consolation to me, but at all events I shall have that of knowing that according to my own opinion I have acted rightly.

Devonshire.[C]

CHAPTER XII

Her Grace of Devonshire — 1809–1811

Among her friend's papers at Chiswick, Bess found a fragment of an Italian poem which she and Georgiana had recited together more than twenty years before — four lines telling of actions, thoughts, and affections shared in common,

'E al fine it nome ancor'.'

'and at last the name also'.

On her second wedding day, October 19th, 1809, she remembered these lines and copied them at the head of her Journal. 'How little I thought', she writes, 'when we first repeated them, that they would be realized, and how my heart would have grieved at the thought of surviving her, though its sole comfort and joy are to belong to the Duke of Devonshire.' But first she wrote in English

'To Thee O God my grateful voice I raise.'

In moments of emotion Italian poetry and English piety were always apt to rise to the surface of her mind.

I was married this day to the Duke of Devonshire. So many contradictory emotions agitate my heart and soul that I can say no more on this subject, but may I be as grateful as I ought, and contribute to his happiness and his children's as much as I wish. Mrs. Spencer was the only person with me. My son Fred and Mr. Spencer were in the house.

The terseness of this record shows how far the writer had travelled from the emotional fripperies of *La Nouvelle Héloïse*.

Two days later we find an entry which reflects more credit upon the good breeding of Lord and Lady Morpeth and Lady Harriet Cavendish than upon their sincerity.

October 21st.

Yesterday dear Georgiana, Harriet and Lord Morpeth came to Chiswick — nothing could be kinder than their manner to me — I went to town by appointment to meet the Prince. He embraced me and expressed the truest satisfaction and affection but would hardly believe me that my marriage had not taken place before — I am so happy but so nervous!*D*

No wonder she was nervous. She still had to get through the first meeting with Hart, the 'young Marquis' to whom she was truly attached, and whose goodwill might in the time to come be allimportant to Clifford and Caroline.

The Duke showed a curious reluctance to write formally to announce his marriage to his heir, and on October 27th Bess could wait no longer. She wrote affectionately to 'dearest Hart', explaining that she thought it would be wrong in her opinion to write before his father did, yet 'the daily delay of his writing grew very painful to her'.

For myself I can say nothing — my heart must ever be full of gratitude to him as of affection for you all, as it has been from your cradles.

God bless you, my dearest Hartington — I hope you mean to come soon to Chiswick, your father wishes much to see you. He has a painful fit of the gout at present, but I trust in God that he will be better before you come.

——Nobody was ever kinder than dear Georgiana and Harriet have been to me.

Ever yours most affectly

Liz.

In the meantime Hartington has received from his sister Harriet a letter which might well have made him proof against the rather pathetically conciliatory tone of the new Duchess's epistle. Her mind declares Hary-O, was early opened to Lady Elizabeth's character, unparalleled she believed for want of principle and delicacy; but she is certain that her 'dearest of brothers' will feel and act as 'he ought'.[222]

If Hart had arrived at Chiswick immediately after perusing this letter it is possible that his whole future relationship with his stepmother might have been jeopardized. Luckily for her, however, he received three more letters from Hary-O before Bess wrote in her Journal:

Hartington has been at Chiswick, and my heart is now at ease, as his conduct to me is as kind as possible. God bless him and preserve him to us.*D*

In the first of these three more temperate letters, all written from Chiswick, Hary-O confessed that the state of things there was better than she could have expected. The Duchess's manner was less offensive from no longer being a perpetual struggle to put forward claims and demand attention to which thenceforward nobody could dispute her right. F. Foster, for the first time in his life, Hary-O believed, had shown good taste, and what was better, and natural to him, good feeling. He was neither elated nor 'significant', he was more attentive in his manner to her and her sister and exactly the same to his mother; Caroline, as always, the best and most amiable of human beings, but impenetrable as to what she thought or felt on the subject. Lady Spencer was talking 'like herself' and recommending moderate conduct in terms of coarseness and violence that would astonish Billingsgate.[223]

On November 4th Hary-O assured Hart that his patience would not be so severely tried as he expected. On the morning of the 15th she wrote again, mentioning incidentally that Lord Granville Leveson-Gower, who had come down to dinner on the previous evening with the Bessboroughs, Lord Duncannon, and Charles Ellis, was still there.

She reiterates her appreciation of F.F.'s 'quiet and considerate' demeanour. 'He has', she says, 'good principles and good feelings, which I think Heaven in mercy to mankind gave to everything belong to her' (the Duchess); but 'the other Caroline' is 'like a volcano on the subject'.[224]

It is clear that Lady Harriet feared that her brother had rather 'too much o' the milk of human kindness'; she reminds him that there was a distinct line to be drawn in their conduct to Bess and assures him that he has the sense to see it and the strength of mind to follow it. But she does not tell him the real reason why she is so eagerly awaiting her 'own adored brother'. It is given in Bess's Journal under the date of November 15th:

> Lord G.L. proposed yesterday evening to Harriet and was accepted by her. He asked me to tell the Duke and to request if he was well enough that he would see him. D.D. saw him late at night, and all is settled.[D]

'Lord G.L.', a diplomat both by disposition and training, had chosen his own 'distinct line'; it led him straight to the new Duchess. He had imposed a brief period of secrecy upon Hary-O so that he might first make some communication to 'part of his family': but subterfuge and dissimulation were soon at an end, and as Lord Granville's wife she ultimately found it easier to bear with Bess than it could ever have been while she was still merely the Duke of Devonshire's daughter. It may have been on the occasion of this betrothal that Lord Granville gave Bess the opal ring which she later bequeathed to F.F.

Lady Sarah Spencer, writing to her sailor brother Bob a week before the actual date of the ceremony at Chiswick, took the line that her mother's daughter might be expected to take. She even uses the word 'vice' to describe the long, quiet liaison soon to be blessed by the Establishment in the person of Mr Preedy. It was a mortifying thing for poor Harriet, to be sure, as it would give Lady Elizabeth a sort of legal right of domineering over her; but otherwise the long-expected wedding of Clifford's 'venerable parents' seemed to the youthful Lady Sarah the 'most uninteresting of events'. It never occurred to any of these good Christians that Bess might be forgiven as Mary Magdalen was forgiven — because she loved much.

She heard that the lovely bride was not to have 'in soft sound Your Grace salute her ear'; but she hazards a prophecy that before her brother receives her letter 'the Duchess of Devonshire's parties and the Duchess of Devonshire's perfections will be talked of in London'. They were indeed. And written of as well. *La Belle Assemblée* for February 1810 contained a gushing article in which Her Grace is credited not only with the accomplishments which she really possessed but also with a skill as an amateur actress of which no evidence appears anywhere else. The portrait accompanying these rhapsodies shows an opulently blooming lady quite unlike the delicate, ethereal beauty painted by Angelica Kauffmann in 1785 and drawn by Lawrence in 1819, but the head-dress is of interest, with its effect of a pearl-clasped veil, for it resembles that in one of her last authentic portraits, and, according to a tradition transmitted by Clifford's descendants, it was thus that she was *coiffée* on her wedding day in 1809.

On Christmas Eve, 1809, Bess records the marriage of Harriet and 'G.L.', in the presence of the Duchess of Beaufort, Lady Harrowby, Lord Hartington, Caro and George Lamb, the Duke and herself. 'Everything went off perfectly well', she writes, 'and they are gone to Walmer.[225] May she be as happy as I wish her and believe she will be.'[D]

In the whole course of her Journals there is never a trace of acerbity in Bess's allusions to Hary-O, but neither did she croon over her cradle as she did over that of Lady Georgiana. This may have been because she had herself an infant daughter of almost the same age over whose cradle she could croon only with difficulty and some danger.

The Journal soon assumes its old patchwork aspect, anecdotes, political reports, and personal records jostling each other. On February 2nd there is a clever quip by the Princess of Wales, who had recently thrown her handkerchief to the Whigs by canvassing for Lord Grenville at Oxford.

Lord Eldon reproached the Pss of Wales for having canvassed for Lord Grenville as Chancellor of Oxford, he [Eldon] having 'attended to her interests[226] before.' 'Oh, very good, my lord,' she answered, 'As it was not a place of profit I thought you did not care about it.'[D]

When the Duke's kinsman, Henry Cavendish, scientist and millionaire, died in March 1810 and bequeathed £100,000 to Lord Bessborough, 'D.D.', writes Bess, rejoiced in this legacy,

> but was disgusted to see the disposal of so vast a property in a few lines, as if to save trouble and not with the intention of doing all the good he could with it.

The Duke and Duchess did not move from Chiswick to Piccadilly until the 26th of April. On the previous day she wrote:

> Tomorrow we intend going to town. It is not without regret that I quit this dear place so full of strong regrets, endearing recollections and present comforts — but still to go to town with D.D. free from all those unkind misconstructions of society, to be there with him without the alloy to which I have been before exposed, is a comfort for me.[D]

Laure, her French maid, was still with her. During January 1809 Bess had been too much taken up by the Convention of Cintra and the retreat to Corunna to record, as Hary-O did, the heroic conduct of this Abigail in grappling with one of the American deer at Chiswick when it attacked her and a fellow-servant in the gravel walk. After this episode F.F. was said to 'walk with his sword drawn'.[227]

There is then another long gap in the Journal, from April 25th to October 12th. When it is resumed, the Duke and Duchess, with F.F. acting as their courier, are setting out on a visit to Hardwick and Chatsworth. Bess was very nervous. She was conscious that she 'had urged D.D. to this journey', and should it disagree with him she would be miserable. It did not disagree: and when the Morpeths breakfasted with them at Bugden they said they had not seen him look so well for a long time.

On the 19th they reached Hardwick, which they had not visited for seven years. Hart, looking well though thin and pale, met them at the door. On the way memories had crowded into Bess's mind, but she was afraid to give them utterance, feeling that D.D. was 'affected in the same way'.[D]

Georgiana's ghost must surely have haunted the 'Gothick' gloom of the old house; but no shadow from the past could dim the joy and pride of her friend when the first anniversary of her 'blessed marriage day' was marked there by a dinner to nineteen poor children. F.F. and Caro and George Lamb completed the family party. Two days later they were all at Chatsworth. Bess had 'almost forgot how very magnificent it is and how comfortable in the midst of its grandeur'.[D]

News of the victory of Busaco and the safe withdrawal of Wellington behind the lines of Torres Vedras reached them there, causing George Lamb to think well of his conduct and to entertain 'more hopes of success than he had a little while ago'. Then, as so often in the old days, the Bard became a topic of conversation. 'D.D. remarked truly', writes Bess,

> that Garrick's famous speech which gained him so much applause — 'off with his head, so much for Buckingham' — was not in Shakespeare. He also said there was a short speech about conscience which he had asked Garrick about, and he told him that it was not in Shakespeare, and that he had never found anybody who knew where it was, nor whose it was.[D]

It seems strange that Mr Garrick should not have known that both these excrescences were the work of Colley Cibber.

As the year waned, the poor old King's sanity waned with it. Once more a Regency was on the horizon — and this time it broadened into dawn. On November 28th the Duke thought it was his duty to return to town, but he would not let Bess go with him, 'as he travels all night, which would fatigue me, he says'. He must have written to her immediately on his arrival in London, for on December 3rd she received from him a letter which caused her to exclaim, 'Happy, happy me!'

On January 6th, 1811, she joined her husband in London, where the air was buzzing with conjecture. Mr Preedy, with a levity which would have shocked his patroness, the Dowager, laid an even bet of a hundred guineas with F.F. that the King would survive the Prince of Wales.

There would have been dismay at Devonshire House if the bet had been won. The Whigs, whose *état majeur* was concentrated there, regarded the Prince of Wales as their man, the self-styled head of their party, chosen by a Whig-minded Providence to turn out the Tories, recall Wellington from Spain, and make peace with Bonaparte. Only by degrees did they become aware of the conflict raging between old allegiances and new alignments in the breast of Fox's former disciple.

On January 12th Bess reported that Grey had seen the Prince, who was 'extremely gracious' but that Sheridan had been 'behaving worse than ever'. Grenville as well as Grey had been at Carlton House for three hours attempting to assist the Prince in drawing up a letter[228] in reply to the Parliamentary Deputation which would shortly invite him to assume the Regency; but their suggestions failed to please, and Sheridan and Moira were called in. It was they who drafted the speech actually delivered on February 6th. The Prince resented the resolutions, embodying the proposed restrictions on his exercise of authority, which the deputation was to communicate to him, and in his speech declared that every feeling of his heart would have prompted him to have shown all the 'reverential delicacy' towards his royal father inculcated in these resolutions.

Grey thought very poorly of the draft, and considered the phrase reverential delicacy 'like a novel'. But D.D. had heard it so abused that it seemed 'less bad' to him.[D]

The unfortunate Prince, under fire from the Queen, who was persuading him that if the King should recover and find a Whig Administration in office the shock might well be fatal either to his wits or to his life, and torn asunder by incompatible inclinations, was not yet ready to break with the Whigs and alienate himself from Devonshire House. Bess's diary for January 15th, 1811, is an historical document of great value to all who are interested in this stormy and pregnant period.

> Today the Prince called on me. He was uncommonly kind and affectionate and said that he wished to tell me all that had passed: also to thank D.D., and to express his gratitude to him for coming to Town on the question of the restrictions. He then said that he hoped I did not dislike his answer as much as other people did. I said that I could not. He added 'I will tell you all that has passed.
>
> I had asked my friend Moira to give me the sketch of a letter. He did so, but I was not satisfied with it. If I was not with *his*, my Lords Grenville and Grey need not be so angry that I did not like *theirs*: and I could not like theirs, into which Lord Grenville, for the sake of his own consistency, had thrust a phrase which I would not write. Well, Duchess, I said that I would write my own letter, and Sheridan being with me, and more in the habit of that style of writing, he reduced my words into the form of a letter. This I had the imprudence to send to Lords Grenville and Grey in Sheridan's writing, and here their dirty jealousy of Sheridan influenced them, and they sent me a most unprovoked and consequentious [*sic*] letter, as if they had already been my ministers and I obliged to act by their advice.
>
> I did not mind their ill humour, but sent my letter. I have been to Holland[229] and explained everything and it is made up now; but they were in too great a hurry, Lord Grey with his d—— cocked-up nose and Lord Grenville with his pomp and consistency. They want to tie me hand and foot.'[D]

Asked by Bess what he meant to do, the Prince said he had not determined; he did not know if he could or ought to change his father's Ministers. 'However,' he said, 'I have begged it of them to "cast their parts" — in short to have an administration ready to come in and act, if the moment should call for it.'

A week later the Whigs met at Devonshire House to 'build up their administration'. Grenville was to be First Lord of the Treasury; Grey, Foreign Secretary; George Ponsonby, Home Secretary; Whitbread or Lord Spencer to take over the Admiralty. Sheridan, Bess supposed, would be Secretary of the Navy again, in spite of the reluctance of many of the more responsible Whigs to serve with him. Later accounts named Whitbread for the War Office and Lord Holland for the Admiralty. Brougham is not mentioned, though report said that he was all agog to go to the Foreign Office.

On January 30th Grey had seen the Prince, whom he found 'very nervous', and whom he had advised to 'change the Administration' — in other words, to eject the Tory Government pledged to support of Wellington and to a vigorous prosecution of the war against French Imperialism. He told the Prince that 'if he was firm, he thought he had the Government for life in his hands'. Flushed with the prospect of an early return to power, he bade Bess rely on him for Clifford's immediate promotion.[D]

Presently the Prince's reluctance to toe the old party line became visible. It was charitably attributed to his 'great nervousness', and to his feelings for the King being 'worked on'.

Then on the morning of February 2nd Sir Thomas Miller called on Bess. 'I am come', he said, 'to relieve all your anxiety about our friends, for the Prince has notified his intention of keeping his present Ministers.' She was thunderstruck, not so much on political grounds as from fear that this decision would adversely affect the prospects of dearest Clifford. Hartington, with great good sense, said he thought the Prince was 'right as from Son to Father to keep the Ministers for a time, but wrong to our party in having gone so far in consulting them'.[D]

Two days later Lauderdale and Grey appeared. They held that the Prince could not well do otherwise, considering the accounts he had received from Windsor of an improvement in the King's condition.

All fears on behalf of dearest Clifford proved to be completely groundless, as the following entry shows:

> Feb. 11th
>
> This has been one of the happiest days I have known. I dined alone with dear D. Devonshire. I received a letter from the Prince telling me that in an audience given expressly for that purpose to Mr. York Lt. Clifford of the Navy was made Master and Commander by a special commission from the Board of Admiralty. He adds every kind assurance to the Duke and me of the pleasure which he felt in doing what was agreeable to us. I am inexpressively happy at it. The Duke, too, is so happy at it; we drank to dear Clifford's health.[D]

The Regent did nothing by halves. Two days later he wrote to inform his 'Dearest Duchess' that he had assented to the nomination of Augustus Foster to be Minister to the United States of America — a most unlucky choice, for relations between the Americans and ourselves were being severely strained by the Orders in Council restricting seaborne trade with Napoleonic France, and

Augustus Foster was not the man to handle the situation with the right balance of tact and firmness. At Melbourne House on February 14th,

> The Prince remarked that the only favour he had (or should) ask from the present Ministers was the promotion of Clifford.
>
> He took them all off: said that Perceval was the one whom he liked best, the Chancellor (whom he hated) the one whose manner was the most agreeable to him.[D]

This passage proves yet again the excellence of the diarist's verbal memory. Nobody familiar with the epistolary style of George IV could fail to recognize here, and elsewhere in the Journal, his characteristic turn of phrase.

In the course of a visit on March 2nd, lasting from five o'clock till seven-thirty, the Prince was characteristically confidential, loquacious, amiable, and disingenuous. He told Bess that the King was not so well again, and tried to throw the blame upon the medical gentlemen at Windsor for the line he himself had adopted.

> He walked about in great agitation and said that the physicians had deceived him — that they were d—— fools, not to use a harsher term.
>
> The Prince seemed uncommonly well, talked principally on private things, but said that he had written a letter to settle some point between the War Office and the Commander in Chief which he hoped would serve as a precedent for ever. — He expressed a great wish to come to D. House the first time that I gave a party, and also wanted me to fix a day for his dining with us. I said that, happy as I should be to do so, — D.D. had the gout and he must allow me to send to him when the Duke was better.[D]

It really seems as if by harping on the string of Clifford, His Royal Highness sought to deflect from his own head the possible lightning-stroke of D.D.'s indignation at his abandonment of the Whigs.

> He came in saying 'Have I not done your business well for you?' I showed him Lord St. Vincent's letter of congratulation which said of Clifford he was 'the most exemplary character he ever witnessed', etc. The Prince then said, 'Why did not Grey promote him?'[D]

This was a clever side-kick at the possessor of the 'd—— cocked-up nose'. When Bess explained the difficulties in Grey's way, the Prince asked, 'But Mulgrave, why did not he?' 'Because, sir,' answered Bess, 'he is a brute.' 'He is a brute,' agreed the Regent; and then went on to prophesy that Clifford would come home, and in a year would be 'made Post'; then 'his own talents and the opportunity of distinguishing himself would do the rest'.[D]

The 'Mulgrave' thus summarily dismissed was her Cousin Henry, second son of Constantine Phipps, Lord Mulgrave, and Lepell Hervey. A staunch Pittite, he was Foreign Secretary, 1805–6, and First Lord of the Admiralty, 1807–10. He then became Master General of the Ordnance, a post in which he so acquitted himself as to win words of praise from his successor, the Duke of Wellington. It is a curious commentary on the Prince Regent's ready acquiescence in Bess's estimate of her kinsman's character that when Mulgrave resigned from the Ordnance Department His Royal Highness insisted that he should retain his seat in the Cabinet.

In conclusion the Regent related a curious anecdote illustrating the mixture of shrewdness and confusion in the mind of his unhappy father.

> His Majesty asked Willis when he would be King again. Willis said, not yet; that it would endanger His Majesty's health. 'Then', said the King, 'I am, however, a gentleman. And one of two things must be right. Either that I go to the Prince's levee or that that Prince comes to mine; so I shall go to the Prince's.'

This was probably the happiest period in Bess's chequered, uneasy life. All ambiguities were removed, old scandals had become old stories; she was the châtelaine of Chatsworth, Chiswick and Devonshire House, she was the admiring companion of D.D. Princes and politicians were cordial and attentive to her. Her four children were as well conducted and affectionate as any parent could desire.

She had other sources of comfort. Hary-O's unfriendly presence had been removed and at the same time the *vent de bise* of Selina Trimmer had ceased to breathe coldly on the company. It was the young Cavendishes who had invented the nickname, but its appropriateness is underlined by Bess's remark that Miss Trimmer affected her 'like the North East wind which in the brightest sunshine still has some chill in it'.

It was autumn sunshine now with Bess, tranquil and golden, if lightly filmed with mist.

The Duke being only in the sixty-third year of his age, and having suffered from nothing more alarming than an occasional sharp attack of gout, his devoted Duchess may well have hoped that they might still enjoy a few years of each other's society. Yet on July 26th, 1812, she had yet another sorrowful anniversary to record in her Journal, and it was recorded, as was her wont, in Italian.

> *questo giorno del anno sarro era l'ultimà di mia felicità! Non temera nulla: ed il giorno sequente fui precipitata nel dolore ed agonizia, che non so come mi trovo in vita.*

(This day last year was the last of my happiness. I feared nothing: and on the following day I was plunged into sorrow and agony so that I do not know how I find myself alive.)[D]

Contemporary accounts of the Duke's death give July 29th, 1811, as the date, and mention that his illness began about a fortnight before his death. For five nights he had to sit up in a chair owing to 'spasms on the chest and difficulty in respiration', but he was 'considerably better on the day preceding his demise', was able to walk on the terrace in front of Devonshire House and to eat a hearty dinner.

The first indications of extreme danger appeared says *The Gentleman's Magazine* 'on Monday afternoon'.

> On Monday evening he exclaimed to Mr. Walker the Apothecary. 'I cannot stay in bed.' His extremities were then getting cold. At 9 p.m. difficulty in breathing increased. A few minutes before 10 Mr. Walker bound up his arm for the purpose of opening a vein, but just as he was preparing the lancet the head of the patient fell back and he expired without a groan in the arms of the Duchess.

That this last statement is correct we know from the letter Bess wrote to her son Augustus a month later: we may therefore assume that the other circumstances were approximately as set forth here. It seems a little strange to find the Duchess saying that on that last happy day she 'feared nothing'; perhaps the stroll on the terrace and the hearty dinner had reassured her, or, at any rate, removed any sense of imminent danger. The shock was proportionately great when the end came almost suddenly.

This time she kept no hour-to-hour record of the last sad chapter. The hatchments were hoisted up, the lugubrious pageant of pall and plume began on August 5th, but a blank space breaks her chronicle until March 26th, 1812. She did, however, write very fully from Chiswick on August 10th to her elder sister, Lady Erne, describing how Hartington and Caroline went again and again into the room where their dead father lay, and how she sat up late, but, feeling her inability to sustain 'this trying, distracting ceremony', had suffered herself to be put to bed and given something to make her sleep. The same Mrs Spencer who was the sole woman witness of the marriage in 1809 scarcely left the Duchess during these hours of distress. Madame Palli, her maid, was not less devoted. F.F. hurried over from Ireland to be with his mother. Lord Bristol had been kinder to her than she could tell. Chiswick, she said sentimentally, was 'tranquil but heart-breaking'. Already she was thinking of it as a Dower House.

We get a glimpse of the Palladian Villa in letters from Lady Bessborough[230] written about this time, a few weeks after the Duke's funeral (followed 'as far as the stones' end'[231] by twenty-one royal and noble carriages) had set out on its slow

'Canis', the Fifth Duke of Devonshire, from a miniature by Hone.

journey to the Cavendish vault at Derby.[232]

Though the Duchess dined alone, she disregarded the etiquette which demanded that a widow should go into a sort of purdah; she mingled with the family, met with composure and even with apparent cheerfulness the friends who came to condole, and encouraged rather than repressed the riotous high spirits which were the reaction of Hartington[233] and George Lamb from the solemn scenes they had witnessed so recently.

Lady Bessborough, still determined not to be unjust to Bess, feared that 'everything was turning against her'.

It was deplorably insensitive of the widowed Duchess to bring forward at this juncture the question of her marriage settlement, and the provisions of a codicil which she believed the late Duke to have made but which his man of business, Mr Heaton, was unable to produce. The young Duke might well have said with Henry V,

> The mercy that was quick in us but late
> By your own counsel is suppressed and killed.

But he later relented. Writing to her sister Lady Erne[234] on October 10th, Bess revealed that 'Hartington, dear Hartington', had fulfilled to her children and herself 'his adored Father's kind intentions, at least as far as circumstances allowed'. She adds that she does not mean to hold as nothing the advantages of an easy fortune, but exclaims 'how unavailing are all things to comfort for such a loss as mine'.

Sorely against her will, Lady Bessborough had undertaken to break to the Duchess that she 'could not have Chiswick'. When she tried to make her chafing nephew see how ill his stepmother looked, he answered dryly, 'I see that she wears no rouge'. It was through Caroline George that he informed Bess that, understanding that she did not at the moment desire to have a house bought for her, he would 'make up her jointure to £6000 a year, the same as the Duchess of Bedford's'. Bess, who had promised herself the pleasure of handing over the Cavendish family jewels to 'Hart's wife', handed them over to Hart instead,[235] a little ungraciously, as Sir Samuel Romilly was deputed to decide to whom the more important items should belong. The less important were returned to her.[236]

The conduct of the Duchess about this time is excusable only if we think of her as a tigress fighting for her cubs.

At the end of August the Duke broke away for a time from the Chiswick circle and sought relief for his asthma in sea-bathing. There is no hint of any friction between them in the letter which Bess wrote to him on the 26th. She fusses over him in a maternal manner, urging him not to bathe when heated and to be careful about the sands, because the tide comes up upon one by surprise when the rocks are almost perpendicular; and she concludes,

> My love for you is as though you were my own son——
> so is my pride in you and for you.
> God bless you, my dearest.[C]

Most unfortunately she soon lapsed into her old, tactless, self-assertive ways. In September she shocked Hary-O and affronted the Duke by writing in her own name to Lady Morpeth to suggest that she should go to Chiswick for her approaching confinement. She let it be known that she herself expected to remain there for a year. Worst of all, she suggested that Clifford and Caro were 'in some measure legitimate', and expressed a rather wild wish that Clifford might use the Cavendish arms. At last the young Duke, goaded beyond endurance and exhorted to firm action by his sisters, his Aunt Spencer, and his once-passionately-loved cousin, Caroline Lamb, issued a stern and abrupt decree that his stepmother must limit her stay under his roof to 'a single week'.

'Thank God', he wrote to his grandmother the Dowager in November, 'I have got rid of the Duchess at last.' His Cousin Caroline showed how perfect was her understanding of his character when she told him that he felt as if he had 'ferreted a maimed fox out of its last hold'.[237]

In his reply he reveals that he would have been glad for the fox to remain in her den 'on less wonderful expense than what had gone on, but she wouldn't'. He rejoices that this riddance was an amicable one,

> being moreover certain that through life I shall much cherish, assist and support the poor body in her old age and crepitude.[238]

He was a true prophet.

CHAPTER XIII

Mercer Elphinstone — Byron — Pope — Madame de Stäel
1811–1833

Far away in Washington, Augustus Foster was full of very proper solicitude as to the fortunes of his widowed mother. On November 6th Caroline George wrote to him from Devonshire House that the Duchess had come to town to pack up her things and leave that house for ever. 'It is', she said,

> a moment I have always dreaded for her. I think a widow's situation is at all times a most dreadful one: at the time that she wants most comfort and care she is obliged to leave her home and the comforts she has been used to all her life. There are a thousand little things too which have annoyed and worried her. It grieves me to the heart to see her so unhappy.[239]

Lady Bessborough, too, was conscious of the difficult situation in which the widowed Duchess was placed by the young Duke's stern decree. The house Bess had rented at 13 Piccadilly Terrace was not ready for her occupation; the Bessboroughs were 'travelling about'; and even if they had been at Roehampton, she would have disliked a 'kind of confession' that she was not, after all, to enjoy the delights of Chiswick for a year.

Bess herself found a solution to the problem, the best possible one. Taking her daughter with her, she went to Portsmouth. Clifford was there, in his ship, the *Cephalus*.

During the autumn following the Duke's death the delicate question of the parentage of Caroline and Clifford swam to the surface. Lady Holland astonished Lady Bessborough in October by saying that George Lamb had told them that his wife had been 'informed of who she was — that is, who her father was, for she had long known that the Duchess was her mother'. Nearly four years had passed since Hary-O had conjectured from a certain agitation, a certain transient aloofness, in her half-sister's demeanour that George himself had in some measure 'opened her eyes':[240] and it might have been expected that the princely marriage-portion of £30,000 would have completed the operation. Be that as it may, the inevitable difficulties now rose up, only to sink out of sight in due course under the pressure of general good feeling and good will. The love of the Duchess for her son and daughter led her into some strange waters before that time came.

In that same month of October 1811 Lady Bessborough was fated to be astonished much and frequently. She wrote to her new nephew-in-law, Granville Leveson-Gower, that for the first time Bess had entirely and circumstantially confided to her the account of her two children's births. 'And, strange as it may seem', she says,

> she is so unconscious of how this would be looked on in the world that she thinks it a stronger claim upon Hartington, and asked me whether I did not think her subsequent marriage made its being suspected immaterial. She fancies ... that they would by this marriage be legitimate in Scotch law.[241]

Lady Bessborough was much more sensitive upon the subject than Bess, whose visit to Portsmouth she deprecated because 'like all places of that kind it is such a very gossiping one'; but, in addition to the greater part of the London social world, Lord St Vincent, Captain Hallowell, and the officers of the *Argo*, the *Tigre*, and the *Cephalus* must have long been well aware as to the origin of the good-looking young man whose leave was usually spent at Chatsworth, Chiswick, or Devonshire House, and who, before he entered the Navy, had been with Hartington at Harrow.

One hazards a guess that it was not until this time that Clifford himself knew for certain that the late Duke was his father. Nothing but the reaction following upon such a sudden accession of knowledge could explain the conduct of the normally well-mannered and right-thinking possessor of the 'beautiful, delicate face' praised by Lord Nelson. Poor Lady Bessborough was 'in a taking' at the folly he 'let himself be induced to commit' at Portsmouth in December 1811. This 'folly' consisted in his walking out of the room several times in front of Lord Duncannon, William Ponsonby, and Lord Balgowrie. Worse still, when they were all four invited to dine with General Whetham, Lieutenant-Governor of Portsmouth, a message was sent to beg it might be understood that Clifford took the rank of a Duke's son. This naturally made a noise in Portsmouth, and caused offence, but the Admiral had decided to speak to him about it.

Bess, alarmed at the results of this unlucky message, hastily declared that it had 'not been intended as a formal one'. That she herself was the instigator is shown by her remark that 'she had never meant Clifford to do as much as he had': but General Whetham made some rather caustic comments and the Admiral's reprimand was duly delivered.

Lady Bessborough was present a few days later when George Lamb commented upon the fact that Lord Keith had taken Miss FitzClarence first into dinner. The Duchess maintained that in this his lordship was perfectly correct, but George

saw no reason on earth for it, and added that he himself would walk out before
the male FitzClarences 'without the least scruple' till an Act of Parliament gave
them 'a rank they could have no other claim to'. He had, he said, told Caroline
'all this' the other night. No wonder poor Caro look confused, and blurted out
hastily, 'I think George is right — at any rate, it is better not to try a doubtful
thing, especially one that signifies so little.' Bess added the profound reflection
that 'all rank but a Peer's is courtesy'; and Lady Bessborough, though pitying the
embarrassment of Caro and Clifford, thought that all this might do good.[242]

There is no hint of any of these cross-currents in the long and lively letters
which the Duchess wrote from Portsmouth to her stepson as the year waned to
its close. The weather was rough. A large party from Purbrook never put to sea at
all. The Duke of Clarence himself was aboard the *Royal Oak*: 'music playing but
alas, wind blowing'. F.F., apparently preferring dry land to the bounding main,
kept a shade over an inflamed eye as a pretext for going nowhere.[C] And Clifford
was flirting with Miss Margaret Mercer Elphinstone, only daughter of Admiral
Lord Keith, stepdaughter of Dr Johnson's Queeney (*née* Hester Maria Thrale) and
friend and confidante of Princess Charlotte.

Here we have one of several curious points of contact between Bess and Byron.
Her son, Clifford, was attached for a time to Mercer Elphinstone, who would
later inform the poet that he ought to have married *her*; her son Augustus Foster
was in love, though briefly, with Annabella Milbanke, whom Byron actually did
marry. And as the years pass the Byronic thread weaves itself in and out of the
fabric of her life, not disappearing entirely until the very end.

'Only think', wrote Bess to the young Duke,

> of poor *Cephalus* going out with all the workmen still on board, rubbish on
> her decks, etc. People kept saying that 'Clifford would not go out today.' 'Oh,'
> said Commander Grey, 'I know that young man better than you do. He will go
> out, I'll answer for it.' And she went out, and sailed so rapidly that if they had not
> slackened sail all the little boats must have been sunk.[C]

The Duke's answer confirmed what Bess had heard of 'Miss M.'. I can't be
too thankful', she wrote, 'that that modest pride and dignity of feeling which I
think is a marked feature in dear Clifford's character should have kept him from
saying anything to her as yet tho' she certainly had given him every opportunity.'[C]
Caroline George believed her to be a flirt. Clifford's comment was, 'I am afraid it
must be so — she is a coquette, a flirt, yet she has done more than mere flirting
should have made her do.' 'He is', wrote his anxious mother,

> in earnest in liking her and wishes her fortune was less that she might the
> more fully know the sincerity of his admiration and liking. I really shan't forgive

her trifling with such a heart as his. Did you ever hear of her having been attached to Sir J. Moore?

Bess's own theory was that 'Peg', as she scornfully calls her, still had 'hopes of the D.'. Peg's determination to flirt with Clifford continued, but she was more elusive now. Presently she showed 'great condescension'. She took him with her to Purbrook in the carriage, and offered to let him ride her favourite horse, 'Windsor', the gift of the Princess Charlotte. When they were out riding,

> Clifford started the subject as to whether one would change situations, character, etc., with anybody. 'Would you?' he said to her. 'Yes,' she answered directly, 'with you. I would immediately change to be in your situation. I would be Captain of the *Cephalus.*'[D]

There spoke the Admiral's daughter: and it is easy to imagine her as she spoke, her red hair lifted by the sea wind, and her hazel eyes turned towards the sea. More than forty years later Clifford wrote[243] of his once admired Mercer:

> She was by many persons thought handsome, and being heiress to a large fortune was of course an object of considerable attention; but at the end of the war she decided on marrying Count Flahaut, whom she had often met at Holland House, the great resort of distinguished foreigners, particularly followers of Napoleon.

When the widowed Duchess resumed her Journal in March 1812, it is her daughter who usurps the first entry.

> Caroline George sang Campbell's *Lord Ullin's Daughter* which she sings so well and with such constant success. Ld Byron was delighted with it, and praised Campbell. He says Caroline George is like *Thyrza* —— the semi — if not wholly — mythical mistress, whose kiss was:

> > so guiltless and refined
> > That love each warmer wish forebore.

The supposed resemblance even produced a jejune set of verses *To the Honble Mrs. George Lamb* — verses which might very well have provoked the spleen of Brougham, the writer of the original review which started all the trouble, had they not been dedicated to a lady whom he so profoundly admired.

1812 was Byron's year, *Childe Harold's* year. He was, as Bess told her son Augustus Foster, 'courted, visited, flattered and praised' by everyone: and he found himself obliged to mingle, at Holland House and elsewhere, with some of the very people whom he had trounced so vigorously in *English Bards and Scotch Reviewers*. Lord Morpeth held aloof, for his father, Lord Carlisle, had been Byron's rather remiss guardian, and was pilloried in the satire as:

Lord, rhymester, *petit-mâitre* and pamphleteer:

but with a view to 'conciliating everybody' the poet bought up the third edition, and many ruffled feathers were smoothed.

George Lamb's connexion with the *Edinburgh Review* won for him the disdainful label of:

Gay Thalia's luckless votary, Lamb;

and Sydney Smith had been curtly dubbed 'smug Sydney'. George proved placable; not so Sydney, as the ensuing extract shows.

> When Sydney Smith asked at Lord Holland's who Byron was they pointed to the poem, *Childe Harold*. This did not inform him, and they pronounced his name. He gave a great shudder and made off. And Lord Byron, when he saw Sydney Smith, said, 'Who is that good-natured, jolly-looking man whom everybody is so glad to see that he must be happy?' And yesterday morning at Caroline's, just before Lord Byron came in, Sydney Smith asked if he was to be there and was told not. 'Oh, yes,' he said, 'I feel a shudder, a creeping chilliness. He must be coming.' Lord Byron had named S. Smith in his satirical Poem along with the other Edinburgh reviewers who had been so severe on him.[D]

The noble lion was now roaring like any sucking-dove. Even the *Edinburgh Review* critique of *Childe Harold* satisfied him, though, says Bess, 'he dislikes their praising him at the expense of Walter Scott'— whom he himself had touched up pretty sharply in his petulant satire. 'Lord Byron', she wrote on April 6th, 1812,

> is impatient to know G. Lamb, and is shocked at having satirized him — and unjustly too — in *English Bards* etc. He admires Mrs. G. Lamb and asks each time for what he calls *his* song — *Lord Ullin's Daughter*: but when in answer to his question whether she ever waltzed she answered, 'Yes,' 'Oh, then,' he said, 'Nothing is perfect.' Her hair is like *Thyrza* he says.
>
> But he is odd — very odd. To cure himself of some fright or ill-founded horror he once sat surrounded with human skulls which he had had dug up and placed in his room. — he lives chiefly on Tea and Vegetables.[D]

Her own first meeting with Byron did not take place till the February of the following year — 1813. She then wrote:

> Lord Byron, though I had heard so much about him, exceeded my expectations. I thought his countenance beautiful, and his conversation, even in the short time I saw him in, most strikingly agreeable. He looks about 20.[D]

In the meantime riots and tumults tore the country asunder, and the authentic news of the victory at Badajoz was dimmed by a baseless rumour that Wellington had lost an arm. George Lamb suggested putting the Prince Regent in a boat, sending him off anywhere, and proclaiming Princess Charlotte Queen.

The assassination of Spencer Perceval by an unfortunate madman who mistook him for Lord Granville Leveson-Gower led to a fresh outbreak of Cabinet-planning. Bess, once more in the thick of things, drove round from house to house collecting the latest information. She had strong personal reasons to be interested in the course of events. On May 21st her nephew-in-law, Mr James Stuart Wortley, husband of 'Lal-Lal', carried against the Government by a majority of four votes a motion praying the Prince Regent to form a strong and efficient Administration without delay; and when the Regent answered that prayer in his own way (which was not Mr Stuart Wortley's way), her brother-in-law Lord Liverpool became Prime Minister.

The Duchess now had a London house of her own at 13 Piccadilly Terrace; but she was restless and ill at ease. At the beginning of the year she had been at Walmer with the Liverpools; thence she went, wretched in health and melancholy in mind, to the Bessboroughs at Roehampton. Yet ill or well, sorrowful or gay, she always loved to keep a delicate finger on the pulse of events. Morpeth now joins the group of MPs sending her notes straight from the House of Commons. On July 1st the young Duke comes direct from the House of Lords to dine with her and then returns there. On July 23rd, as news of Napoleon's Russian adventure trickles in, she writes:

> People seem to look on this contest in Russia as to what is to decide the enslaving or liberating of Europe. If Bonaparte succeeds, can we ourselves resist much longer? Yet never I think can England be conquered.[D]

In the midst of these alarms the Duchess found time to correspond at great length with her harassed son, Augustus, who between the intransigence of President Monroe in America and the aloofness of Miss Annabella Milbanke in England was in dire need of maternal sympathy. To Bess, as to many people before and since, Annabella was a mystery. 'I hope', she wrote 'that you don't make yourself unhappy about her; she really is an icicle.[244] Of his sister Caroline she tells him that she is more than ever liked and admired and yet is not happy.

At the end of July, Bess was taking the waters at Tunbridge Wells. She received good news there, both public and personal. Clifford was made a Post-Captain. And the cottages of the Kentish-Sussex border villages were gay with boughs of trees by day and twinkling lights by night in honour of the happy tidings from Spain — the victory of Salamanca.

Bound up in the Journal of September 4th is a little note forwarded by Lady Liverpool. A square of red chalk is roughly drawn round the message:

> *By Telegraph*[245]
> Wellington in Madrid on 13th ult.
> took 1700 Prisoners
> & 1800 pieces of cannon.
> *By the Niobe*

'The Tower guns are firing,' comments Bess, happily.

Chiswick being barred, she very sensibly decided to build herself a small house at Richmond, and by the autumn of 1812 it was well ahead. Walking alone in the adjoining meadow she thought wistfully of friends departed.

> Two such friends as I had no one ever had before — all that has extended comfort under the severity of their loss I still owe to them. O, dear, adored husband and friend, may Heaven grant my prayer and suffer me to be reunited to you both in another world!*D*

From this it is clear that even as Sir Thomas Browne's idea of Heaven was a quincunx, Bess's idea was a triangle.

At the end of the year dear Clifford was 'chose at Brooks's', his sponsor being Lord Duncannon. The young Captain was on leave, and had planned to go with his brother the young Duke to Althorp and thence to Chatsworth, 'but,' writes Bess, 'this my dear stepson is not well, and I feel an inexpressible anxiety at the words "irregular action of the heart" — yet Farquhar assured me he had not disease'. Her anxiety and her affection were both sincere; but the death of the young Duke would have wrecked all the hopes she built on his regard for her children.

Early in 1813 she was at Combe Wood with the Liverpools, collecting miscellaneous patches of information. Lord Liverpool, who was now beginning to have a high opinion of the Regent, praised his attentions to the Queen, and observed that he could do anything with Princess Charlotte 'did he but take the right method'. He also told his sister-in-law that

> before the Prince's marriage the King wished him to send for the pictures of different Princesses who were Protestant, but the Prince, who was then military

mad,[246] would marry the Duke of Brunswick's daughter. 'Anybody', said Mr. Wallace, 'might have told him how loose her conduct was.'

It was during the month of February 1813 that the Whigs began their systematic vilification of their one-time patron, the Prince Regent, using as a knotted scourge for his shoulders the alleged wrongs of his preposterous wife. When what Lady Charlotte Campbell rightly called a 'letter in masquerade, forced and unnatural' appeared in the *Morning Chronicle* over the signature of the Princess of Wales, Brougham was soon perceived to be the real author. 'I believe him', wrote Bess, 'to be clever, but a cold-blooded, mischievous and malicious man.'[D] Her son-in-law George Lamb told her that the Princess's party intended to 'bring forward the business of the Prince's marriage — as it is called — with Mrs. Fitzherbert'. Caroline reported that Michael Angelo Taylor had 'unguardedly enough' said, 'Oh, the man is dead' — the man who read the ceremony.[D] Bess, who hated vulgarity, would obviously see little to admire in that arch-vulgarian the Princess of Wales. On April 3rd, after various deluded civic bodies had presented congratulatory addresses to the foolish woman, she wrote:

> the singular thing in all this business is that there does not seem to be anybody who has a doubt of the Pss having had attachments and even intrigues. I have never heard anybody for this last 7 or 10 years, I think, express any doubt as to the Princess's imprudence of conduct, indelicacy of manner and conversation, and criminal attachments.[D]

She was soon, and rightly, sickened of the whole subject. 'How foolish' she remarks, 'all these people will look if anything ever comes out against her past all contradicting.'

They did indeed, in posterity's eyes if not in their own.

Though she savoured *Childe Harold* and *Marmion*, Bess was at heart an Augustan; she was therefore keenly interested when Samuel Rogers told her that at Twickenham there was still living an aged ferryman who remembered rowing Pope on the Thames. Frederick Foster, also interested, resolved to seek this ancient out.

> He went accordingly to Ham Walks and this very man had just ferried over a party from the other side. My son asked him if he remembered Pope. 'Yes, Sir.' 'Did you ferry him across the river?' 'I helped my father to ferry the boat, and we often rowed Mr. Pope to Chiswick to see Lord Burlington, and there was always a little chair brought to carry him up to the house.' 'Do you remember Dr. Swift?' 'No, Sir, — but we did row Mr. Pope to see one Mrs. Blount' 'Was she handsome?' 'She was a comely woman.' This man's name I think is Horne. He is 88 and still very hale and strong.[D]

Some three weeks later Bess 'went on the water' with F.F. to Twickenham and herself questioned the aged ferryman about Pope. Horne had apparently heard vague rumours about Pope's collaborators in the translation of Homer, and his interpretation of the poet's friendship with Martha Blount was what one would expect it to be. 'He gave me', she writes,

> much the same account as he had done to Frederick before, but when I said to him that Mr. Pope was a very famous person, he said, 'Yes, Lady, he was a famous person — but Lord bless you, those were not all *his* works — there was a company of them.' He said Pope was a little man, 'deformed but not much': that his chair had a desk to it to write upon. His house, he said, 'was but a bandbox', but had been much enlarged afterwards. He had often rowed him to 'his favourite woman, Madam Blount.'[D]

The shadow of Bonaparte now projects itself once more upon the pages of the Journal. Narbonne's son-in-law, the Comte de Sabrail, suspected in some quarters of being a spy, related the following anecdote:

> The report of a badly executed manoeuvre by Marshal Victor was read aloud to Bonaparte by an officer of whom he demanded whether in the same place he would have done the same thing. '*No, Sire. And at one time I doubt whether he would have done it either. But this campaign has made old men of us.*' Bonaparte glanced at him in some surprise, for he himself had just made some sort of blunder. He answered, '*Perhaps.*'[D]

A year later, when the horrors of the retreat from Moscow had become a chapter in the history of the age, Bess gathered up a few anecdotes from people who had somehow survived. The Comte d'Asté de Grammont related how

> once, when he felt incapable of thought or movement, he saw a little fire, to which he made his way. From his pocket he drew half a potato, which was frozen stiff, and, holding it over the flame, thawed it out sufficiently to be able to nibble at it. A friend gave him a drop of brandy — '*never*', he said, '*shall I forget that mark of friendship!*' It revived him so much that he was able to cover another five miles that day.[D]

General Belliard,[247] whom she met at Spa in 1814, told her that extreme cold was beyond all comparison worse than extreme heat. In Egypt, though the heat was dreadful, they were certain of being refreshed by the night, but that no words could express what they suffered in Russia. 'In the evening you would see regiments gathered round fires — by the morning they were frozen stiff.'[D]

For the benefit of Lady Bessborough the Duchess recorded three or four patches of Bonapartiana, on the authority of Monsieur de Montargnac. He was, said de Montargnac, very brutal in his manners, particularly to women. '*I am not*', he remarked of himself, '*a natural man. I care neither for women nor children*' — a curious avowal from the one-time ardent lover of Josephine de Beauharnais and the still adoring father of the King of Rome. When he went to Fontainebleau to persuade the Pope to marry him to Josephine, he ran up to the Holy Father 'with a clenched fist'. The Pope, raising his eyes and hands, said, '*My son, you are lost!*'[D]

Finally, when he returned to Fontainebleau after his second abdication, he heard himself addressed for the first time simply as 'General', and the following dialogue took place. It showed how implicitly he believed that Marie Louise and his son would share his banishment.

'*Where am I to go with my family?*'

'*To the Island of Elba.*'

'*Does anybody know it?*'

They named an officer, but he pretended ignorance. He [Bonaparte] called for maps and sat on the floor, as was his custom, to examine them.

'*Is there any hunting?*'

'*No.*'

'*Oh, well, it can at least he fortified; for if they*[248] *have any wit they will carry me off. My wife will be bored there — but then she was not much amused in Paris.*'

Of Caesar he said that he was merely an intriguing tribune. Alexander he considered the greatest of all Captains. On the eve of the Moscow campaign he remarked, '*This old Europe bores me.*'

In May and June 1813, when the tide was actually running strong against Napoleon, gloom prevailed in England. Bets were laid not as to whether Danzig was taken but whether he had not gained a complete victory over the Powers allied against him. It was even rumoured that Lutzen was a defeat for the Allies, and the official accounts suggested nothing more heartening than a draw.

Yet in the midst of all these alarms the Regent gave a ball for his daughter, the blooming, slightly bouncing Princess Charlotte. 'The D. of Devonshire', writes Bess, 'danced with her a great deal, was quite at his ease with her, and she seemed to enjoy it very much.'[D] There could have been no stronger contrast than that between the young Duke's first love, his delicate, diminutive cousin, Caroline Ponsonby, and the jolly, obstreperous royal girl to whom he now began to send presents of game from Chatsworth, and also to pay other more marked attentions. Charlotte herself certainly believed him to be *épris*. She liked him, even though she found him very plain;[249] she flirted with him, and was suspected by her fuming papa of giving a political turn to the flirtation. The caricaturists pounced with rapture upon the supposed romance, and in the print-shops the staring public could see a languishing Cavendish dancing with a coyly simpering Princess. The Regent dismissed it all as 'complete stuff and nonsense', but he was flustered, and it was not until after his daughter's death that the breach between him and the Young Duke was happily closed.

The Duchess in her Journal makes no direct allusion to these things, but when the tragic news from Claremont reached her at Rome in November 1817, she hastened to write a kind letter to her stepson, knowing that he would be 'so much affected'.

Caro George had been present at Caro William's waltzing party when Byron met Annabella Milbanke for the first time. Fate laid its hand upon them both, to their undoing: and by the end of 1812 he was gravitating slowly, almost it seemed reluctantly, towards that mysterious icicle, whose aunt, Lady Melbourne, was soon active again in her character of Mistress Overdone.

Byron wrote to her ladyship that he certainly wished to cultivate Annabella's acquaintance,

> but Caroline[250] told me she was engaged to Eden[251] and so did several others. Mrs. L.,[252] *her* great friend, was of opinion (and upon my honour I believe her) that she neither did, could, nor ought to *like* me; and was moreover certain that E. would be the best husband in the world and I its antithesis.[253]

A little later he wrote to Lady Melbourne:

> My terrific projects amount to this — to remain on good terms with Lady Cowper and Mrs. Lamb and on the best terms with you, being the three pleasantest persons in very different ways with whom I am acquainted.[254]

Caro George, like the rest of the Bessborough-Melbourne circle, was later deeply dismayed by Caro William's unbalanced passion for Byron. It was probably for the sake of her languishing half-brother, and because she felt 'a great horror at the possibility of an American Mrs. Foster', that she first cultivated Miss Milbanke, but their friendship was soon dyed in grain and it stood wind and weather.

By Byron's subsequent marriage to Annabella he became Caro George's cousin-in-law, Sir Ralph Milbanke being Lady Melbourne's brother. During the sinister and tragic honeymoon at Halnaby the bridegroom wrote to his new aunt, 'Pray, how many of our new relation (at least of mine) intend to own us? I reckon upon George and you and Lord M., and the Count and Countess of the Holy Roman Empire.[255] As for Caro and Caro George and William, I don't know what to think — do you?'

It could hardly be expected that Byron's early liking for Caro George would endure when he found her ranged among the most loyal friends of his unhappy wife. He wrote from Rome in May 1817 that Lady Byron was surrounded by people who detested him, among them 'Brougham the lawyer — who never forgave me for saying that Mrs. Ge Lamb was a damned fool.'

When it became clear that the child of this lamentable alliance would be born towards the end of 1815, Byron set about finding some furnished quarters in London where the potentially important *accouchement* might take place. His choice fell upon Bess's home, 13 Piccadilly Terrace, and it was there that his daughter Ada saw the light, while he himself was flinging soda-water bottles about the room beneath. It was thence that Annabella fled back to her parents, and thence that he wrote his desperate and seemingly genuine appeals to her to return.

The rent fixed was £700 for a year's tenancy, and in view of the tenant's insolvent condition it is hardly surprising that this rent was not paid regularly, nor in full. In May 1817 Bess met Byron in Rome, near the Colosseum, but 'he just alighted from his carriage and darted by'.[D] In November he wrote to her from Venice to assure her that until very lately he had not been aware that Her Grace was so unlucky as to have him still among the number of her debtors, and to promise that he would do his best to have the remaining balance of the debt 'liquidated'.[256]

Four years later he sought her intercession on behalf of 'the two Counts Gamba', the father and brother of his golden-ringleted last love, the Countess Guiccioli. In spite of her considered opinion that his lordship was 'either mad or a Caligula', she returned a gracious reply. He had certainly shown great adroitness in appealing to the memory of their late friend Lady Melbourne: 'I say *friend* only', he wrote, with some bitterness, 'for my *relationship* with her family has not been fortunate for them nor for me.' He also mentioned the testimony afforded by the recently published letters of Gibbon as to the 'high and amiable qualities' of Bess's character. The spell worked. She promised to do her best with 'the present Government of Rome', and in a postscript she says that she gives up the Austrian Government to all he chooses to say of them.[257]

There seems to have been only one more point of contact between Byron[258] and the lady whose fate at one time bid fair to be involved with the woman he might have married and the woman he did marry. In the event both Augustus Foster and Augustus Clifford found amiable wives with whom they were probably happier than the diplomat would have been with Annabella Milbanke or the Admiral with Mercer Elphinstone.

By the middle of 1813 Bess had re-established friendly relations with the Young Duke and with the Morpeth family. In June, the most hay-feverish month of the year, she was much concerned about her stepson's health when she and Caro were staying with him at Chiswick. On the King's birthday she records, 'I had all my grandchildren (as I call them) with me to see the Mail Coaches pass by.'[D]

These must have been the little Howards, Georgiana Morpeth's numerous brood. From their stepgrandmama's windows in Piccadilly Terrace they would

Madame de Staël.

get an excellent view of a most attractive sight, the annual parade of mail coaches, horses, harness and paintwork groomed, burnished and polished in the highest possible degree. It is a pity that Hary-O's devotion to these small people never softened her heart towards 'Lady Liz', who also held them very dear. Bess's detractors have more than once compared her to Becky Sharp, but there was one respect at least in which she differed from that arch-*intriguante*. She not only loved children; she loved to have them with her, and was loved by them in return, which, as William IV used to say, is 'quite another thing'.

During this same month Bess was able to give active proof of friendship to one of the numerous distinguished foreigners then present in London. This was Madame de Staël, whom she had known slightly at Passy and with whom she had never lost contact. There was a link here with her old admirer, Edward Gibbon, who had once wanted to marry Suzanne Curchod, the predestined wife of Necker and mother of that remarkable woman so often called, after her most famous book, 'Corinne'. There was also a link with the unfortunate Count Fersen, between whom and his dark, ugly, brilliant daughter Necker had once sought to arrange an alliance. In the end Corinne did marry a Swede — the Baron de Staël-Holstein, from whom she was formally separated in 1798.

Hearing that Madame de Staël was staying at Brunet's Hotel in Leicester Fields, Bess went to call on her, accompanied by Augustus Foster and Caroline George. She found that the former redness of Madame's face had disappeared, while the brilliancy of her eyes was undiminished.[D]

The authoress of *De l'Allemagne*, the book which had been suppressed by Napoleon and was soon to be published by John Murray, might well have expected to be received with enthusiasm in London; but there was one person whose iron virtue recoiled from the presence of the mistress of so many notable lovers. This was the Prince Regent's reigning Sultana, Lady Hertford, who, according to Bess, remarked to Lord Granville Leveson-Gower that Madame de Staël 'ought to be made to leave the country'.[D]

There was, however, a practical reason for the interest felt by the Government in the visitor. She provided a point of contact with Marshal Bernadotte, who, after having been nominated by Bonaparte to succeed Charles XIII on the Swedish throne, had had the audacity to set the interests of Sweden above the desires of his imperial patron and was now ranging himself with the enemies of the Empire. It was because Fersen was falsely suspected by the Stockholm mob of having poisoned Bernadotte that he perished so cruelly at their hands.

Bess flung herself generously into the fray on behalf of Corinne.

> Lady Hertford's abuse alarmed me, for fear it should influence the Prince not to invite her to Carlton House, and finding that Lord Melbourne held the same language I determined to write to the Prince — I went Tuesday to Richmond and was not very well. Wednesday early I sent the Prince my note. About half after six, as I was dressing, the Prince Regent was announced. By the help of a shawl I came very soon to him, and he said, 'My dear Duchess, I am come to answer your note myself' and embraced me. He then said that he would invite Madame de Stael, that he begged I would tell her that he hoped to have the honour of seeing her but that he thought it was *plus dans les formes* to send a card only after he had been presented to her which he hoped to be at Lady Heathcote's, where he understood she was invited. This was perfectly kind to me and civil to her. He then talked a good deal about her and about different things, stayed a great while, but finding company were to dine with me, he said he would go away.[D]

'I do hate ill-nature, and to a foreigner, too,' was Bess's comment on Lady Hertford's tirades; but the Hollands and the Liverpools were less austere, and in the end the Sultana, probably at the urging of the Sultan, relented also.

The triumph of Madame de Staël was complete. Even Queen Charlotte condescended to receive her. But English politicians may have been slightly disconcerted when this vigorous, voluble, ungainly woman proceeded to make long speeches, and to harangue with impartial energy both the Whigs and the Tories.

One of Bess's likeable traits was her absolute freedom from petty jealousies. She was an intelligent and beautiful woman; she knew that Madame de Staël excelled her in intelligence as Madame Récamier did in beauty; yet her friendship for Corinne and Juliette never moulted a feather.

CHAPTER XIV

Bernadotte — Moreau — The Bourbon Princes — The Regent and his Wife — The Young Duke — 1813–1815

It was characteristic of Bess that she should have taken immediate advantage of her renewed acquaintance with Madame de Staël to collect from her some anecdotes of Talleyrand, Bonaparte, and Bernadotte.

Talleyrand, declared Corinne, was in conversation the wittiest person she had ever known,

> but he could not write. When Mirabeau died, and Talleyrand was chosen to pronounce his funeral oration in the *Assemblée Constitutionelle*, he came to her and said, '*My child, you must prepare this speech for me, and have it ready for tomorrow.*' She did as he wished, and when he supped with her on the following evening, he told her that the speech had been *the most complete success.*[D]

Of Bonaparte she related that he went up one day to Madame Condorcet,

> a very handsome woman who had taken great part in the politics of the day, and, placing himself before her, he said, '*Madame, I do not like women to meddle in politics.*' '*General,*' she replied, '*the fact is that in this country people are accustomed to cut off women's heads — and one does like to know why.*'[D]

Bess was greatly interested when Madame de Staël told her that the famous prophetess, Mademoiselle Normand, had assured Bernadotte that he would some day be King of a Northern Country.

> It was for that reason that he named his son Oscar, though he pretended that it was after a character in Macpherson's *Ossian*.
>
> M. Rocca[259] reminded Madame de Staël that the same sybil had foretold that a famous and persecuted woman would some day come and seek refuge with him. It was not until Bernadotte saw Madame de Staël that he recollected this.[D]

'It is all', adds Bess, 'in the Swedish archives at Stockholm.'[D]

A second foreign lady to whom the Duchess was showing much attention that year was Madame Moreau the wife of that other Marshal, who after rendering great services and receiving great rewards had fallen out with his Imperial master and had finally gone over to the Allies. During their temporary exile in America both the Marshal and his wife had established friendly relations with Augustus Foster, and when the Tsar Alexander I called Moreau back to Europe to act as Adviser to the Allies nothing could be more natural than that *Madame la Maréchale* should settle for the time being in England — at Wimbledon, to be precise — and that Bess should visit her there.

Madame Moreau was said to have encouraged her husband in his vaulting ambition and when he o'er-leapt himself her overweening arrogance was held to be in some degree responsible: but from Bess we hear nothing of this, and it was she to whom Castlereagh sent the letter written by Moreau to his wife after he was severely — and as it proved fatally — wounded in the Battle of Dresden. Bess chose Madame de Staël as her messenger, but a few days later Castlereagh dispatched an express to her so that Madame Moreau should not learn 'suddenly or by the papers' of the Marshal's death, and she then drove straight to Wimbledon, where 'the scene of misery was great'.

The Foreign Secretary's letter is bound up with the Journal.

> St. James's Square,
> Saturday, 3 a.m.
>
> My dear Dss,
>
> I grieve to report that a messenger just arrived from the Headquarters confirms the intelligence of General Moreau's death. He died on the 31st at Laun, in perfect possession of himself and after dictating a letter to the Emperor full of manly sentiments. His remains were embalmed and to be immediately removed to St. Petersburgh.
>
> Forgive me for asking you to assist me in communicating to his unfortunate wife the melancholy event.
>
> God bless you, dear Duchess,
>
> Ever affectionately yours,
>
> Castlereagh.[D]

On October 4th Bess, accompanied by Lady Bessborough, Lady Melbourne, Caroline George and F.F., attended the Requiem Mass for Moreau in the black-draped French chapel. Bess was much overcome, but recovered herself sufficiently to offer up her own thoughts and prayers to God and her hopes of being united to him whom she had lost. The absence of the French princes caused unfavourable comment but there was general satisfaction when Count Lieven announced that just as he was setting out for the service a messenger arrived bearing a letter to Madame Moreau from the Tsar, who had settled a pension of 100,000 roubles on her, and intended to assign a house to her in St Petersburgh.[D]

In the meantime Clifford had become engaged to Lord John Townshend's daughter, Elizabeth Frances, and the Young Duke was entering whole-heartedly into the arrangements for his half-brother's wedding. They all dined at Devonshire House on October 16th, and Bess stood the return to that mansion of many memories better than she had expected. Her dear stepson's kindness and affection bore her up in the morning, and when she returned to dinner the happiness of 'Cliff' and 'Lizzy' still more supported her. On October 20th the Tower guns were firing to announce the entry of Wellington into France, and the same evening Clifford and Elizabeth Townshend were married.

> The Duke gave a magnificent dinner, and the whole thing was well managed and very handsome. Lizzy looked very pretty and my Clifford quite beautiful.[D]

So wrote the bridegroom's mother, at the close of a day which must have been closely packed with poignant memories.

In his privately printed *Sketch of the Life of the Sixth Duke of Devonshire* Clifford commented on the Duke's love of splendour, and contrasted it with the simple tastes of their father, who when told he was to have a blue riband said that he would prefer a blue great-coat.

The honeymoon was spent at Chiswick where Bess went with Lady John Townshend to visit the young couple two days after the wedding. Ten days later she was there again:

> ——I found my kind stepson well. He received me at the door. The Townshends are here, and my dear Clifford and Lizzy.[D]

Public and national events were soon sufficiently exciting to banish even the delightful vision of Clifford's happiness from his mother's mind — at any rate for the time being. One day when she was at Wimbledon with Madame Moreau, Monsieur was ushered in.

'He is', she wrote,

> much altered, is grown very thin, and his looks bear the stamp of suffering. He hoped Lord Wellington would not invade France. '*For you know what the French are like, Madame — if they are invaded, Royalists, Republicans, Bonapartists, everyone, will march either under Soult or Suchet to deliver France.*'[D]

In this Monsieur proved himself as poor a judge of the French people as most of his House were wont to be.

Even in October 1813, when the Bonapartist Empire was visibly foundering, there were Left-wing Englishmen who could not bring themselves to face up to a fact which accorded so ill with their long-held theories. Among these was Tierney. 'He still', writes Bess, 'believes that Bonaparte knows what he is about, and can extricate himself.'[D]

Then came the news of the glorious victory at Leipzig, when in the Battle of the Nations the Allies inflicted a crushing defeat upon the man whom quaking Europe had once believed to be invincible. Bess's first thought was of her dead Duke. 'Oh, that such events could have happened when his Patriot mind and mild nature would have rejoiced at the prospect held out by it of peace and repose!'[D]

Yet at a garden fête in the grounds of Chiswick, Lord Holland characteristically belittled both the successes of the Allies and the losses of the French, thereby casting a damper on the spirits of a large, distinguished and optimistic gathering. The Duchess was among those who stoutly refused to be daunted. Her faith was justified by the good news which did not cease to pour in; and the fact that she soon begins to jot down miscellaneous anecdotes shows that her equilibrium, never seriously shaken, was now perfect once more.

Bonaparte, she notes, once said of Metternich,

> '*He asked to leave the room. He did well, because he stank.*' Of Lannes, his favourite, he said, '*When that rascal began to talk about God and Eternity I knew that it was all up with him.*'

On November 24th we have this glimpse of Wellington through the eyes of a cautious British officer:

> When Major Brown was sent with a flag of truce to Soult, the Marshal asked him how Lord Wellington was dressed. Major B. said he often changed his dress, sometimes his uniform, sometimes in plain blue or brown. 'Where was he, chiefly?' 'Oh, he changes his place also frequently.' '*Monsieur,*' said Soult, '*you were well chosen.*'[D]

Spain was much in the mind of most people at this time, and Bess inserts a brief anecdote to illustrate the pride of the Spanish people in their country. A priest, preaching on the Temptation in the Wilderness, said, '*My brethren, let us bless God that He did not permit Satan to show Andalousia to Jesus Christ.*'[260]

In the midst of all this excitement Clifford's young wife frightened everybody by falling downstairs. 'Thank God nothing broke,' wrote Bess, 'and no inward injury — but they bled her to be more secure.'

A pithy saying of Madame de Stäel's is recorded *à propos* of the liberation of the Netherlands: 'as Stadholder', she said, 'the Prince of Orange would be the successor of William III, as King, the successor of Louis Bonaparte'.[D]

After dinner with the Liverpools at Fife House, Bess recorded some opinions of her brother-in-law, the Prime Minister, who 'would like Lord Wellington to restore the Bourbons' but spoke disparagingly of the Duc D'Angoulême. Bernadotte he really admired, though he believed he was 'a little cracked'.

> I said, 'Oh, no — a little dramatic, if you will, but that suits the circumstances.'
>
> Lady Hertford feared that Bernadotte desired to make himself King of France. 'Now,' said she, 'Another adventurer — for adventurer he is — is surely not desirable. He spares the French. At first he could hardly be brought to fight them. He even gave orders not to fire upon *les petits bleus*' — the French soldiers.
>
> I told Lady Hertford that I had heard that Bernadotte had said that he never could hope to found a solid dynasty in France, but in Sweden he could. She thought I had all my impressions from Madame de Stäel and said that she knew she swore by him. I said my son Augustus had given me the same character of Bernadotte and that I myself knew him in Paris in 1802.[D]

As the year waned to its close the Tower guns hardly ceased to shake the windows in London, and to re-echo like thunder through a looming fog.

Corisande Ossulston, on the authority of her odd little atomy of a husband, described to Bess the anxiety of the French princes to cross the Channel and land in France.

> Monsieur had an interview with Lord Liverpool and the scene was a violent one. Lord Liverpool refused his consent to Monsieur going. The latter grew warm, complained of the cruelty of this proceeding and talked of going to some part of France and appearing among those who demanded him.
>
> Lord Liverpool then in a vehement manner said that he should not only refuse him all means of going but should send such a description of his person that no one should dare to facilitate his escape — in short, he gave him to understand that he was as a prisoner here, and interrupted still his discourse by saying, with a half-bow, '*Monseigneur, I am grieved to speak to you like this.*'
>
> Poor Monsieur is quite in despair, and he and the Duc de Berri are capable of doing some desperate thing.[D]

There is unfortunately a gap of three months in the Journal at this point, but when it begins again the hard-worked Tower guns are thundering to proclaim the capitulation of Paris, and white cockades are blossoming in the streets of London.

At Devonshire House incredulity alternated with relief and joy; but when 'D.' came home from a long walk Caroline was able to confirm that the news was true as well as glorious. At Holland House there was less exultation, and Lady Holland characteristically 'treated Tierney as a dupe' because he believed in the freedom of the new constitution granted to France.

> Tierney said, 'Upon my word, I came here thinking it as pretty a finish as ever I heard, and I find I am all wrong!'
> 'All a humbug, my dear Tierney,' said Lady Holland.[D]

Bess proceeds to fill her Journal with somewhat disconnected notes upon the sayings and opinions of her family and friends during these pregnant days. 'Dear Clifford', she notes, 'has a sort of feeling for Bonaparte which is occasioned by admiration for his military talents and from having seen French officers devoted to him. Caro only rejoices at the idea of the return of the Bourbons from a feeling for Corise and my friendship for them.' The Duke of Argyll declared roundly that Bonaparte's acceptance of a pension and the sovereignty of Elba showed 'the dunghill in him': but Clifford and Caro contended that he 'could do nothing else'.[D]

'It turns my thoughts', wrote Bess,

> from the greatness of his fall which, if he had shown magnanimity in it or even a rash attempt to recover his power, had shed a kind of ray of glory on his setting, but to meanly stoop to be pensioned by the nation whom he has tyrannized over — to secure his miserable life by a retreat to a barren island, are circumstances so extraordinary that he becomes little better than one of the poor wretches whom we send to Botany Bay.

A year later he made the rash attempt, and was forced to retreat to an island even more bleak and inhospitable than Elba: but in 1814 he was in his first eclipse, and the white cockade of the Bourbons was sprouting even on the greasy hats of the London 'coachees'.

Bess was pleased by the delicate conduct of the Allies in Paris. The sovereigns lodged in Talleyrand's house instead of at the Tuileries, and the Tsar begged that *La Vestale* might be substituted for the more topical *Triomphe de Trajan* at the opera. The audience would have preferred Trajan; they also

> begged that the Eagles might be pulled down which Bonaparte had set up in the Opera House. These were so firmly fixed that it was found necessary to cover them with the *drapeau blanc*.[D]

It was reported that Lucien Bonaparte on hearing of his brother's abdication remarked, 'I always said that he would blow the bubble till it burst.'

In honour of the visit of the Allied sovereigns to England in the summer of 1814 the Prince Regent with his habitual flair for showmanship planned a variety of pageants. His 'Dearest Duchess' enjoyed many of them, though she seems to have held aloof from the more rowdy scenes of revelry. What she liked best was to meet famous people at close range, as when at Combe Wood she was presented to the Tsar Alexander and King Frederick William of Prussia. The Tsar was benignant, as he always was unless in the company of the Prince Regent; and Bess records proudly that when sitting next to the King at dinner she overcame what she kindly calls his 'shyness'. A less tolerant chronicler described him as being 'as surly as a bear'.

It was a trying summer for her flamboyant friend, the Prince Regent, but her Journal proves conclusively that several of the stories about him generally believed both then and since were without foundation.

The Regent was to go to the Opera ten minutes or quarter of an hour in advance of his guests.

He came up to me rather in a nervous manner and he seemed to have drank rather more than he ought. It was known that the Princess of Wales was to be at the opera and it made him nervous, but he was determined to meet it, and Lord Liverpool attended him. He was however well received the sovereigns were, of course.

Many stories were put about afterwards of the extreme paleness and terror of his countenance and the Princess came into the House whilst the applause was going on to the Sovereigns and Prince. There was a distinct applause for her, but nothing to offend the Regent. He bowed to her, I am told.[D]

Later Bess emphatically denied that the Regent had requested the sovereigns not to visit the Princess of Wales.

On the contrary, the first few days over, which he certainly wished should be in visits between himself and them, Lord Liverpool, whom I asked about it, said he authorized me to quote him a being the bearer of a message from the Prince to the Sovereigns begging that they would do exactly as they wished, and to be assured that he did not wish to be an obstacle to their visiting the Princess, to which he had not the least objection: that in consequence of this the Emperor intended calling on the Princess and went next day to consult with the King of Prussia. The rupture of the Princess Charlotte's marriage then took place, and the King of Prussia said that this circumstance had altered his feelings on the subject of the Princess:[261] that, though her nearest relation, he would not go. The Emperor then said he would not go either.[D]

It is indeed difficult to imagine why the Prince should have tried to deflect his Imperial and Royal guests from Connaught Place. Half an hour spent with that bold-eyed, rouged, and raddled, indecorously and inadequately clad creature would probably have erased from their minds any lingering impression of the virtuous martyr of Whig propaganda.

The Young Duke and Clifford went to the celebrations at Oxford, admired the illuminations, attended the State banquet in the Radcliffe Camera, saw the Prince wearing his academic gown and for the first time *not* wearing hair-powder on his wig, and returned delighted with everything.

Giving free rein to his love of magnificence, the Duke next planned a 'supper and waltzing party' at Devonshire House, but his principal guest, the unpredictable Alexander, excused himself on the plea that couriers had arrived from the Empress.

In spite of his annoyance with the Duke, the Prince Regent duly appeared at the ball. 'He was', says Bess,

> exceedingly amiable and kind and spoke with a feeling about D. House which makes me quite love him. I believe he don't like the Emperor very much — he said to me, 'He is like a weathercock; one never knows what he will do.[D]

On their way to the coast the sovereigns were entertained by the Liverpools at Combe Wood, where Bess had 'much conversation' with the Tsar and his Mongolian-looking but attractive sister the Grand Duchess Catherine.

> He told me he had left a bad impression on one person — the woman who showed the Crown Jewels at the Tower. '*I lost patience. I said I had seen enough, and I confessed that the two hundred and fifty thousand muskets ranged round the armoury seemed far more beautiful to me.*'[D]

When they returned to the drawing-room Lord Bristol's children were there, and once again Bess shows her real and tender love for the young.

> Seeing me caress Arthur both the Emperor and his sister caressed him also, and were kind to all the other children, though little Arthur alone was kissed and his little hand asked for, which he stretched out.[D]

'Little Arthur', then six years old, lived to become Bishop of Bath and Wells, and thereby forged yet another link between the Hervey family and the Church. These children, like the crowd gathered round the gates, had the pleasure of contemplating the Tsar's heavily bearded coachman in his picturesque Cossack livery.

Though Wellington never appealed to Bess's heart as Nelson had done, she watched with interest from her window in Piccadilly when on the evening of June 23rd an open carriage with six horses attended by gentlemen on horseback drove up to Hamilton Place, and when crowds collected shouting, 'Hurray the Duke of Wellington!' Early on the following day she saw even greater crowds gathering to cheer him when he set out to pay his respects to the Prince Regent at Portsmouth. The Prince, shattered by the numerous awkward incidents attending the visit of his Allies, had gone down to the coast to bid them farewell. The arrival of the great soldier whom he had backed steadily against the Whigs must appreciably have fortified his morale.

'It is curious', remarks Bess, 'to know the secret bickerings that were going on behind the appearance of harmony and mutual admiration.' The Tsar 'grew impatient under the etiquette of Court parties'; and the Prince so far overcame his habitual dislike of Lady Spencer as to confide to her that His Imperial Majesty was 'as obstinate as a mule'.

Just as she had done when the Peace of Amiens made the Continent accessible in 1802, the Duchess now hastened to take advantage of the changed conditions resulting from the restoration of the Bourbons.

On August 6th, accompanied by her daughter and squired by Lord Gambier, she crossed from Dover to Calais in two and a half hours, and found on disembarking that a letter from the Comte de Chartres 'made everything easy'. The first thing which struck her was the improvement in the people's manners — 'none of that familiarity which they had in 1802'. Their destination was Spa, where she had stayed twenty years before with 'the dear friend who made every place a place of happiness' to her.[D] The Morpeths visited them there, and when they left it was to their 'very great regret'. 'G.' was evidently less implacable than Hary-O.

In November the Duchess and her daughter were in Paris, where many of the famous figures of 1802 were floating about rather like phantoms — La Fayette, Lally-Tollendal, Madame Récamier, Lady Bessborough. The Paris of Louis XVIII seems to have lacked some quality which the Revolution had failed to destroy and which Napoleon, consciously or unconsciously, had kept in being. Perhaps this was because most of the actors and actresses in the comedy were ageing, disillusioned men and women; the fiddles were a little out of tune, and the dancers did not always keep time to them. Whatever may have been lacking it was something which Bess had hoped and failed to find.

By the end of the year she and Caroline were in Marseilles, another place of many memories. Marshal Masséna lived in the same street, and the opportunity to collect some fragments of Bonapartiana was not allowed to pass.[262]

The susceptible Augustus Foster, then English Minister in Copenhagen, was once more in love, and consulting his mother as to his prospects of happiness. This time the object of his *flamme* was Clifford's sister-in-law, Audrey Townshend, whose 'beautiful clean hair and light little figure' were continually before his eyes. A year later his heart finally came to anchor when he married Albinia Jane Hobart, grand-daughter of the third Earl of Buckinghamshire. It was their third son, Vere Foster, whose book, *The Two Duchesses*, published in 1898, has been until now one of the principal sources of information about his charming grandmother, Dearest Bess.

With her knack of being near, if not upon, the scene of great historical events, Bess was at Marseilles when Napoleon escaped from Elba and landed at Fréjus, near Cannes. F.F. was with her; and with his habitual good sense he wrote to his younger brother that he thought it would soon be over with Bonaparte: but Augustus was confounded, and in London the news was received with equal dismay at Court and on 'Change.

Bess made no attempt to escape from the Continent, and most unfortunately her Journal for the year 1815 is not among the Dormer family papers. It seems to have been sent to Augustus Foster. She was to return to England more than once before her death, but Italy was the home of her heart, and she found there devoted friends, intelligent interests, and even a touch of slightly theatrical adventure.

In February 1815 she wrote a letter to her stepson which suggests that she was then uneasy about both her health and her money affairs.

My dearest D.,

In case I should die abroad before I have paid my debts towards which I have given up half my income, I earnestly request of you to allow that half to be continued another year as though I were alive, as that will clear them. I recommend to you my poor, faithful Madame Palli and Jacquey and Loton — the others are excellent servants, but I have not known them so long.

Above all, I do implore you to continue your affection and kindness towards my darling Caroline — she will need your comforting and assistance. Be still, as you have been, a kind brother to her and Clifford.

I hope you will continue friends to my dear sons and never quite forget me, who loved and adored both your parents with an entire and faithful affection.

God bless you and make you happy, my dearest D., let me be laid next my dear husband.

Elizth Devonshire.[D]

The Duke responded to this appeal with all the generosity of a singularly generous nature. He missed no opportunity of showing kindness and even of paying honour to his half-sister Caroline; and the friendship between him and Clifford ended only with his life.

After 1828 'Cliff' was not actively employed afloat, but the Duke soon found him other seas to sail. He was returned to Parliament in the Cavendish interest first for Bandon Bridge, then for Dungarven, then for Bandon Bridge again. He was knighted in 1830 at St James's Palace by King William IV, whom he had once had the honour of attending when Royal Tarry Breeks was Lord High Admiral. A baronetcy followed eight years later.

In 1852 the Duke of Devonshire as Lord Chamberlain appointed him Gentleman Usher of the Black Rod, a post which he held till his death at the advanced age of eighty-nine: and on various occasions he deputized for Lord Willoughby d'Eresby as Lord Great Chamberlain of England. To these ceremonial duties he brought the undoubted assets of a fine figure, a charming presence, and a bearing in which the simplicity of the sailor was, as it were, lightly gilded by golden rays from Chatsworth. Sad to relate, the 'beautiful, delicate face' was, before it vanished from the eyes of men, adorned with a Newgate fringe.

Admiral[263] Sir Augustus Clifford shared his mother's taste for objects of art and antiquity. His house at Westfield in the Isle of Wight was a show place, and the cards of admission bore a notice exhorting the visitors not to damage 'the marbles'. Some part of his leisure he spent poring over his mother's Journals, which he page-numbered and annotated evidently with a view to publication. Any small errors in names of ships or other naval matters he amended; but he left unedited the rather numerous passages where his own good looks and good character are fondly commented upon.

Jean Victor Moreau.

Another act of family piety was the writing of *A Sketch of the Life of the Sixth Duke of Devonshire*. In this are printed some deliciously playful and affectionate letters from the Duke, showing a strong community of tastes and interests between those two sons of Canis, who inherited the lively temper of their respective mothers rather than the phlegmatic turn of their common father. Clifford dwells with loving pride upon the Duke's enlightened patronage of art, architecture and landscape gardening, his skill in dancing the mazurka, his courage in addressing a public meeting held in Derby in 1821 to deprecate the recent proceedings in the House of Lords against Queen Caroline, though at the same time expressing, a little paradoxically, inviolable loyalty to the throne. Of his speech on this occasion he sent a copy to his stepmother in Rome, and she received it with enthusiasm.

By one person it was naturally received with anything but enthusiasm. This was George IV. But he was an amiable creature, and Clifford tells us how the breach was closed.[264]

> Shortly afterwards the Duke and the King met at the house of Prince and Princess Lieven, where H.M. was to stand sponsor to their child. The Duke asked the King if he must wait for such an event to hope to have the honour of His Majesty dining with him — the King said he would do so with the greatest pleasure and promised shortly to name the day.

The Duke then arranged a grand rout, dinner, concert, and ball for the King at Devonshire House, when seventeen footmen wearing the Cavendish livery, yellow and azure laced with silver, lined the crimson-carpeted hall.

In the list of people to whom copies of this *Sketch* were sent we find many stragglers from earlier days. Even the ghost of Selina Trimmer is called up, for we learn incidentally that, at her request, the Duke placed a nephew of hers in the Navy, and that he went to sea with Captain Clifford on the *Euryalus* in 1821.

It is, however, the closing passage of this artless biography which throws the most endearing light upon both writer and subject.

> There may have been slight shades or aberrations in his character; but who is without? They may be pointed out by others, but not by him who was fondly attached to him and who has written this imperfect memorial.

CHAPTER XV

My Friend the Cardinal

By the first days of February 1816 the Duchess was settled in Rome, a city which she found archaeologically rewarding, socially satisfying, and politically perturbing. The Congress of Vienna had riveted the fetters of Habsburg and Bourbon tyranny again upon the Italian peninsula, and a smouldering discontent filled the land.

One of the very few people who realized the growing evils and dangers of the time was the Pope's Secretary of State, Cardinal Consalvi, of whom Monsieur Artaud, the French Minister, said, 'He is making great progress, and if he had the power he would do great things. But he is in a difficult position. The other cardinals do not like him. They are jealous. And he is accused of being too favourably inclined towards the English.'ᴰ In the introduction to the letters of Hary-O it is categorically and quite unwarrantably stated that in Italy the Duchess 'made herself ridiculous by an affair with Cardinal Consalvi'. The friendship of this remarkable man was indeed the solace of her last years, but no one with even the most superficial acquaintance with his character and career would be likely to misinterpret it. They enjoyed each other's society, and very often after an exhausting day coping with recalcitrant fellow-cardinals, he would call upon her — sometimes so late that she had retired to bed and could not receive him. Once he 'stayed talking in the kindest manner till he forgot he had to go to the French Ambassador's'; but nowhere is there the faintest hint of elderly dalliance.

Hercule Consalvi was the same age as herself; they had many tastes and interests in common; and the very qualities she admired most in 'my friend the Cardinal' were those which would have made an amorous intrigue between them unthinkable. It is true that her admiration verged on the ardent; but that was Bess's way. It is true that she took his portrait wherever she went, and that it travelled with her in her carriage; but what portrait would be more likely to turn her thoughts towards Heaven and away from the world in which neither of them had then many years to live?

This wise and saintly statesman was born in Rome in 1757 and educated at Cardinal York's Seminary at Frascati. He became Chamberlain to Pope Pius VI in

1783; and when the French occupied Rome in 1798 it was he who reluctantly surrendered to them the Castle of St Angelo.

A year later the Pope died and a Conclave was called at Venice to elect his successor. Cardinal York, whom a stubborn remnant of Jacobites still called 'King Henry IX', had lost all his episcopal revenues as the result of the French occupation of Italy, and he would have been unable to attend the Conclave as became a Prince of the Church had not a fellow-cardinal provided him with the needed robes, pectoral cross, and pastoral ring. Yet even in this shabby plight he had sufficient influence to get Hercule Consalvi chosen as secretary to the assemblage.

With the election of Cardinal Chiaramonti as Pius VII, Consalvi's star rose also. The new Pope appointed him his Secretary of State, and in 1800 conferred upon him a cardinal's hat. It was not until then that Consalvi took even minor orders, and he never became a fully ordained priest.

The concordat with Bonaparte was negotiated by him with great diplomatic skill in 1801, but his liberal views and his resistance to French encroachments caused the Emperor to demand his removal from office in 1806, and in 1809 he was summoned to Paris under a military escort. There he was divested of his sacred insignia, and both his personal fortune and his official stipend were declared to have been forfeited. For nearly three years he was kept in semi-captivity at Rheims, and for a shorter period later at Béziers. Then the second abdication of Napoleon set him free. Oddly enough he passed the Emperor on his way to Elba when he himself was *en route* for Italy. They exchanged no words, but when Napoleon recognized him he remarked to an Austrian officer in his escort, '*Yonder man, who would never become a priest, is the best priest of the lot.*'

On his way to represent the Vatican at the Congress of Vienna the Cardinal paid a short visit to London, where he made an excellent impression not only on the Prince Regent but also upon all the English statesmen whom he met there. At Vienna he established friendly contacts both with Castlereagh and Metternich, no small feat of diplomacy.

Other English ladies besides Bess felt the charm of the Cardinal's personality. Among these was Castlereagh's sister, Lady Octavia Law, who was in Rome in 1817, with her husband, afterwards Lord Ellenborough. When she died two years later the Foreign Secretary himself wrote to His Eminence, and the sorrowing widower promised that if he should go to Florence he would make a point of passing through Rome so that he might see again the faithful and honoured friend of his Octavia.

In his Will Consalvi bequeathed a gilt-bronze obelisk to Lady Sandwich and a model of the Column of Trajan to Lady Matilda Ward. To Bess he left a Florentine snuff-box in *pietra-dura*,[265] but as she survived him by only three months she probably did not live to receive a bequest which she would have treasured tenderly.

Her Journal and her letters to the Duke of Devonshire are haunted by the scarlet-clad figure of 'my friend the Cardinal'. In the *Biographical Sketches* privately printed by Sir Augustus Clifford after her death, she describes Consalvi as she knew him between 1815 and 1819 when he filled the honourable and thankless post of Minister of Foreign Affairs to Pius VII.

In person he is tall, thin, of the most dignified yet simple manners, a dark and animated eye, a thick dark brow, a smile of inexpressible sweetness and benevolence, his conversation natural and instructive, his temper mild, forgiving, yet warm and rather impatient of delay.

He took a constant interest in the excavations financed by her in the Forum, and approved warmly when she chose to employ paid workmen instead of the convict labour offered by the Government. In June 1817 Lord Gower, calling on Hary-O on his return from Rome, told her that

the Duchess, Cardinal Consalvi and Souza are digging *à qui mieux mieux,* and that they rout up great curiosities; that the Duchess is adored, that she protects all the artists and employs them and pays them magnificently, and that all the way on the road the inn-keepers are asking, *Connaissez-vous cette noble dame?*[266]

Lady Spencer's remarks were characteristic. 'That Witch of Endor the Duchess of Devon', she wrote, 'has been doing mischief of another kind to what she has been doing all her life by pretending to dig for the public good in the Forum.' In her view she had brought up 'nothing but a quantity of dirt and old horrors', and was also making herself 'the laughing-stock of all Rome by her pretensions to Macaenasship'.[267] Another person who thought that Her Grace 'attempted to play the Macaenas a little too much' was George Ticknor. Being an American he probably deprecated such private and personal encouragements as savouring of 'privilege'. Yet even he admitted that she did a great deal that should be praised and would not, he hoped, be forgotten.

We hear surprisingly little in the Journal about Bess's *éditions de luxe* of new Italian translations from the works of Horace and Virgil. Here, again, she found an encourager — even a collaborator — in the Cardinal. Her first venture was not particularly happy. It was Horace's Fifth Satire of the First Book, describing the journey to Brundisium, and she was unlucky in her choice of a translator. Scholars soon spotted textual and typographical errors, and Consalvi then advised her to have a completely new version made. This was done by his secretary, under his personal supervision and with interpolations from his own hand. It was published in 1818, with illustrations by Carraccioli, and is one of the finest books ever produced by the famous Bodoni Press at Parma. In 1819 followed Annibal

Caro's translation of the *Æneid*, with engravings by Marchetti after drawings by Thomas Lawrence. If Hary-O is to be believed,[268] Bess herself supplied one of the landscapes for the *Iter ad Brundisium*.

On New Year's Day, 1818, she sent the Cardinal a copy of the Bodoni Press edition, containing the originals of the illustrations, and inscribed:

> From the Duchess of Devonshire to her friend, Cardinal Consalvi, as a token of her very sincere and respectful attachment.

Apart from their common interest in art, architecture, and classical literature, the Duchess and the Cardinal shared the cult of friends departed. He had planted a small garden in memory of a much-loved brother who had died about ten years before. It contained a fine portrait-bust by Canova, numerous inscriptions, and many of the rare plants which his brother had loved, arranged in their proper Linnæan order. To this garden he gave Bess the key, 'when he was not able to go there himself' — a discreet qualification.

It cannot be denied that in her admiration for Cardinal Consalvi the Duchess reiterated the tale of his virtues with a persistency which might well have caused cynical persons to draw foolish conclusions. The modern colloquial verb active to 'plug' seems best to describe these activities. Wherever she went, in Italy, England or France, whether her interlocutor were Louis XVIII or Talleyrand, the King of Naples or the Prince Regent, she never missed an opportunity to introduce the Cardinal's name, and if none occurred she contrived to create one. When, as frequently happened, she elicited some words of appreciation from august or famous lips, she recorded them in her Journal with a delight as transparent as it is engaging. 'I think', she wrote once, 'if there is a pure and angelic mind on earth now, it is his.'[D]

Consalvi was not merely a statesman and a patriot. He was a humane and courageous innovator in another sphere. The Roman police, never reliable, were quite unable to cope with the *banditti* infesting the hills about Rome. These robbers were aided by certain ancient sanctuary rights, and they also enjoyed a certain romantic prestige among law-abiding citizens, just as some gangsters do in our own day. The Cardinal got in touch with Masocco, the leader of the most important band, and assured him that if he and his men would surrender, they would neither be executed nor put in chains. All that would happen to them would be temporary imprisonment in a fortress, and on their release the State would 'afford them the means to begin a peaceful existence'.

Bess recorded one day that the Cardinal had set off with a small escort for an unknown destination. And presently three wagon-loads of brigands rolled into Terracina, the place where he had arranged to hold parley with them.

Writing to Bess in his graceful Italian he described the picturesque scene.

They were all, he says, fine-looking men, wearing gold ear-rings, velvet jackets with silver buttons, and hats with coloured ribbons and feathers. Masocco asked for the reward offered by the Government to anyone who should bring him in, dead or alive, and also requested a free pardon for himself and his followers. This, replied the Cardinal, was more than it would become the Government to give, but as they had surrendered voluntarily he would take it upon himself to grant them the Pope's pardon and a mitigation of punishment. It was Masocco's wife who chiefly induced him to capitulate — a very handsome woman who was anxious to share his imprisonment.

A few days later Bess went to see the captives. She admired the good looks of the chief brigand and his wife, but thought that two of his nine *banditti* were 'very ill-looking'. The Signora Masocco spoke with enthusiasm of the kindness and clemency of the Cardinal, and Bess gave her an amber necklace from her own neck. The Duchess also gave a *scudo* to another bandit's wife, who begged her to intercede with the Cardinal so that she, too, might be allowed to share her husband's captivity.

The sequel, not recorded by Bess, was tragic. Masocco was shot dead by another brigand called Cesari, whom he had arranged to meet in order to negotiate the surrender of his band. An orgy of killing followed, in which neither women nor children were spared, and only when Cesari was picked off by a Roman carabineer did the reek of blood disperse.

In December 1816 the Cardinal was greatly amused to hear that the Duchess had received letters from England asking if she had 'turned Catholic'. Such reports persisted for some time. A year later, when the Stuart-Wortleys were in Rome, James Stuart-Wortley received an anxious letter from his father begging him not to hurry home and leave Caroline and the boys with Bess lest she should convert them. 'It is inconceivable such reports should be so credited,' she wrote. 'Every Sunday I go to prayers at Mr. Wortley's and I have never had a religious conversation with Cardinal Consalvi. Now and then I have asked him some question on subjects I had heard variously represented, but that is all.'[D]

The Cardinal's kindness was unwearying, and could not have been greater had Bess been a most devout member of his flock. When F.F., staying with his mother in Rome, contracted a severe ague and 'the bark' would not stay in his stomach, Consalvi sent his own physician, who in turn fetched an apothecary reputed to have 'a famous remedy'. This proved to be the inevitable bark again; but mixed with a different salt and administered in larger doses at longer intervals, it proved efficacious, and before long Fred, whose 'full habit' had temporarily given place to extreme emaciation, was enjoying both his dinner and his books.[D] In 1817 the Cardinal lent his house at Frascati to the Cliffords, who were there with Caroline George; and at the end of the same year we get a charming glimpse of him sitting on a sofa between Bess and her sister-in-law, Lady Bristol.[269]

Diplomats as well as sculptors, painters, and Roman princes teemed in the Duchess's elegant *salon*. Sir Robert A'Court, English Minister at Naples, M. Artaud, French Minister to the Vatican, and Luchesini, the Prussian envoy, were among those whose conversation she found most rewarding from the point of view of the keeper of a diary.

Luchesini had been for more than six years in the service of Frederick the Great, of whose closing moments he gave this vivid description.

> This extraordinary Man preserved his faculties to the last ...When asked to take some repose, he retorted that he was on the throne to serve his country. When told that the gentlemen who usually formed his society had retired, though still near, he said, 'Very well, I will try to take some repose, but tell these gentlemen that I hope to see them tomorrow.' He had a restless night, and on Tuesday night was breathing with difficulty. His physicians entreated him to take some of the cordial which had already given him relief and they brought it to him in his favourite cup, which he always drank out of. Frederick took the medicine, and when he had swallowed it he looked at the cup and flung it away; and leaning his head against the side of the couch, he beckoned to his Page, and saying, 'Cover me up,' he folded round him the for pelisse of 40,000 roubles which Paul[270] had formerly sent him, and died so.

She also recorded Frederick's words that if he wanted to ruin any provinces he would send philosophers to rule over them.

The term 'Philosopher' was indeed out of favour in a world which regarded the French Revolution and all the woes which flowed from it as the result of the sinister influence of such persons. Luchesini related to Bess an anecdote of Louis XV which shows that even in his last years that graceless debauchee was capable of seeing things both as they were and as they would be. On one occasion, when sitting by the fire after a hard day's hunting,

> he heard his courtiers commenting on how few people now came to Versailles except the Ambassadors, who were compelled by their duty to come. The King then turned round and said, 'That surprises you, Messieurs? Don't you see that people don't want a monarchy? They want a Republic. But old and indolent though I may be, I would, if necessary, place myself at the head of my Army, assemble my *noblesse*, and, from the further bank of the Loire, I should, if need were, retreat towards the Pyrenees. The King of Spain would not forget that Louis XIII placed his grandfather on the throne, and he would help me at a pinch. I do not fear for myself   Although I was not fond of the Dauphin I admit that he was a great loss to France. He would have known how to defend himself. But let my little grandson look out for himself; for *him* I am afraid.'[D]

Although Bess was completely disillusioned about Bonaparte she took a lively interest in those members of his family to whom the Pope had magnanimously given asylum in Rome. She notes that the parsimony of *Madame Mère* is proverbial, and also that the old lady was said to have given her imperial son a box on the ear at the time of the judicial murder of the Duc d'Enghien. She is amused when Madame Bacciochi, *née* Elisa Bonaparte, reveals that the Emperor called her his intelligent sister, Caroline, Queen of Naples, his ambitious sister, and Pauline, Princess Borghese, his pretty sister. One evening in February 1816 she met Pauline and Louis in 'the great walk of the Borghese Palace'. The Princess appeared to her 'like a pretty French milliner'; Louis, though pale and sickly, had a look of Napoleon.[D]

Soon after this Metternich was expected in Rome, and Bess records that the policy of the Austrian Cabinet was to protect the Bonapartes. 'If', said Luchesini, 'the King of France should die, there might easily be a French party, supported by Austria, on the side of the little Napoleon.'[D] He was perfectly right. Only the premature death of the Duke of Reichstadt prevented a Bonapartist restoration in 1832.

The news of Metternich's approach made Bess turn her mind back to the previous year, 'about the time of Napoleon's surrender to the English', namely in June 1815. Pauline Borghese then expressed a great desire to see the Duchess, and one of her English friends, Mrs Broderick, conveyed this desire to Bess, who answered that she never refused seeing anybody in distress. If, she added, the Princess Borghese thought she could render her any service, or send a letter from her to Lord Liverpool, she was ready to accompany Mrs Broderick to the Bagni della Villa, but it must be in the morning, as she was 'afraid of the night air'. Mrs Broderick wrote to say that she was to hear on the following day at what o'clock the Princess would be returning from her bath; and in due course the two Englishwomen kept the appointed rendezvous. Not so Pauline Borghese, who failed either to appear or to send any explanation of her failure to do so.[D]

Bess was later informed that the Princess had that very day been taken ill and blooded, 'but', she adds, 'a little sense of propriety, or she having been born to her situation, would have told her that she ought to have written her regrets, or some civil expression to anyone she had requested to see, but particularly to a foreigner of distinction'.[D] This omission rankled: and it is with obvious disapproval that she notes in 1816:

> Our English here however are going to her, though she and her mother and sister sit on a sofa to receive their company, with footstools, — and their company ranged round the room on small chairs and no footstools.[D]

Completely new light is thrown in Bess's Journal upon the curious and complicated transactions which ultimately led to the transference to the Royal

William, Sixth Duke of
Devonshire, engraving
after a portrait by
G. Hayter.

Archives at Windsor of the Papers bequeathed by the 'Bonnie Lass of Albany' to her
uncle, Cardinal York. Using all the available materials with their wonted fidelity and
skill, Alistair and Henrietta Tayler told the story some years ago,[271] but, lacking the
evidence supplied by Bess, that story could be neither authoritative nor complete.

In January 1817 it became known in Rome that a certain rather shady Scot,
called indifferently 'Doctor' or 'the Chevalier' Watson, had possessed himself
of these Papers, which Brougham had tried to purchase from Prince Charlie's
daughter to serve as source-material for his projected *History of England from 1688
to 1789*. Consalvi, as an intimate friend of Cardinal York, was called into council,
and in the event Bess herself, accompanied by a Mrs Dennis, ventured into a
room on the first floor of a house in the Vicolo delle Tre Cannelle, where the
documents were piled up. This must have required some courage on her part, as it
was rumoured — not without reason — that Watson was a fugitive from English

justice. He was, she remarks, 'a short, ill-looking man'.[D]

In reply to her questions he told her that the papers had belonged to a bishop who, as he could read neither French nor English, 'parted with them'. When she asked him if there were no legal heirs to them, as formerly belonging to Cardinal York, he turned aside without answering. Mrs Dennis then inquired whether he had informed Cardinal Consalvi, as Secretary of State. 'Yes,' answered Watson, 'eight days ago', but Bess noticed that he avoided her eyes which were fixed upon him. 'I never', she writes, 'saw a worse countenance.'[D]

The Chevalier then became more communicative. Mr Brougham, he said, had not offered enough. He hoped to get £2,000 for the papers, together with a small picture of James II, and some letters from Clementina Walkinshaw and her daughter.

This seems to have closed the interview.

In the meantime Consalvi had been making independent inquiries. It appeared that the person who had 'parted with' the papers was the Abbate Cupo, claiming to be authorized by Tassani, *homme de confiance* of Charlotte of Albany. The Cardinal asked Bess what sort of man Watson was, and she told him her opinion. He then suggested sealing up the papers, provided this action did not compromise him with the English Government. Bess approved. As Tassani denied having given any authority to Cupo to dispose of the documents, Consalvi suggested that the Abbate should be 'put up in San Angelo for a time'.

It was highly improbable that the Cardinal's action would compromise him with the English Government. He was *persona grata* both with the Prince Regent and with Lord Castlereagh, neither of whom would be unmindful that it was through his active intervention that the jewels and other Stuart relics bequeathed by Cardinal York to George III were transmitted to England.

The egregious Watson later declared that he had breakfasted with Consalvi about a week previously, and had then told him about the papers, both statements being equally untrue. When the Italian police called at the house and sealed the papers up, he asked, and was allowed, to affix his own seal as well as the official one. Calling on the Governor to thank him for this concession, he buttonholed the secretary on his way out and offered him a bribe if he would let him have the papers again. 'The Governor heard the Secretary answering in loud and indignant tones, came out, and heard the whole affair.'[D]

The Chevalier Watson must bitterly have regretted that he did not close with Mr Brougham's offer, however inadequate it may have appeared at the time.

Soon after the episode of the Stuart Papers, Bess left Rome for Naples with Clifford and his Lizzy, Caro George being also of the party. At Herculaneum Caro and her brother 'went down quite', but the other two ladies preferred to remain on the balcony. As Lizzy gave birth to a daughter less than three months later she was wise not to go scrambling among ruins. At Naples, Bess dined with the King, and was told by the Duc dei Medici that 'her' Cardinal was 'rather obstinate'. She flew to the defence of the 'purest and most unselfish character, the most noble conduct', that could possibly exist. When the royal and distinguished company expressed their surprise that an Englishwoman should espouse the Papal cause, Bess, never at a loss for an answer, reminded them that when all the other sovereign princes had obeyed Napoleon's behest the Pope alone had refused to close his seaports to England.[D]

Lizzy's baby was born on March 3rd: on the 16th her husband and sister-in-law ascended Vesuvius, Caro in a sedan-chair. Bess stayed at the Hermitage, and watched the two beings most dear to her as they made their way up the mountain. The summit was burning brightly, and sending up what the guides proudly described as *un bel pino*, a column of smoke shaped like a stone-pine. Thirty-two years had passed since she wrote in her Journal, 'the sky is clear, at a distance blazes Vesuvius — oh, were I happy!' Then she had sat by the seashore,

> of ladies most deject and wretched,

peering forward into a future untouched by any gleam of hope. Now she was a wealthy woman, a Duchess, an enlightened patroness of the arts, the centre of a brilliant Roman *salon*, the mother of devoted children, and, in spite of all that the Spencer-Cavendish clique had said and done, the valued friend of her stepson, the Young Duke.

Added to all these solaces was the friendship of Cardinal Consalvi, with whose many tribulations she sympathized with an ardour that must have been heart-warming to a lonely and overburdened man.

Among these tribulations was the visit of Caroline, Princess of Wales, to Rome in the summer of 1817. He confessed to being 'teased and plagued' by the Princess, who every day asked for something new 'and in so inconsiderate and strange a manner that it was difficult to content her'. Her two main demands were:

> one, that His Holiness would give, as being Chief Supreme of the Order of Malta, the Cross to her Baron,[272] the courier; and the other that he would confirm the Order of St. Caroline, instituted by her to commemorate her visit to Jerusalem.[D.]

The consequent embarrassment at the Vatican was great; but the unpredictable creature, though 'vexed' at the Pope's refusal to grant either request, announced cheerfully that she proposed to return to Rome in February 1818.

Always kindly disposed towards Princes of the Church, Bess supplied the Pope with arrowroot during the severe illness which resulted from a fall about this period. The compassionate streak in her nature had not been rubbed out by time or — a still more potent eraser — prosperity. Whether its object were a weary Cardinal, an ailing Pope, a team of overdriven post-horses or the 'poor labourers' working on her excavations, her pity always rose quickly to the surface, and, whenever possible, expressed itself in action.

During the greater part of the summer and autumn of 1817 Clifford and Lizzy were with Bess. Fortunately they both shared her passion for instructive expeditions, and these loom large in the Journal. One reads with some surprise that of the temples at Paestum 'the cork models give the best idea', those neat cork models which, under square glass cases, once adorned the libraries of so many noblemen and gentlemen.

The eldest grandchild, three-year-old William John Cavendish Clifford,[273] was of the party, together with his sister, Isabella Georgiana Camilla. Their grandmother took them to see the cascade at Tivoli, where the sight of three rainbows in the foam delighted 'Willy'. After the whole family had departed, Bess wrote in her Journal:

> Civita Castellano, September 29th
>
> How different does this place look, returning without my dear Clifford and Lizzy. Many tears were shed, many projects were formed for meeting again — Even the dear little boy seemed sorry and to know something of parting. Clifford, but of him who is ever present to me, tho' the first and long bitterness of grief is softened into deep-felt regrets.

She records fondly that her dear Clifford was now the father of three children — the number would ultimately rise to seven — and she adds that her son is,

> as he was from his infancy, everything that is lovely and lovable in mind and body. Lizzy feels his merit and is really deserving of him. May God in Heaven protect them both![D]

A fortnight later Augustus Foster, his Albinia and two very small infant sons, arrived in Rome and were received with much affection, though without the rapture which accompanied the appearance of Clifford and Lizzy.

The Duchess had always kept alive her old friendship with the Prince Regent, whom she had known so well as Prince of Wales and during the early, difficult days of the Regency. When she heard of the death of Princess Charlotte, she wrote a letter[274] of condolence, recalling incidentally the kindness and feeling he had shown her on her two irreparable losses,[275] and the many proofs she had seen of the warm and affectionate feelings of his heart. Lady Octavia Law and her husband were in Rome when the shattering news arrived, and Bess, calling on them, thought they were both equally affected.

Mr. Law maintained against us the want of affection in the P. Regent for his daughter, but I am certain of the kindness of his heart — so she said she was.[D]

She was also shocked at the 'strange and harsh sermon' which she later heard had been preached in London, ending with a verse from Jeremiah of which the parson said he dared not quote the whole, 'but bid the congregation on their return to read the end of the verse'. It was the thirtieth verse of the twenty-second chapter:

> Thus saith the Lord, Write ye this man childless, a man that shall not prosper in his days: for no man of his seed shall prosper, sitting upon the throne of David and ruling any more in Judah.

In March 1818 it was the Cardinal's turn to offer consolation to Bess. This was when Caro George wrote from London:

> Though it may worry you I must tell you that all London is occupied with the strange story that you have written to the Prince Regent that the Duke is not the real heir, not the Duchess's son: that being turned Catholic, you had confessed it to a priest, which priest had sent an affidavit of it to Lord George, and that Croft being implicated in it he had shot himself.
> Strange and absurd as this story is, nothing else is talked of in London.[D]

Galignani's and the *Gentleman's Magazine* both hinted at the scandal in their obituaries of the unfortunate Sir Richard Croft, but Caro's letter to her mother provides a new clue to the conjectural motive for his suicide — possible action by Lord George Cavendish,[276] the heir to the dukedom, if the holder of the title should be proved to have no legal claim to it.

The Cardinal remarked that the story showed no one could be exempt from calumny, but that he hoped it would not vex her. He urged her to do nothing — excellent advice which she appears to have followed. She was soon sufficiently tranquillized to begin jotting down anecdotes in her Journal again. She received a visit from Junot's widow, the Duchesse d'Abrantès, who emphatically stated her opinion that Ney deserved his fate.[277] He had certainly kissed the hand of Louis XVIII, promising at the same time to bring him back 'the wild beast', Napoleon, bound hand and foot. During the Hundred Days, when the King was hesitating whether to leave Paris, news was brought to him that Ney had deserted him for Napoleon. He was 'much overcome'. The Duchesse added that Napoleon had asked to see her, but that he had used her and her husband so ill, she refused to go.

Misgivings were felt about the evacuation of France by the troops of the Allies. Charles Ellis considered that the alternative was the bankruptcy of that country or 'the danger to the Bourbon dynasty from being left to themselves'. Apropos of Josephine the Cardinal told Bess that he believed Napoleon had married her 'only in civil form', which was quite true; that on the day of his coronation 'some sort of ceremony' took place; and that the Emperor then remarked to Talleyrand, '*We really must pacify the Pope.*' Consalvi called on Josephine at La Malmaison after the divorce, and she said to him, '*Would you ever have thought of seeing me here?*'

In June 1818 Bess tore herself away from Rome, not to return till the beginning of the following year. At parting the Cardinal gave her a beautiful cameo, and it must have been of him that she was thinking as she cast wistful backward glances at Mount Albano while her carriage bore her away through the summer air laden with the scent of Spanish broom.

During a brief halt at Parma she learned that Marie Louise was much loved by her subjects in the little principality. She also recorded Talleyrand's quip on the improvement in the health of Louis XVIII. '*He is better. He will live to inter the monarchy.*'

Passing through the Jura she was sorry to find that the people were already speaking French instead of Italian; the fireflies crept on the ground instead of soaring like the *luccioli* of Italy; not an olive tree was to be seen, hardly a single vineyard. At Coppet, she wanted to visit the tomb of Madame de Staël, but was deterred by an intimation that Auguste de Staël knew his mother did not like anybody going to the tomb of her father, Monsieur Necker, which was in the same place, and that they must be guided by 'what she did or wished done'. At Dijon she recognized a fragment of wall as being 'antient', and found that it was in fact Roman. And in Paris she records joyfully on July 17th that 'her dear D.' arrived yesterday and came and dined with her that night.*D*

Louis XVIII received her in audience at St Cloud — a rare honour — in order to thank her for the copy of her Horace, which she had sent him. She found him looking well, and the swelling of his legs reduced; and she had the happiness of recording His Majesty's opinion that Cardinal Consalvi was '*distinguished alike by his talents and by his most agreeable manners*'.*D*

By the beginning of September 1818 the Duchess was back in her riverside cottage at Richmond, whither she removed her fast-failing sister-in-law, Lady Hervey, whom her sister Lady Liverpool helped her to nurse until the end came without a pang on September 3rd. The poor lady, to whom Bess was much attached though Hary-O found her 'odious', desired to be buried at Esher, the place made both sorrowful and sacred by memories of her only child, the unforgotten Eliza.

Bess does not allude to the fact that her son-in-law George Lamb was returned for Westminster in June 1818 to fill the vacancy created by the tragic death of Sir Samuel Romilly. Byron, far away in Venice, was scornfully derisive about it, and described the Lambs as a 'cuckoldy family'; but even the frequent and prolonged absences of Caroline George from England never caused a breath of scandal to touch her name. She had, as she wrote to her mother-in-law, Lady Melbourne, in 1817, 'struggled for seven years' and her courage at last had failed her. George could not be brought to say that her absence made him unhappy, only that it fidgeted him and unsettled him, and that he got through less business in consequence.[278] Perhaps his ineradicable hatred of Brougham was his nearest approach to the lover-like attitude which Caroline would have wished to continue to the end. At the close of October 1818 their marriage was still in jeopardy. She was then with her mother at Walmer, staying with the Liverpools. 'Caro and I', wrote Bess,

> walked and sat long on the beach. The past, present, and dimly seen future all passed before us. To do as far as one can see what is right and leave the rest to Providence — that is our determination.[D]

Two years later Lady Cowper wrote to her brother Frederick Lamb that George was 'very happy and well employed', and that he would not hear of Caro going to see Queen Caroline as she had '*half* a mind' to do. In the end they settled down, as might have been expected with a husband so essentially good-natured and a wife so gentle and withdrawn.

Cardinal Consalvi, drawn by
Sir Thomas Lawrence.

During this stay at Walmer, Bess savoured again the once familiar pleasure of hearing confidential political talk. Lord Bathurst and his lively daughter Lady Emily[279] were there. They spoke of St Helena, the personalities and the conditions on the island. O'Meara was said to have been sent away because he was 'a rogue and behaving very ill'. Benjamin Constant was suspected of having written the memoir supposed to have been dictated by Napoleon to Las Casas. Wellington thought no military man could have written it.[D]

Bathurst and Liverpool agreed that Sir Hudson Lowe was 'only too much inclined to give way' to his difficult prisoner; and they both declared that St Helena was a healthy island, and that everything Napoleon wanted was sent out to him. 'Lady M. Erskine', writes Bess,

> answered my saying that I thought all unnecessary severity should be carefully avoided, 'As if *he* never used any to those in his power.' I could not help saying that the conduct of a person whom one blamed ought not, I thought, to be any rule for one's own.[D]

'I don't like her,' adds Bess. But she found Lady Emily an 'open-hearted and good-humoured girl'. 'Oh, do attack my father again,' she said, 'I like to hear him answer the attacks.'[D] Always ready to humour the young, Bess continued to harry the Minister for the Colonies, from whom she elicited the interesting opinion that Napoleon's defence of Paris in 1814:

Madame Récamier.

was amongst the most brilliant of his military efforts, but that his conduct after the Battle of Waterloo was very flat. No heroism about it.[D]

In the autumn of 1818 Caroline Stuart-Wortley was seeing her Aunt Bess every day, often in her box at Drury Lane. As she 'always contrived to have a few men about her' besides Lizzy Clifford and Caro George, the Duchess had a 'pleasant little *société*'. She seems to have been fond of this niece, though never as fond as she was of her godchild, Eliza Ellis, and she went with her to see that old friend of the family, 'poor dear Farquhar', lying on his couch in a silk gown and cap, yet well and cheerful.

Among the men whom Bess 'contrived to have about her' was the Prince Regent, whom she found 'most kind and affectionate' when he called upon her. With obvious pleasure she writes that

> he praised Consalvi excessively, and said that he most particularly liked him besides the esteem due to his character and conduct and great talents. I asked the Prince to grant the plasters of the Elgin Marbles for Rome. 'Certainly,' he said, 'May I write this to Rome, Sire' 'Yes, you may, and tell Canova to write to me, and they shall be sent directly.' I thanked him most sincerely and then urged a little the sending a Minister to reside at Rome. 'Sir', I said, 'when nobody would believe it you said you should restore Louis 18. Decide only that you will remove this prejudice about a Minister from England to Rome, which an Act of Parliament can do, and it will be done. We are the only Protestant power who does not.' He said there were difficulties but he hoped it would be done. —Then we talked of D. He complained that D. had not invited him, and I told him that D. thought himself neglected. He assured me he never meant this but that at one time there was a sort of flirtation between him and Princess Charlotte, and that it was necessary on his part to discourage it.
>
> We talked over everything. He was very amiable.[D]

The active, prehensile mind of the Duchess soon found a variety of objects to record: the discovery of hippopotamus bones at Plymouth; the excavation of a temple between the paws of the Sphinx; the publication of *The Heart of Midlothian*. Her verdict on the latest Waverley novel suggests that she had the good taste to prefer the Laird of Dumbiedykes to the Duke of Argyll. It may even be that in the last volume, which she dismissed as 'bad', the return of the lovely, frail Effie Deans as the wife of her former lover reminded her of another lovely, frail creature who, like Effie, had given birth to her child in squalid and sinister surroundings, and, again like her, had finally married the child's father.

CHAPTER XVI

Roman Sunset — 1818–1824

When the ship bearing the Duchess back to the Continent sailed from Dover at the end of October 1818, 'poor F.F.' stood sadly on the pier. It is surely to her credit that her affection for this plain, portly, slightly uncouth first-born of hers should have remained so active to the end. Augustus Foster had become an established if not particularly successful member of the Diplomatic Service; Clifford was making a distinguished career for himself in the Navy; but F.F., apart from representing Bury St Edmunds rather passively from 1812 to 1818, had achieved nothing. The Cavendish sisters, who had found his ponderous pleasantries so hard to bear, little guessed that he was contributing to the support of his mother right up to the time of her marriage to their father. Now his circumstances were easier. He had chambers in Albany, a property in Ireland, a place in Sussex; but he was soon to fade into the background, and his name gradually vanished from the Foster, Cavendish, and Hervey chronicles after the death of the Duchess.

On arriving at Calais Bess found the streets full of rattling artillery, martial music in the air, and people crowding on the beach to watch the embarkation of the British occupying forces in process of being evacuated. 'It is now to be seen', she remarked, 'whether France can settle into being a free country.'[D]

In Paris she was received in private audience by Monsieur, who exhorted her to 'get things settled' at Rome, thereby opening the sluices to a flood of pro-Consalvi propaganda. He was, as royalties were wont to be in her society, 'very amiable'. Even when she pointed out that the ceiling of the room had been 'painted in honour of the birth of the King of Rome', he merely replied, '*Yes, but he has been re-christened Louis XIV*': and he was 'very complimentary' about her looks.

If Lawrence's drawing, made a year later in Rome, is to be believed, she had indeed retained a surprising measure of her beauty. The heart-shaped face had still its delicate, almost youthful, lines, the eyes were still melting and expressive. Near the very end of her days her nose seemed to lengthen, her cheeks hollowed, and she became a little haggard and spectral, as Lawrence depicts her in the character of a Sybil, dimly draped, a goblet in one hand, a scroll in the other, an antique temple in the background: but even then, and even in the last portrait of all,[280] the beautiful bone-structure of the skull prolongs the story. Of the medal struck by the grateful City of Rome in her honour it need only be said that its Witch of Endor profile would have pleased Lady Spencer.

The Young Duke and Clifford were in Paris that autumn, and they took Bess to see Napoleon's one-time mistress, Mademoiselle Mars, in *Le Tartuffe*. No warnings, no exhortations that his younger sister could utter broke the concordat between the Duke and the Lady whose signature had gradually evolved from 'Liz' into 'E. Devonshire'.

'My fears', wrote Hary-O in September 1817, are on your part the difficulty of ever saying to her "No, you shall not."'[281] it does not seem to have occurred to her that he might not invariably desire to say 'No.'

While she was in Paris Bess collected some further fragments of Bonapartiana. From Madame de Genlis she heard how Napoleon had once remarked to Josephine '*You have a soul of lace, I have a soul of adamant*': and this former royal mistress (and preceptress of royal children) related how

> Once a woman came to solicit pardon for a man who was her lover, and condemned to death. Bonaparte tore himself from her and got into his carriage. She fell flat on the ground and the carriage was near passing over her. He said, '*The man who knew how to make himself loved like that must deserve pardon,*' and granted his life to the woman.[D]

In spite of Talleyrand's flattering anxiety that she should remain in Paris till the spring, the Duchess decided to set out for Rome early in 1819. She was missing her friend the Cardinal, her excavations, her sculptors and her *soirées*. In the light of later events it seems that she also desired to be on the spot when Thomas Lawrence, dispatched by the Prince Regent, began to paint the Pope — and the Pope's Secretary of State.

On January 12th she bade farewell to Madame Récamier, who told her that she was adored in that *petit cercle* and whom she was to meet again in Rome; the next day she left Paris; a week later the Young Duke joined her at Lyons, to accompany her on her journey to Italy.

At Orange they visited the Roman ruins together, and as they travelled south she recorded with delight the distant glimpse of olive trees which showed that she was indeed nearing the place where she would be. With her she took 'the most beautiful book that ever was', the gift of her stepson during her last days in London. The binding, she said, put her out of conceit with her others; but she would be proud to show it to 'her' Romans.[C]

Before leaving Paris she wrote to Sir Thomas Lawrence about his imminent visit to Rome. She is anxious that he should do justice to Consalvi, Vicard having 'entirely failed by painting him in profile. I feel assured', she adds, 'that you will agree with me that a three-quarters or nearly a full face is what will best do justice to the beauty of his countenance, so peculiarly suited to your happy talent of giving that expression which best suits the character of the person.'

Lawrence took the hint, and she later expressed great admiration of the 'countenance', though finding the position of the arms a little stiff.

It was an interesting and happy summer. The Young Duke was in Rome, where there were many things to delight both him and Bess. Their admired Canova was at work on a statue commissioned by Lord Liverpool, and when she invited Lawrence to dine with her, or to visit palaces, temples, and galleries in her company, 'the D.' often made a third.

Always anxious that any *protégé* of hers should do her — and himself — credit, she wrote to Lawrence:

> Canova must not do too holy a figure for Lord Liverpool, who is a great admirer of female beauty and would like a Nymph or a Venus better than a Magdalen.

Canova continued firmly to model a Magdalen. During this same summer the Duchess's 'poor labourers' unearthed a porphyry column which she bestowed upon her stepson, urging him to accept it 'without scruple'. And after he had returned to England she wrote:

> I really cannot bear to look at the Palazetto Albani — there is no saying how much I miss you and how much I want you. Never shall I forget your most dear and amiable manner to me and generous conduct.[C]

Canova was working for the Duke as well as for Lord Liverpool at this time, and Bess was eager to know what the subject of his newest statue would be. The sculptor remained strangely reticent, perhaps on the instructions of his patron with whose ideas he was perfectly well acquainted. 'Canova', wrote Bess, on August 15th, 'came last night — he had worked with such ardour that he was quite exhausted, but he won't yet tell me what he is modelling for you, but I think we are certain of liking it.'[C] Her enthusiasm was unbounded when the mystery was divulged. It was the Sleeping Endymion, which, according to her, he considered the best of all his works, and which was long to be regarded as one of the finest pieces of sculpture in the Gallery at Chatsworth.

When Canova died at Venice in 1822 both the Duke's Endymion and Lord Liverpool's Magdalen were still in his Roman studio. He had, as Bess assured Lawrence, 'completely finished' both, but doubts seem later to have been felt upon this subject, as the Duke writes in his *Handbook to Chatsworth and Hordwick*:

Bess in 1819, drawn by Sir
Thomas Lawrence in Rome.

If evidence were wanting of its having been completely finished by Canova
I have plenty of letters in my possession that establish that point; but none can
be required when you contemplate the admirable perfection of the work. — I
had really attached myself to him very much, and it was with mingled feelings
of grief and exultation, of boundless admiration and recent bereavement that
I first saw my group in the well-known studio where I had passed so many
happy hours with the most talented, the most simple, and most noble-minded
of mankind.

To that studio Bess could hardly bear to go; but at last, as she wrote to Lawrence,
'D.' took her there.

Hary-O, now Lady Granville, would much have preferred that her 'adored
brother' should not correspond with the Duchess, but their correspondence
flourished, and with so many interests in common it is hardly surprising that they
should have found much to say to each other. Her letters are full of affection and
archaeology, solicitude about his health and day-to-day Roman intelligence, most
of it revolving round Consalvi. His were to her, as she wrote in February 1823,
'such a comfort and such a pleasure'; and one at least she called 'a perfection of

letters'.[C]

Bess needed all the comfort that he and her children could give her, for her old friends were quitting the stage one by one. In June 1821, died Lady Liverpool, to whom she had always been much attached; but the death of Lady Bessborough in November of the same year was a heavier sorrow, seldom though they had met of late. The ghost of Georgiana would not let either of them forget the other while they still remembered her; and the Young Duke wrote to Lord Duncannon that 'the Duchess was very much overcome indeed'. A year later the tragic exit of Castlereagh broke yet another link with the unforgotten past.

With her elder sister, Lady Erne, now living in semi-retirement at Hampton Court, Dearest Bess had never been on quite such affectionate terms as with her younger, Lady Liverpool. Hary-O recorded with a touch of compunction[282] how F.F., returning from a visit to Walmer in November 1806, 'said out loud before Lady E. that Mary[283] was an odd old girl, for she did *not* like her and was not kind about her': but if 'Lady E.' were really as insensitive as Hary-O believed her to be, compunction was hardly indicated.

This imperfect affinity with Lady Erne did not cloud Bess's steadily increasing affection for Lady Caroline Stuart-Wortley, to whom she wrote charming, playful letters, one of them describing her 'Roman morning', when even before she had finished her breakfast engravers, musicians, play-actors, Roman Princes and English peers were on her doorstep. Apparently she fled from them to the garden of the Villa Pamphili, which was then covered with violets, crocuses, and 'enemonies'.[284]

Her last years in Rome were spent in a suite of apartments in the Palazzo Spada. To Lawrence she wrote on April 20th, 1820, that Prince Piombini, who had bought the Palazzo, had made a new kitchen for her, and had given her three fine rooms — presumably in addition to those described by Ticknor as 'an endless suite of enormous rooms', with a 'comfortless antechamber'. 'I shall', she says, 'be excellently lodged, thanks to Consalvi, who has made a lamb of Piombini.'

At the end of 1821 she was in England again, her last visit. In London she stayed with Lord Liverpool at Fife House, Whitehall; at Chatsworth she was deeply touched by 'the kind and feeling attentions' of her 'Dearest D.'. She wrote to him from Fife House on September 27th:

> The King came the 27th — sent the D. of Wellington to tell me he would walk across the park to see me yesterday — not being well he desired him to ask me to come to him. He never was more kind and affectionate — told me all about his reconciliation with you, cried, quite *cried*, in telling me of your amiable, delightful thought and manner of giving him the snuff-box — he kept me above two hours, sending Ministers etc. away — today we dined at the Palace in town with him.[C]

She saw him more than once before she left England, and the last occasion was also her last meeting with the Prince whose kindness and affection she had never found wanting. It was a long friendship, going back to his flamboyant early manhood when his whole personality seemed to be epitomized in his Garter-blue silken umbrella sprinkled with Prince of Wales's feathers in gold.[285]

As we hear so much about George IV's unwieldy immobility in the first years of his reign and his nervous reluctance to expose himself to the gaze of his people, it is worth remarking that on one occasion at least he proposed to walk across the Park to Fife House, Whitehall, even if he did not carry out his intention.

During the brief triumph of that meretricious martyr, Queen Caroline, in 1820, Bess had been forced to admit that the excesses of the London mob proceeded from their instinctive love of fair play. The cry about the Queen's innocence and purity, however, struck her as 'almost ludicrous', and her sympathy was with the King, so cruelly assailed, so bitterly humiliated, by the partisans of his impossible wife. She importuned Lawrence to send her news of him. How was he bearing up, amid these tumults? But now, in 1821, Caroline's popularity was guttering down like a cheap candle, and the King's reconciliation with the Young Duke seemed to matter far more than the fizzling out of the Queen's trial for adultery.

Before leaving England at the end of the year the Duchess sent to Wellington what he described as a 'beautiful present'. He promised that he would have the addition made to it of her own picture, and would keep it in his own Library as a memorial of her kindness to him. It was indeed a beautiful present — a copy of her Æneid, in two volumes, bound in green half-morocco with marbled sides; and it is still in the Library at Strathfield Saye House, though it does not appear as if the Duke ever carried out his intention to insert a portrait of the donor. 'The blessed Hero', as she called him, had asked the Duchess for a copy of the book when she met him at dinner at Fife House. She was naturally 'too happy to give it to him', together with a little pencil sketch of Napoleon: but she lamented that, in accordance with 'the terrible English custom' by which the ladies were compelled to leave the gentlemen in the dining-room over their port-wine, she had to sit talking about ruffs and caps in the drawing-room while Wellington delighted Lord Liverpool and his other male guests by 'relating his battles'.[286]

Once back in Rome, the Duchess flung herself with her usual ardour into all her wonted pursuits. She corresponds vigorously with Lawrence. His portrait of George IV, brought to Italy aboard the *Euryalus* under dear Clifford's command, is, she informs him, hanging on a cold, light green wall. If he would prefer red, and would wish it changed, he must tell her. Her interest in Sir Thomas's pictures of Pius VII and Cardinal Consalvi was great. She would like to see mezzotints made of both. She is anxious that the engraver should 'touch with caution' the drawing of herself which has had 'such a success'. She confesses that she is rendered quite vain by it; and she adds, 'it is your peculiar talent to extend the term of looks which may have been reckoned good'.

The Young Duke visited her frequently, and in his absence letters flew to and fro between them.

'My Dearest D.', she wrote on July 23rd, 1823,

> You end your letter saying 'I wonder where my letter will find you' — it found me in the Duc de la Val's summer apartment, he eagerly reading the paper, his Sec. and company the same — he always asks a great deal about you and says how nobly you enjoy your riches.
>
> The Duc de La Val is like the kindest brother to me. He flirts with *la petite* Dodwell, but he says he comes to me '*as a stream follows its course*'.[c]

Adrien de Montmorency, Duc de la Val, was Louis XVIII's Ambassador to the Court of Madrid. The Duchess describes him as 'noble in all his actions, chivalrous in all his thoughts and feelings, invariable in his friendship, inconstant in love'.

The death of Pope Pius VII two months later filled her with deep concern, chiefly on account of its possible repercussions upon Cardinal Consalvi, who was worn out by his constant attendance on the dying Pontiff, and whose future status and fortunes depended entirely upon the decision of the Conclave summoned to elect a new Pope. Unluckily for him the lot fell upon Cardinal della Genga, who took the name of Leo XII. Between this zealous but ultramontane churchman and Consalvi there had in the past been a certain amount of friction. 'My friend the Cardinal', with his liberal views, his large tolerance and his flexible wisdom, was not likely to commend himself to the party which in our own time would be stigmatized as 'reactionary'. The people of Rome had short memories. They showed no disposition to resent the petty slights put upon the dead Pope's Secretary of State almost before the dust of His Holiness had been consigned to its sepulchre in St Peter's. There were many in all classes who had resented his abolition of monopolies, feudal taxes and exclusive rights: and even those who had approved were silent now.

The Duchess was furious. She poured forth her feelings to the two people most likely to sympathize with them — the Young Duke and Thomas Lawrence: and through Lawrence she enlisted the ready assistance of George IV.

During his stay in Rome Sir Thomas had become sincerely attached to Consalvi. When writing to him that the King's portrait was on its way to the Pope, he had described himself as the 'Cardinal's English Painter' and had declared that he owed the happiness of the most beautiful chapter in his life to his graciousness, munificence and kindness. He now threw himself promptly into the plans of the Duchess.

Her first demand was that an article doing justice to Consalvi's fine and disinterested character should be inserted in the English press: if any expense be incurred, she will reimburse the painter as soon as she knows the sum. But above all things she wants 'some sign of esteem' from the King.

His Majesty considered — no doubt quite correctly — that the gift of his own portrait, accompanied by a friendly letter, would be the best possible way of meeting the wishes of the Duchess and reviving the drooping spirits of the Cardinal.

Everything was at once put in train, and the delighted Duchess was in a fever of impatience to let the Cardinal know what was in store for him. Etiquette forbade that she should anticipate the royal action, but when it became obvious that the thread of her friend's life was fast wearing thin she threw etiquette to the winds and told him. 'He knew,' she wrote later to Lawrence, 'and was touched to the extreme by the King's mark of friendship for him.'

At this eleventh hour the Pope made a conciliatory move — the offer of the honorary post of Prefect of the College *de Propaganda Fide* founded by Gregory XIII for the benefit of non-Catholics, whether heathen or heretical. Consalvi accepted the post — a token acceptance of a token offer. As a good if not a perfervid son of the Church any sign of favour from its Head would be grateful to him: but during his last days and hours the constant affection of the Duchess must have given him solace of another sort. It was not the first time that she had watched by the death-bed of a beloved friend; she would know instinctively when to speak and when to be still; and we hear of no other woman among those who watched beside him.

On January 23rd, 1824, she wrote to the Duke:

> This morning that pure, noble spirit, that kind, benevolent heart ceased to exist. God bless you, dearest D. — I know how you will feel for me.[C]

A few days later she wrote again:

> While he was ill — I saw him every day, sometimes twice a day. Some days he was well and cheerful, always patient and courageous, but generally with a conviction that he could not recover. He thanked me for all the kindness and interest I had shown him only about three hours before I lost him for ever.[C]

To Lawrence she wrote that the Cardinal had expired without a struggle. His last words were a message to the Pope, who had sent him his blessing: 'tell him that I am at peace'.

George IV's letter did not reach Rome till after the Cardinal's death. Bess begged that the portrait might be sent all the same: it would be prized by the Comte Parisani, Consalvi's nearest relative and joint executor. She immediately busied herself about commemorative bronze medals of the Cardinal, and invited subscriptions of one *louis de France* each from five hundred of his admirers.

All her friends, she assured the Duke, were 'quite perfect' in their kindness and sympathy: she mentions de la Val, d'Artaud and Madame Récamier. She was seeing a good deal of the still charming Juliette, of whom she had recently written that she had 'taken to the theatre' since she had found that one might talk a little 'except during the favourite airs'.[C] But her own health began to fail almost at once, and the Young Duke, hearing this, hurried to her side — thereby causing foolish persons to opine that his only motive was anxiety that she should not on her death-bed be received into the Church of Rome.

In October 1812, the Duchess had made a long and complicated Will. To this she added not only a number of after-thoughts and interlineations, but seventeen codicils, with the result that before probate could be granted 'the most noble William, Duke of Devonshire' had to appear in person before the Prerogative Court of Canterbury and swear an affidavit that all these addenda were in order. Even this was not enough. Two gentlemen from Devonshire House also had to swear that they were 'well acquainted with the above-named most noble Elizabeth, Dowager[287] Duchess of Devonshire, and with the manner and character of her writing' and to confirm His Grace's evidence as to the genuineness of every part of the document.

The preamble to the Will of 1812 sets forth that she believes her sons Frederick and Augustus Foster to be her heirs-at-law; that she trusts to them 'for not disputing' her last Will and Testament; that she thinks it right that such property as she inherited from her family should go to these sons and that almost all that she possessed from her beloved husband, the late Duke of Devonshire, and his family should go to his children, Augustus William Clifford and Caroline Lamb. The £4,000 on which Sir Hervey Bruce[288] pays her interest is to be divided between her Foster sons. If she has repaid Lord Bessborough the £1,000 he lent her, the 'old South Sea annuity' which she made over to him is to go to Frederick Foster.

From these clauses in the Will it is clear that Bess, like her 'angelic friend' Georgiana was apt to get into financial difficulties, though, unlike Georgiana, she kept a firm grasp upon the details and was methodical both in lending and borrowing. Any money in the bankers' hands beyond the sum of £5,000 bequeathed to Caroline Lamb is to go to her son Frederick Foster, 'who left himself poor to increase my income before I became Duchess of Devonshire'.

This revelation throws a completely new light upon the relationship between her and Canis. The Cavendish family probably believed that the hated 'Lady Liz' was in receipt of a substantial allowance from her lover. And all the time it was 'poor F.F.' who, after the death of her lavish benefactress Georgiana, was bringing up her income to the sum appropriate to a lady whose principal habitations were Devonshire House and Chiswick, Chatsworth, Hardwick, and Bolton Abbey.

The personal bequests also throw light on Bess's character, on her strong family affections, her tenacity in friendship, her care for faithful servitors. Her house and garden at Richmond are to go to Clifford, whom, if he died unmarried or childless, she desires to leave it to Caroline Lamb. Her plate is to be divided between the two Fosters, except that her daughter is to have 'the little silver tea-pot' and four silver dishes with covers. To Clifford she leaves her table linen and her silver coffee-pot.

With a touch of characteristic self-deception she says that, as she has made the Duke of Devonshire 'a present' of the 'fine jewels', including 'the fine yellow diamond', she feels at liberty to leave her trinket-box and all it contains to Caroline Lamb, who is to hand the diamond Maltese Cross to Clifford 'for his wife'; the pink topaz, his own gift, to Augustus 'for his wife'; and the 'opal ring set with diamonds which Lord Granville gave me' to Frederick Foster 'for his wife'.

> My diamond watch to my dear Caroline Lamb — it was the last gift of her dear father to me and is never out of my sight.
> The enamel portrait of the late Duke by Boni to Lady G. Morpeth.
> The enamel miniature in my pocket of D.D. in uniform to Lady Harriet Leveson-Gower.
> The hair bracelet on my arm to my dear friend Lady Bessborough — it is her sister's hair — she knows how I loved her.
> The one I wear round my neck of the Duke and Duchess I leave to Caroline — she always said she loved her as her own.
> The locket with the Duchess's hair which I wear round my neck to Corisande, Lady Ossulston.

From this it would appear that round her neck, on her arm, or in her pocket Bess habitually carried about with her bracelets and lockets to remind her — if such a reminder were necessary — of her departed friends.

Her clothes were to go to her faithful personal maid, Madame Palli, but Caroline was to have the Indian shawls and Lady Ossulston the red one, which was the gift of her dear mother, the Duchesse de Grammont. To Lady Erne she bequeathed the bronze tripod she brought from Paris; to Caro William, a picture of her mother, Lady Bessborough; to Lady Hervey, Cosway's portrait of her husband, Bess's 'dear, dear eldest brother'. She commands her servants, 'very, very good servants', to her children.

It may be remembered that a certain Mrs Spencer was the only witness of Bess's marriage, and afterwards hardly left her on the night of the Duke's death. A clause in the Will reveals that Midshipman William Spencer, presumably this Mrs Spencer's son, was 'fitted out' by the Duke and Duchess in 1809. He receives an annuity of £20.

A month later the testatrix indulged in a few of those afterthoughts which were later to cause so much confusion and delay. The Young Duke is to have the bust of his father, also the lapis-lazuli snuff-box given by the old Duke to Bess on their marriage. After another two years, small diamond ear-rings are assigned to Clifford's wife.

In 1818 she returns to the task — not uncongenial, one feels — of distributing her belongings. Her great-niece, Eliza Ellis, is now remembered. And Cardinal Consalvi is to have £600 'to continue the Impression of Virgil by Anibal Caro'. If she should die abroad she desires to be 'sent home' and buried, 'according to her right', in the vault next her dear husband. She had already stipulated that her wedding-ring should not be removed from her hand.

After a three years' interval she inserts a bequest to her brother, Lord Bristol — Lawrence's drawing of Consalvi, to be carefully preserved as that of 'one whose friendship has stored my mind and whose constant kindness makes Rome delightful to me'. This is the drawing which she was reputed to carry everywhere with her, the same to which Hary-O referred when writing to her sister G. in September 1821, *à propos* of a possible visit from Bess and her daughter: 'I think we must have the Duchess. Mrs. Lamb I shall be charmed to see. I do not know where we can hang Consalvi.' In April 1822, Madame Palli's successor, Adelaide, Madame Javamal, is named as the recipient of the Duchess's wardrobe. The India shawls, as before, are to go to Caroline George, except the fine gold one which is to be Albinia Foster's.

'My friend the Cardinal' makes his last appearance in this codicil: but now he is neither 'Cardinal Consalvi' nor simply 'Consalvi'. He is 'dear Consalvi', and he is to have as a memorial of her the little gold ring in the mosaic box which he gave her.

In the last codicil of all, written at Naples only four months before her death, the Duchess records that she has promised Adelaide 2,000 francs to portion her daughter 'who is going to marry M. Pallier in Paris'. It is, she explains, about £80. She begs that this money may be paid, adding simply, 'I am very much attached to Adelaide.'

It is not clear whether Madame Palli ceased to be the Duchess's maid through death or through retirement; but it seems at least possible that the 'M. Pallier' mentioned in this codicil was really 'M. Palli', and if this be so he was probably the son of the older Abigail.

In his letter to George IV,[289] informing him of the Duchess's death on March 30th, 1824, the Young Duke remarked that he was just beginning to hope that she was 'recovering her spirits which had almost left her since the great loss she had in Consalvi'; but it is more likely that the pleasure she showed at seeing him masked the lassitude which was taking hold of her. She was ill for only a week, but it was found impossible to subdue the fever accompanying 'a most violent inflammation of the lungs'. Writing to Lady Caroline Stuart-Wortley the Duke said that the Duchess appeared to suffer very little pain, and 'constantly expressed her comfort and satisfaction with her attendants'.

Her whole conduct was remarkable from the fortitude, good sense and composure which she showed, as well as the most touching consideration for all around her. She knew her danger, made every arrangement, and charged me with affectionate remembrance to those she loved.

As if to confute the gossips who whispered of her imminent conversion to the Church of Rome, she asked for a clergyman, and when he came he unconsciously provided the last of those slight yet curious points of contact between Dearest Bess and Lord Byron.

He was Dr George Frederick Nott, once Princess Charlotte's sub-preceptor, and now one of the poet's rather numerous *bêtes noires*. He had for a time occupied the lower floor of the Tre Palazzi di Chiesa at Pisa, with Edward and Jane Williams over his head, and Shelley and Mary Shelley over theirs. Every Sunday he read the Church of England service and preached a sermon for the benefit of the small English community there. It was tactless in him to choose atheism as the theme of his discourse on the three successive Sundays when, at his personal invitation, Mary Shelley was a member of the congregation. His denial that he had been aiming his shafts at Shelley did not convince her, and Byron, regarding the episode as 'a shabby example of priestly malice', declared that Dr Nott had revised the Ninth Commandment so that it should read: 'Thou shalt, Nott, bear false witness against thy neighbour.'

Such was the man who was summoned to the Palazzo Spada to give ghostly comfort to the dying Duchess.

Four days after her death he penned a full and circumstantial account of what the Young Duke called (in his letter to Lady Caroline Stuart Wortley) their 'most interesting conversation'. Without throwing any doubts upon Dr Nott's sincere piety, it is difficult not to perceive that somewhat in this fashion would Mr Collins have written if he had had the honour of attending the death-bed of Lady Catherine de Burgh.

When I approached the bed where Her Grace lay, I remarked that her countenance, though it showed extreme debility, was expressive in the highest degree of composure and resignation. She was perfectly collected, and perceiving me near her, she addressed me first by enquiring after some of my Friends — Having answered her generally I paused, while her Physician gave her something to drink, to enable her to speak with more ease. I then asked Her Grace how she found herself — She moved her head slowly, as if to say that she was very ill — On which I said 'I perceive, Madam, but too clearly that you are in a state of great debility, and that your present illness is such as cannot but excite much fear and apprehension — I trust however that you do not suffer any bodily pain, and that your mind is in perfect peace and composure.' She replied that she was in perfect tranquillity and that she felt no pain or agitation either in body or mind.[D]

This reply does not seem to have pleased Dr Nott. He must have been well acquainted with the history of the once-lovely being who now lay at his mercy, and he may have felt that a broken and contrite heart would better become her than a state of perfect tranquillity. He exhorted her with some vehemence and at great length to prepare herself, as far as lay in her power, to appear as she ought in the presence of God. 'When', he continues

> I began my conversation with Her Grace I had taken hold of her hand. She seemed pleased with my having done so, for she made no motion to withdraw it — At this moment however the Physician was holding her hand having taken it to feel her pulse. She made an effort to withdraw it from him, and once more taking hold of mine she pressed it feebly, evidently to let me understand that she felt the force of what I had said, and then looking at me stedfastly, she replied, 'I have long endeavoured to fix my thoughts wholly on God and am perfectly resigned to His will, whatever it may be' — I then said, 'Should it be his Holy Will to take you hence now, what is the ground you have for believing that you may be able to stand before Him in Hope?'

The tone of voice in which she spoke was so low that Dr Nott was uncertain as to the gist of her reply, but the physicians again gave her something to drink, and she was able to follow, looking at him earnestly, his exhortations to her to ground her hopes upon the Atonement. At last she said in a clear and distinct voice that this was the foundation of all her hopes.

From the next part of his discourse — as reported by himself — it would seem that Dr Nott was anxious that she should make an open and categorical confession of all that she might have done at any time displeasing to God. 'Yes, Madam,' he said, 'such is indeed our duty, a duty binding upon us all, seeing we all offend, even when we are placed in situations the least exposed to danger, — how much more, then, when in those which are particularly open to temptation.' He understood her to reply that she had long turned her mind to this and had endeavoured to put all things in order.

The watchful physicians now intervened again, and Dr Nott offered to retire 'for the present', but he begged her to inform him first whether there were anything she wished him to do for her. What he was hoping to extort from her was a request that she might receive the Sacrament; but she either did not understand or did not choose to respond. She had no wishes, she said, but that she might be spared long enough to see some of her family who, he understood her to say, were on their way from England.

Dr Nott then invited her to reflect upon what a blessing it was that she should be surrounded by so many friends, adding, in the best Collins tradition,

> 'and particularly that you have one part of your family who watches over you with such care and tenderness.' As I said this, I looked towards the Duke of Devonshire, who was kneeling at the other side of the bed, his face reclined upon it — Her Grace followed the motion of my eyes, and made an effort to turn her head towards the Duke, saying, 'I am indeed most truly sensible of the goodness of God towards me in this particular, and am most sincerely thankful to Him for the blessing.' I then repeated my former question whether I could be of any use to her, or do any thing, that could administer comfort and consolation — She now spoke with great difficulty and replied, I think, in these words — 'I thank you — but not now.'[D]

These were the very words in which Charles II, dying in his mother's faith, evaded partaking of the Sacrament according to his father's: but the coincidence does not seem to have struck anybody, and after the physicians had almost peremptorily put an end to the colloquy, and Dr Nott had withdrawn, baffled, to the adjoining room, the Duke told that pertinacious divine that he was sure the Duchess would 'accede to his proposal' — the proposal he had never made — should her strength be equal to the effort:

> that latter point however was one on which the physicians alone were competent to decide, and to them therefore it must be referred.[D]

These gentlemen consulted a considerable time together. They went to the Duchess's bedside, and having observed her attentively, and remarked her increasing weakness,

> they gave it ultimately as their opinion, that if the sacrament were to be then administered, the effort might remove the small remaining hope there was of recovery. Upon this I felt it my duty to urge the point no further then and retired.[D]

Though Dr Nott's report[290] was not addressed to the Duke, it was obviously intended for his perusal. He expresses the hope that it may hereafter be a source of consolation to His Grace to revert to it, since he would dwell with lasting pleasure on whatever might tend to strengthen the 'consolating assurance'

> that the Person whom he loved so much and honoured so sincerely has entered full of Christian Hope into a state of Everlasting Peace.[D]

That report was written in a hotel in the Piazza di Spagna, not far from the house where, almost exactly three years before, the 'fiery particle' of John Keats's mind had been snuffed out — though not, as Byron supposed, 'by an article'. This circumstance provides the final link in the chain of Byronic association.

Two days after the death of the Duchess Monsieur d'Artaud wrote a brief memoir which the filial piety of Sir Augustus Clifford gathered up in a privately printed collection of her *Anecdotes and Sketches*[291] many years later. Tribute is paid to the success of her excavations (including the discovery of the Column of Phocas), the splendour of her editions of the classics, her bounty to the poor of Rome, the grace with which she did the honours of her house, but above all to her unfailing *douceur*. 'Those who saw her die', writes Artaud, quoting Bossuet's funeral oration on Henrietta of Orleans, 'might say of her — she was gentle with death as she was wont to be with all the world.'

Even the implacable Hary-O was not proof against the cumulative effect of this *douceur*. Old wrongs had receded, old jealousies and suspicions had withered away, when she wrote to Georgiana Morpeth that the news of the Duchess's death had shocked them very much, 'she had so much enjoyment of life'.[292] Later she even declared, with a touch of something like kindliness, that she was 'glad the poor Duchess had friends about her'[293] when the end came.

If Lady Spencer troubled to read the obituaries in the English, French, and Italian Press she must have been greatly annoyed to find that the 'dirt and old horrors' she had so foolishly scorned included many things of great archaeological interest, such as the long-hidden stones of the Via Sacra where it entered the Forum, to say nothing of the Column of Phocas: but harder still to swallow would be the intelligence that when the dead Duchess was brought back from Italy for burial she would lie in state at Devonshire House upon the way to the Cavendish vault at Derby.

Neither effigy nor epitaph marks the last resting-place of the fifth Duke and his two Duchesses. Bess probably desired none. It was her wish that they should be reunited in death as it was her prayer that they might be in the world to come, and the wish at least has been granted.

APPENDIX I

Copy of a fragment contained in a scrapbook at Chatsworth connected with Georgiana, Duchess of Devonshire.

List of a few things in Lady Elizabeth Foster's Apartment with the places where they are to be found.

Watches — 2. One, that is sometimes wound up, on the green baize table — the other is only an old Gold Watch, and usually lies on one of the Marble Slabs.

A Parcel of Small Bank Notes behind one of the Cushions of the Sopha — if they should happen not to be there it will scarcely be worth while to make any great search for them, as they will probably have been torn to pieces by Sidney, who sometimes expresses his resentment of my leaving him by destroying (poor dear little wretch) whatever is most valuable in the room: at least, that is the only rational way of accounting for the various Bank notes which have disappeared. If a Guinea is by accident left on the Table, he never fails to swallow it, but seldom touches the halfpence, tho' my Inkstand is generally covered with them.

A handsome red morocco box containing memorandums — N.B. the Key was lost long ago and never has been found.

Another, covered with green leather, full of letters from my Friends — it is always open.

Portfolio of Drawings, etchings etc., by the most eminent Masters Under the Vase that holds water for Sid.

A Portfeuille of my own Drawings, on a very high shelf, for fear of accidents.

Manuscript Poetry, French and Italian, in my strong-box, screwed to the floor.

Johnson's Poets, Tasso, Ariosto, Danté, Petrarch and other bound books on tables and chairs all over the room.

A bunch of Seals, among which are some valuable Cameos and Intaglios, on a table close to the door.

42 locks of hair of my most intimate friends, in the drawer of the Ink Stand.

My own Memoirs in Cypher upon the Marble Table.

The Poker, Tongs and Shovel upon the Pianoforte.

A very small parcel of Bills with receipts always laying on my writing Table.

Unsettled Do in 12 different parcels of the same order in which they were brought in, with the respective dates of the Year, commencing in 1789 — in a secret drawer.

Miniatures of the Polignac family somewhere about the Room.

Attorneys' Letters made into allumettes on the chimney-piece.

A breakfast Service of plain Wedgewood ware.

Several very fine Dresden and Sèvres China Saucers holding Indian Ink, Gumboge, etc.

Camels' hair pencils to sweep the hearth.

Contrât de Mariage d' Henriette——

Pearce avec un Nègre de la Guadaloupe.

A view of Monaco *par l'aveugle de Spa.*

Shawls, handkerchiefs, a Bottle containing Magnesia, several pairs of buckles and scissors, pieces of Dresden lace and other similar articles in the wicker Basket with the Green Satin covering, lilac border.

My Night things in the brass coal-scuttle.

Hervey's *Meditations among the Tombs*, Bath guides, Tissot's *Avis au Peuple*, Mazzinighi's Sonatas, Blair's *Sermons*, Roote's farce of *The Nabob*, all bound up in one large quarto volume. Busts of the Kemble family on a Table with Castors that they may always be placed in the best light.

[One hazards a guess that this fantastic and satirical inventory was the product of one of those *petits jeux* with which people amused themselves in great houses like Chatsworth. Lady Elizabeth had a dog called Sidney with her at Bath in the autumn of 1803. The general impression of modish squalor seems more in character for Georgiana, who was apt to be sluttish (*teste* Fanny Burney) than for Bess, who was inclined to be fastidious: but there may be an ironical twist here. Some of the items suggest Lydia Languish's instructions to Lucy in *The Rivals*, Act I, Scene II.]

APPENDIX II

Posthumous 'Anecdotes and Sketches'

Sir Augustus Clifford, realizing that his mother had envisaged the preservation of parts of her Journal in the form of Memoirs but recoiling from the task of editing for publication the whole mass of papers in his possession, compromised by printing privately in 1863 what he entitled *Anecdotes and Biographical Sketches by Elizabeth, Duchess of Devonshire*. The frontispiece is a lithograph from the miniature reproduced in Chapter XVI of the present book and the preamble includes M. d'Artaud's elegant obituary.

It cannot be said that anything in this piously garnered sheaf of notes is of outstanding interest. The *Sketches* are less lifelike than those in the Journal, the *Anecdotes* have for the most part found their way into other memoirs of the time: but they all reflect the wide range of the writer's tastes and her quick eye for character, to say nothing of her lifelong eagerness to instruct and to be instructed.

Though both Sir Augustus in this little volume and his nephew, Vere Foster, in his bulky *Two Duchesses* quote these *Lines addressed to Lady Elizabeth Foster by Georgiana, Duchess of Devonshire*, neither gives the date which would enable us to understand to what phase of that ecstatic friendship these outpourings belong:

> Untutored in the pencil's art
> My tints I gather from my heart,
> Where truth and love together trace
> The various beauties of thy face.
> Thy form, acknowledged fair and fine,
> Thy brow, where sense and sweetness join:
> Thy smile, the antidote to pain;
> Thy voice, that never spoke in vain;
> As diamonds on crystal trace
> In lines no efforts can efface
> To please for ever is thy lot
> Once seen, once loved, and ne'er forgot.

Vere Foster also prints the lines which gushed from the too-facile pen of the Duchess in 1796, 'when she was apprehensive of losing her eyesight', and adds for full measure some undated verses in the French language entitled *Portrait d'Elisabeth* and beginning

> *À la beauté enchanteresse*
> *Elle unit l'attrait de l'esprit.*

Neither gentleman seems to have seen anything ridiculous in these rather cloying fragments of amateur versification; and no doubt the flutings of Bess's own Muse were very similar. That her Muse did flute sometimes we know from the circumstance that Lord Byron was good enough to remark that he liked a poem of hers, though unkind enough to add that this did not make him like her any better: but Sir Augustus confines his extracts to prose. Popes, poets, painters and sculptors, ancient Romans, Greeks and Phoenicians, all these seemed worthy to march through this slender, gracious volume, and even Bess of Hardwick is deemed not below its dignity. Yet the compiler unwittingly produced the impression of a pedantic, dryasdust blue-stocking, and that this impression is not a faithful one will be obvious to anyone who reads the story of Dearest Bess to the end.

END NOTES

1. Born, 1748. Educated at Eton and Cambridge. Married first (1774), Lady Georgiana Spencer; secondly (1809), Lady Elizabeth Foster. Died, 1811.
2. *A New Ballad to the Tune of Molly Mog* by Pulteney, Chesterfield and Swift.
3. Third son of John, Lord Hervey (1730–1803).
4. The *D.N.B.* says 1759, but the above is the date given on her coffin-plate.
5. John Augustus, Lord Hervey, died 1796.
6. Afterwards fifth Earl and first Marquis of Bristol.
7. The Duke and Duchess of Devonshire.
8. *The Two Duchesses.*
9. See the *Anglo-Saxon Review*, volume II, 1899.
10. Quoted in the *Anglo-Saxon Review*, volume II, p. 66.
11. Lady Bristol alludes to her twice as 'Louchee', but the nickname does not seem to have been used by Bess either in her letters or her Journal.
12. Yolande Marie Gabrielle de Polastron, Duchesse de Polignac, 1749–93.
13. For example, the Prince of Wales and his sisters, and Georgiana and Harriet Cavendish with their 'adored Hart'.
14. An Englishwoman like an Angel.
15. The galley-slaves.
16. Simon André Tissot, 1728–97. One of the most famous physicians of the time. Appointed to the Chair of Clinical Medicine in the University of Pavia, 1780. Among his numerous publications was an *Essai sur les Maladies des Gens du Monde* (1770).
17. Constantly associating, not cohabiting, with.
18. *The Two Duchesses.*
19. François Joachim Pierre, Cardinal de Bernis (1715–94). poet, statesman and diplomat. On the strength of his *Épitre à la Paresse* he was admitted to the French Academy, but Frederick the Great thought poorly of his Muse and disparaged his *stérile abondance*. In 1752 he became French Minister at Venice, largely through the influence of Madame de Pompadour, to whom

he had dedicated Madrigals. He negotiated the Franco-Austrian Treaty of May 1st, 1757, but later lost the good will of the Pompadour clique by his efforts to obtain a negotiated peace with England and Prussia. His last years were spent in poverty, owing to the confiscation of all ecclesiastical revenues after Napoleon's conquest of Italy.

20. The Abbé Raynal (1713–96), French historian and philosopher, once a frequenter of Madame Geoffrin's *salon*. His *Historie Philosophique* was banned in France, and he himself sought sanctuary with Frederick the Great and Catherine II. Subsequently he retracted his unpopular opinions and the Directorate rewarded him by making him a Member of the Institute.

21. Now at Ickworth; reproduced in this book.

22. Paraphrased in *The Face Without a Frown*.

23. 'Mrs Brown', the Devonshire House pseudonym for Marie Antoinette. Louis XVI was, of course, 'Mr Brown'.

24. Charlotte William was married to a nephew of Heaton, the agent at Chatsworth, and not, as stated by one authority, to Signor Perconto.

25. D. of D———e — The Duke of Devonshire.

26. D. of D. — The Duke of Dorset.

27. Lord Hervey. He and his wife and their little daughter were with Bess throughout the first months of her stay abroad.

28. This passage seems strange when we recollect that she could not possibly have married the Duke of Dorset, her husband being still alive. The Duke was Minister Plenipotentiary in France from 1786 to 1789.

29. All sorts of people. *Macbeth*, Act I, Scene VII.

30. Where the greater malady is fixed, the lesser is scarce felt. *King Lear*, Act III, Scene IV.

31. In such a sea of troubles what shall I, unhappy, do?

32. Horace Walpole's friend, the Countess of Upper Ossory, divorced in 1769 by her first husband, the Earl of Euston, later third Duke of Grafton.

33. In a letter to the Duchess she says they eat oranges and drank iced water, and her brother ate half a fowl.[c]

34. Perhaps Elizabeth Ashburne, later Madame Perconto.

35. *Nessun maggior dolore*
    Che ricordarsi del tempo felice
    Nella miseria.   Dante, *Inferno*, V, 121.
    There is no greater sorrow than remembering happy times in misery.

36. The past makes me despair, the present overwhelms me, the future appals me.

37. Harriet Elizabeth, afterwards wife of the first Earl Granville (1785–1862).

38. Probably the miniature of Duchess Georgiana which she is wearing in the portrait by Angelica Kauffmam painted a year before at Naples.

39. A little town on the Gulf of Salerno.
40. The Queen of Naples and the Two Sicilies.
41. Including a shipwreck.
42. The Duchess of Devonshire.
43. *The Tempest* Act I, Scene II.
44. Frederick North (1766–1827) later Lord Chancellor of the Ionian Islands. He succeeded his father as fifth Earl of Guilford in 1817.
45. One could — by his wife, as appears from a later entry.
46. The Duke.
47. General the Hon. Richard Fitzpatrick (1747–1813) son of the first Lord Ossory: later MP for Bedford. A noted Whig and a close friend of Charles James Fox.
48. Frederick Fawkener. He was married to Lady Spencer's niece, who eloped later with Lord John Townshend.
49. See, however, Chapter X of the present book.
50. Sheridan.
51. Her dog. The Duke had a bitch of the same name in 1807.
52. Charles Alexandre de Calonne (1734–1802).
53. Jacques Necker (1732–1804) Director-General of Finance (1771–81 and again in 1788–90). Father of Madame de Stäel as well as 'of the People'.
54. General J. A. van der Merch (1734–1792). Bess misheard his name and called him van den Bosch. I am indebted to the distinguished Belgian historian, M. Carlo Bronne, for kindly setting her and me right, and also for giving me these and other particulars of the General's career.
55. In *The Face Without a Frown*.
56. This was the second son of Louis XVI and Marie Antoinette, the 'Louis XVII' of the French Royalists (1785–95).
57. Trophime Gerard, Marquis de Lally-Tollendal (1751–1830). After acting with the Third Estate in the States General in 1789, this son of an Irish Jacobite allied himself with the court party in France, and did what he could to protect Louis XVI. In consequence he had to flee to England. After the Bourbon Restoration he was made a peer.
58. *i.e.* that Lady Elizabeth was to be of the party.
59. It was he who had conducted the fugitives back from Varennes. Later he paid for his moderation with his life.
60. La Fayette, the Marquis de (1757–1834). Fought against the English in America: Member of the National Assembly: formed the National Guard. Driven out of France by the Jacobins.
61. In Berlin.
62. The Earl-Bishop.

63. The notorious milliner and dressmaker, Mademoiselle Bertin, who insinuated herself with such lamentable results into the confidence of Marie Antoinette.

64. This ceased to be so after she and Nelson met at Naples seven years later.

65. Muzzle, 'phiz'. *The Two Duchesses*.

66. See Lord Bessborough's *Georgiana*, Chapter XVI.

67. Sir Samuel Granston Gooda. In April 1793, he commanded one of the divisions of the Mediterranean Fleet, hoisting his flag in the *Princess Royal*.

68. Caroline Ponsonby.

69. Ferdinand IV. King of the Two Sicilies (1751–1825). His wife was Marie Antoinette's sister and Lady Hamilton's warm friend.

70. The second Earl of Bessborough had died in March of this year, and was succeeded by his eldest son, Lord Duncannon.

71. Small donkey.

72. Comité du Salut Publique.

73. The King's valet.

74. The Executioner.

75. After Robert François Damiens had stabbed him with a penknife to give him an *avertissement salutaire*: January 1757.

76. At the fierceness of the fire.

77. Apparently without a third garment, *i.e.* a pair of breeches.

78. 16th? See *Lady Bessborough and her Family Circle*, p. 1.

79. Jane, daughter of Sir William Maxwell of Monreith. Married Alexander, fourth Duke of Gordon, by whom (or during her wedlock with whom) she had numerous children. She was Queen of the Tories, a termagant yet energetic Queen.

80. Under Sir John Warren, with a view to reinforcing the Chouans, led by Georges Cadoudal.

81. *The Two Duchesses*.

82. The Ponsonby ladies.

83. Presumably on account of Bess's delicate state of health, but the Duchess, too, had been ailing since the previous August, when the trouble in her eye seems fast to have declared itself.

84. Born 1773: created Viscount Granville, 1815: Earl, 1833: died 1846.

85. *Julius Caesar*, Act I, Scene II.

86. Francis, fifth Duke of Bedford, died 1802.

87. Lord fitzWilliam, who apparently followed hard upon the Duke of Bedford's heels.

88. See *Hary-O*, p. 14.

89. Arthur Connor (1763–1852), one of the United Irishmen and a close friend of Lord Edward Fitzgerald. He later became a naturalized Frenchman,

but his Republican sentiments were not congenial to Napoleon, and though he was given the rank of 'General' he never saw active service with the *Grande Armée*. His wife was the only daughter of Condorcet, the encyclopædist.

90. William, first Marquis of Lansdowne (1737–1805). Called by George III 'the Jesuit of Berkeley Square'.

91. Alexander Vasilivitch Suvarov (1729–1800).

92. At their First Communion in the Abbey.

93. Act II, Scene II.

94. Act III, Scene III. The actual words are "'Twas fit I should be rebuked——'

95. August Kotzebüe (1761–1818), author of the original German play.

96. Leveson-Gower Correspondence, volume II, pp. 3, 5, 7, 17, 32. Bess does not mention these letters in her Journal, though she received at least one.

97. See Lady Bessborough's heart-rending account in the Leveson-Gower Correspondence, volume I, pp. 125–6.

98. For many years his mistress and since 1795 his lawful enough not-yet-acknowledged wife.

99. A less detailed account of both escapes in given in the Leveson-Gower Correspondence, volume I, p. 150.

100. The Comte d'Artois, later Charles X.

101. The 'Corise' of Hary-O's letters. She married Lord Ossulston ('little O'), eldest son of the Earl of Tankerville, whom we shall meet later in Bess's Journals.

102. Lady Wellesley, Hyacinthe Gabrielle Roland; Lady Yarmouth, Maria Fagniani; Lady Ferrers, Elizabeth Mundy. None of these ladies enjoyed a reputation likely to commend itself to Queen Charlotte.

103. Fox and King George, for once of one mind, must have been thinking of the much-misunderstood case of Caracciolo, of whom the late Sir Henry Newbolt wrote (in an unpublished letter) that he was 'a traitor well served', and that his 'life was forfeit by the laws of every civilized nation'.

104. William Ponsonby (1787–1855), created Lord de Mauley in 1838. In the Leveson-Gower Correspondence, volume I p. 280, there is a charming letter from Lady Bessborough describing Lord St Vincent's kindness to 'poor Willy and Clifford', whom he hoped to 'live to see Post-Captains'.

105. Lord Morpeth and Lady Georgiana Cavendish were married on March 21st, 1801. It was a happy and very fruitful marriage.

106. More familiar to most of us as Horace Walpole. This anecdote was inserted by Sir Augustus Clifford in *Anecdotes and Sketches*. See Appendix II.

107. The alienist in attendance upon George III.

108. When the Regency came into being in 1811 the original restrictions, as formulated in 1788, were imposed for the term of one year.

109. William Ponsonby and Augustus Clifford. They were later joined by Lord Spencer's second son, Robert.

110. The Ribbon of the Order of the Saint Esprit.

111. *The History of the Revolution of 1688.*

112. Charles Richard Fox (1796–1873) son of Lord Holland and Lady Webster, afterwards Lady Holland.

113. Sir Robert Adair (1763–1855). Hero of Canning's humorous lyric about 'sweet Matilda Pottingen'. Sent by Fox to Vienna in 1806 to warn Austria of the dangers to which she was exposed from France. K.C.B. 1809.

114. Leader, with Pichegru, of the Chouan conspiracy against Bonaparte (1798–1800).

115. For Lady Bessborough's more detailed account see Leveson-Gower Correspondence, volume II, p. 391.

116. *Hary-O*, p. 30.

117. Louis, Comte de Narbonne (1755–1813). Fled to Switzerland in 1792: returned to Paris and offered his services to Bonaparte after the establishment of the new Consular Constitution of the 18th Brumaire (November 9) 1799. Reputed natural son of Louis XV.

118. Camille Jordan (1771–1821), another ex-*emigré*. He was a Liberal of the amiable, unrealistic type, and wrote (but did not publish) a pamphlet against Bonaparte's assumption of the First Consulship for life.

119. Pierre Alexandre Berthier (1753–1815) Marshal of France and Chief of Staff, later created Prince of Wagram and Neuchâtel.

120. Juliette Récamier (1777–1849). Famous alike for her beauty and for the number of eminent persons who fell under its spell.

121. Antonio Canova (1757–1822). His Cupid and Psyche shocked Wordsworth when it was exhibited in London.

122. Now in the Apsley House Museum. It is a colossal nude, the head only being modelled from Napoleon's.

123. Jean François de la Harpe (1739–1803), dramatist, critic and man of letters.

124. Richard Lovell Edgeworth (1744–1817). Bess does not mention his more celebrated daughter, who was with him in Paris and had there for his sake refused the honourable proposals of a Swedish admirer, Count Edelkrantz.

125. Through this marriage the barony of Howard de Walden passed to her descendants.

126. Better known as Sir Henry Halford. He assumed the surname on inheriting the estate of a kinsman, Sir Charles Halford, Bart. As be 'deprecated the physical examination of his patients' no diagnosis made by him had much validity.

127. Caroline Crichton, married in 1799 to Colonel James Archibald Stuart Wortley, afterwards first Lord Wharncliffe.

128. English Minister at Stockholm. He and his clever second wife, *née* Harriet Fane, were Wellington's closest friends in later years.
129. Lady Conyngham, *née* Elizabeth Denison, the last of George IV's old hens. See Leveson-Gower Correspondence, volume I, p. 392.
130. *The Two Duchesses.*
131. Dominique, Baron de Denon, archaeologist, draughtsman and engraver (1747–1835).
132. In the original the word 'cabal' is stroked out and 'party' substituted.
133. Her real name was Marguerite Josephine Weimer or Weymer, and though Lady Bessborough had heard that she was the mistress of Lucien Bonaparte it was the First Consul who was her lover.
134. *Lady Bessborough and her Family Circle*, p. 123.
135. Afterwards chosen by Napoleon to be the governess of his son, the King of Rome.
136. Lord Whitworth (1752–1825), for twelve years Ambassador in St Petersburg. He had great personal charm, and had been known and liked by Marie Antoinette.
137. Henry Quin, son of a well-known Irish bibliophile.
138. Wife of Bertie Greatheed, of Guy's Cliffe, Warwick.
139. The American Minister, whose deafness was a constant source of complications.
140. Androche Junot, later created Due d'Abrantès. He was defeated by Wellington at Vimeiro.
141. This letter is among the Ickworth MSS.
142. During Robert Emmett's abortive rising (July 1803), Lord Kilwarden and his nephew, Richard Wolfe, were dragged from their carriage and butchered by the Dublin rabble.
143. He had applied for a military command, hoping that 'this might excite the loyal energies of the nation'.
144. 1757–1833. Second son of the fourth Viscount Townshend. MP successively for the University of Cambridge and the boroughs of Westminster and Knaresborough. After Mr Fawkener had divorced his wife, Georgiana Anne, *née* Poyntz, on his account, Lord John married her. Their second daughter, Elizabeth Frances, became the wife of Augustus Clifford in 1813.
145. Henry Dundas (1742–1811). 'Retired from Bench of Treasury', 1801; created Viscount Melville, 1802.
146. The English always showed a marked reluctance to call him 'Napoleon'. To them, whether 'Emperor or Caesar, Kaiser or Pheezar', he remained plain 'Bonaparte', usually pronounced with four syllables.
147. 'Ever bitter day, when I lost thee, dear, beloved brother.' Dearest Bess often

dropped into Italian on such sentimental occasions.

148. Finch was the original name of the Earls of Winchelsea: it was later expanded to Finch-Hatton.

149. A curious request, all things considered, but Fox probably did not know the Duchess's secret, and it may be remembered that when the break with Grey came seven years later some people ascribed it to retrospective jealousy on the part of the Prince.

150. Printed in *The Two Duchesses*.

151. The Young Melbourne, pp. 58–61.

152. Afterwards Admiral Sir Benjamin Hallowell, one of Nelson's most trusted officers. A Canadian by birth, he was a man of exceptional height and bulk, and must have towered over the Admiral when they walked together on the quarter-deck. It was he who caused the ship's carpenter of the *Swiftsure* to make from the mainmast of *l'Orient* the coffin which Nelson accepted with so much pleasure and in which he now lies in the crypt of St Paul's.

153. Afterwards Admiral Sir Robert Spencer, K.C.B., the 'beloved Bob' of Sarah, Lady Lyttelton's correspondence.

154. *The Two Duchesses*.

155. Leveson-Gower Correspondence, volume II p. 467.

156. William Henry West Betty (1791–1874). In 1805 the House of Commons adjourned to see him in *Hamlet*.

157. *The Two Duchesses*.

158. When Kemble saw him act at Leicester before the triumphs in London, the comment of the great tragedian was, 'The pooh boy is hoarse, very hoarse.'

159. Amelia Opie (1769–1853), the novelist, wife of John Opie, R.A.

160. Henry Dundas, Viscount Melville (1745–1811). He was impeached on a charge of 'gross malversation and breach of duty' as Treasurer of the Navy, but acquitted by his peers, at his trial in April 1806, 'an all charges involving his honour'.

161. Peniston Lamb. Born 1770. The only one of Lady Melbourne's children who was beyond doubt Lord Melbourne's as well.

162. May that dear girl be happy!

163. Son of William, Duke of Clarence, and Dorothy Jordan.

164. Sir Robert Calder (1745–1818). He was court martialled in December 1805, found guilty of an error of judgement and sentenced to be severely reprimanded.

165. George Bussy, fourth Earl (1735–1805), married 1770, Frances, daughter of Dr Twysden, Bishop of Raphoe. It was for her that the Prince of Wales temporarily deserted Mrs Fitzherbert between 1794 and 1800.

166. Nelson.

167. The future first Earl.

168. To Lady Hamilton.
169. Frederick Foster.
170. Clifford's ship.
171. Robert Spencer, her nephew.
172. Bess wrote *Trinida* but Clifford inserted *Rédoubtable*.
173. General Mack's defeat by Napoleon at Ulm, October 17th, 1805. At an earlier stage in his career his exploits against the French Republicans had impressed Bess so much that she hung a print of him in her room at Devonshire House.
174. Matcham, son of Nelson's favourite sister Charlotte.
175. *Hary-O*, p. 133.
176. The mainmast.
177. There are stains, as if of tears, on this page of the Journal.
178. Not to be confounded with his secretary, John Scott, who perished in the battle.
179. My italics. This paragraph has been pasted over, probably by Clifford when revising his mother's Memoirs with an eye to posterity: but I do not apologize either for holding the page up to the light or for transcribing what is written there. To anyone interested in Nelson it is of great value, and there is nothing *scabreux* about it.
180. Younger brother of the Duke of Devonshire (1754–1834).
181. Dr Pretyman, Bishop of Lincoln, who had been Pitt's private tutor at Cambridge.
182. English Minister at Washington.
183. He was created first Baron Rendlesham on February 4th, 1806.
184. Mrs Samuel (afterwards Lady Elizabeth) Whitbread.
185. A phrase perhaps best rendered by the Victorian equivalent, 'tame cat'.
186. Lady Buckingham. She was the wife of George Nugent Temple Grenville (1753–1813) created Marquis of Buckingham, 1784.
187. No formal separation ever took place.
188. 'Jesuits' Bark' — quinine.
189. So uncouth a figure that nothing but her illness would prevent it being 'laughable' wrote Lady Bessborough. Leveson-Gower Correspondence, volume II, p. 185.
190. And of her own death eighteen years later.
191. Lady Morpeth, who was expecting yet another baby.
192. Leveson-Gower Correspondence, volume II, pp. 184–7.
193. The removal of the coffin on the first stage of its long journey to Derby.
194. See *In Whig Society* by Mabell, Countesn of Airlie.
195. William Adam, successively Attorney-General and Solicitor-General to the Prince of Wales and later Lord Chief Commissioner of the Scottish Jury Court.

196. Dismantled.
197. At the house in Whitehall which still bears his name.
198. Thurlow, Edward, Baron (1731–1806), of whom Fox said that 'no man was so wise as Thurlow looked'. For the rest he was arrogant, foul-mouthed and recalcitrant, even in the dignified position of Lord Chancellor (1778–1792).
199. Volume II, pp. 208–11.
200. 'This,' says Bess in parenthesis, 'is not quite true.'
201. Sheridan.
202. Charles Grey bore the courtesy title of Lord Howick From 1806 to 1807. In the latter year he succeeded his father as second Earl Grey.
203. *Hary-O*, p. 166.
204. *Hary-O*, p. 169.
205. Afterwards fifth Earl FitzWilliam (1786–1857). It was reported that what Sir Leicester Dedlock would have described as the 'necessary expenses' of this election amounted to £100,000 on either side.
206. Henry Lascelles (1767–1841) afterwards second Earl of Harewood. He had caused acute embarrassment to Fox in January 1806 by his motion for a public funeral, burial in the Abbey and a monument for William Pitt.
207. He had married on July 8th, 1806, Mary, fourth daughter of Thomas, first Lord Dundas, but their eldest son was not born till 1812.
208. See Chapter XIII.
209. *Hary-O*, pp. 183, 248.
210. 1777–1822.
211. According to which Junot agreed to evacuate Portugal. If Wellington had had his way, the Convention would never have been signed.
212. In an unpublished letter.
213. To the effect that her shameless selling of military commissions was connived at by the Duke of York to his own advantage.
214. *Lady Bessborough and her Family Circle*, p. 185.
215. Lord David Cecil, *The Young Melbourne*, pp. 34–5.
216. *Hary-O*. p. 232.
217. *Ibid.*, pp. 240, 594.
218. *Ibid.*, p. 174.
219. *Lady Bessborough and her Family Circle*, p. 189.
220. *Lady Bessborough and her Family Circle*, pp. 192–3.
221. *Lady Bessborough and her Family Circle*, p. 195.
222. *Hary-O*. p. 330.
223. *Ibid.*, p. 232.
224. *Ibid.*, p. 334.
225. Lord Liverpool's residence as Lord Warden of the Cinque Ports.

226. At the time of the Delicate Investigation, when the Tories, as King's Men, supported the 'dear daughter-in-law and niece' whom he was backing against his eldest son.
227. *Hary-O.* p. 294.
228. Bess and the Prince both call it a 'letter', but it was intended to serve as a draft for the Prince's speech when he received the Deputation at Carlton House on February 6th.
229. Lord Holland.
230. Leveson-Gower Correspondence, volume II pp. 389, 399.
231. As far as the point where the road leading northward out of London ceased to be paved with cobblestones.
232. In the church of All Saints, now the cathedral.
233. His family continued to call him 'Hart' for some time after he succeeded to the Dukedom.
234. *The First Lady Wharncliffe and her Family*, volume I, pp. 177–8.
235. Leveson-Gower Correspondence, volume II, pp. 390, 394.
236. See Chapter XVI for Bess's Will, and her allusion to this transaction.
237. *Lady Bessborough and her Family Circle*, p. 213.
238. *Ibid.*
239. *The Two Duchesses.*
240. *Hary-O.* p. 282.
241. Leveson-Gower Correspondence, volume II, p. 405.
242. Leveson-Gower Correspondence, volume II, pp. 423, 426.
243. In his privately-printed *Sketch of the Life of the Sixth Duke of Devonshire.*
244. *The Two Duchesses.*
245. Semaphore.
246. He was still 'military mad' in 1812 and for a long time after.
247. General Count Belliard (1773–1832) served in Italy and Egypt, as well as in Russia.
248. Apparently the Bonapartists in France.
249. See *The Letters of the Princess Charlotte*, ed. Dr A. Aspinall.
250. Caro William.
251. George Eden: succeeded his father as Lord Auckland, 1814.
252. Caro George.
253. Quoted by Peter Quennell in Byron: *The Years of Fame.*
254. *Ibid.*
255. Lord Cowper and his wife, *née* Lady Emily Lamb, later Lady Palmerston. There is another link with Bess here, for Clifford was Palmerston's fag at Harrow.
256. *The Two Duchesses.*
257. *Ibid.*
258. See Chapter XVI.

259. Corinne's unacknowledged second husband.

260. St. Matthew, Chapter IV, verse 8.

261. of Wales.

262. *The Two Duchesses.*

263. RearAdmiral, 1848; Vice Admiral, 1855; retired Admiral, 1860; Admiral of the Red, 1864.

264. For Bess's comments on this reconciliation, see Chapter XVI.

265. For her bequests to him see Chapter XVI.

266. *Letters of Harriet, Countess Granville*, volume I, p. 110.

267. *Letters of Sarah, Lady Lyttelton.*

268. *Letters of Harriet, Countess Granville*, volume I, p. 136.

269. In a letter from Lady Caroline Stuart-Wortley. See *The First Lady Wharncliffe and her Family*, volume I, p. 235.

270. The Tsar Paul, son of Peter III and Catherine the Great.

271. In their book, *The Stuart Papers at Windsor.*

272. Well might he be called *her* Baron; this was the notorious Bergami.

273. Second Baronet. Died unmarried, 1882.

274. *The Letters of King George the Fourth*, volume II, p. 214.

275. The death of the Duchess of Devonshire, and of the Duke only five years later.

276. Created Earl of Burlington, 1831. His grandson, the second Earl, succeeded to the Dukedom in 1858.

277. He had been executed for High Treason in December 1815.

278. *In Whig Society* by Mabell, Countess of Airlie.

279. She was afterwards the wife of Frederick Ponsonby.

280. Reproduced in this book.

281. *Letters of Harriet, Countess Granville*, volume I, p. 128.

282. *Hary-O*, p. 174.

283. Lady Erne.

284. *The First Lady Wharncliffe and her Family*, volume I, p. 295.

285. In the London Museum.

286. *The First Lady Wharncliffe and her Family*, volume I, p. 300.

287. 'Dowager' is an error. The Duke being unmarried, his stepmother remained simply 'Duchess of Devonshire'.

288. Henry Hervey Aston-Bruce, grandson of John, first Earl of Bristol, created a Baronet, 1804. He inherited all the Earl-Bishop's Irish property.

289. *The Letters of King George the Fourth*, ed. Dr A. Aspinall, volume III, p. 70.

290. In the possession of Lord Dormer.

291. See Appendix II. There is a copy in manuscript among the Lawrence papers in the library of the Royal Academy.

292. *Letters of Harriet, Countess Granville*, volume I, pp. 269, 276.

293. *Ibid.*